CRITICAL DIALOGUES IN SOUTHEAST ASIAN STUDIES
Charles Keyes, Vicente Rafael, and Laurie J. Sears, Series Editors

CRITICAL DIALOGUES IN SOUTHEAST ASIAN STUDIES

This series offers perspectives in Southeast Asian Studies that stem from reconsideration of the relationships among scholars, texts, archives, field sites, and subject matter. Volumes in the series feature inquiries into historiography, critical ethnography, colonialism and postcolonialism, nationalism and ethnicity, gender and sexuality, science and technology, politics and society, and literature, drama, and film. A common vision of the series is a belief that area studies scholarship sheds light on shifting contexts and contests over forms of knowing and modes of action that inform cultural politics and shape histories of modernity.

LIVING SHARIA

Law and Practice in Malaysia

TIMOTHY P. DANIELS

UNIVERSITY OF WASHINGTON PRESS

Seattle and London

Living Sharia is published with the assistance of a grant from the Charles and Jane Keyes Endowment for Books on Southeast Asia, established through the generosity of Charles and Jane Keyes.

All photos and charts by author unless otherwise noted.

Map of Malaysia by Pease Press Maps, based on "Administrative Divisions of Malaysia." 1:11,000,000. Washington, DC: Central Intelligence Agency, 1998. Courtesy of the University of Texas Libraries, University of Texas at Austin.

University of Washington Press
www.washington.edu/uwpress

Library of Congress Cataloging-in-Publication Data
Names: Daniels, Timothy P., 1960– author.
Title: living Sharia : law and practice in Malaysia / Timothy P. Daniels.
Description: Seattle : University of Washington Press, [2017] | Series: Critical dialogues in Southeast Asian studies | Includes bibliographical references and index.
Identifiers: LCCN 2017007243 (print) | LCCN 2017008658 (ebook) | ISBN 9780295742540 (hardcover : alk. paper) | ISBN 9780295742557 (pbk. : alk. paper) | ISBN 9780295742564 (ebook)
Subjects: LCSH: Islamic law—Malaysia. | Islam—Social aspects—Malaysia. | Islam and politics—Malaysia.
Classification: LCC KPG469.5 .D36 2017 (print) | LCC KPG469.5 (ebook) | DDC 346.59501/5—dc23
LC record available at https://lccn.loc.gov/2017007243

To Rachida, Yusuf, and Aisha

CONTENTS

ACKNOWLEDGMENTS

THIS PROJECT EMERGED FROM PREVIOUS RESEARCH PERIODS IN Indonesia and Malaysia during which the growing relevance of Islamic law and ethics to public discourses and everyday lives became increasingly apparent to me. I would like to thank the Wenner-Gren Foundation for Anthropological Research for its kind financial support of my research project titled "Local 'Shariah' Regulations and Contested Implementation," conducted for six months during 2010 and 2011. I also thank Hofstra University for faculty research grants supporting summer research on this project during 2011 and 2012 and academic leaves in 2010 and 2015. I am grateful for the institutional support I received from the Universiti Sains Malaysia and its Islamic Studies Section that served as my Malaysian sponsor and academic home during this research endeavor. Their assistance in applying for my research visa and providing letters of introduction to libraries, government officials, and sharia courts was indispensable.

Special thanks go out to all my Malaysian interlocutors, including street vendors, taxi drivers, Muslim worshipers, mosque speakers, students, store workers, political activists, NGO members, sharia court judges, and Muslim scholars in government think tanks and departments. Of course, without these discussions, interviews, and welcomed participation, this project would have been impossible. After returning from these productive periods of fieldwork research I organized two panels, one at the annual Association for Asian Studies meeting in Philadelphia during March 2014 and the other at the American Anthropological Association meeting in Washington, DC, during December 2014. I acknowledge the "Sharia Dynamics" panel participants and volume contributors Norhafsah Hamid, Matthew S. Erie, Omer Awass, Ahmad Najib Burhani, Robert W. Hefner, James D. Frankel, Laura Elder, Wajeeha Ameen Malik, Charles Allers, David J. Banks, Meryem Zaman, and Sarah Eltantawi for stimulating discussion and astute work. I also thank the Critical Dialogues in Southeast Asian Studies series editors, anonymous reviewers, and Ustadha Zaynab Ansari for their insightful comments on an earlier draft of this book. I am grateful to Jacob Wilson Zucker and Monica M. Yatsyla from the Hofstra Faculty Support Center for their technical assistance. Final thanks go out to my wife, Rachida, and our children, Yusuf and Aisha, for their inspiration and patience as I produced this text.

NOTE ON TRANSCRIPTION

IN GENERAL, MY TRANSCRIPTION OF SPOKEN AND WRITTEN MALAY and Arabic terms and phrases follows local usage. Key Malay terms in translated segments are rendered as written or spoken in the original texts or statements. When quoting Malay sources, I use the spelling *syariah* (without italics). When referring to particular institutions I use the spelling *shariah* (e.g., the Kelantan *Shariah* Court), with the English usage *sharia* and *sharia* court in most of my other discourse (again, without italics). *Sy* in Malay is pronounced *sh*. In cases in which the pronunciation of Malay terms varies across dialects, I try to represent the local expressions. In-text and bibliographic references to Malay authors generally use their personal or full names, unless an author prefers to use their surname, family, or father's personal name. For instance, Abdullah Alwi Haji Hassan is cited as (Abdullah Alwi 1996) rather than (Hassan 1996). His name is also alphabetized in the list of references under *a* rather than *h*. Malay honorific titles such as *Datuk*, *Datuk Seri*, *Datin Seri*, *Tun*, and *Tun Seri* are used as appropriate.

Arabic words follow Malaysian conventions, and these are multiple in some cases. I also provide information on the spelling of Arabic words and phrases in Modern Standard Arabic, especially key terms that have broad significance for Islamic studies. Arabic terms, such as *sharia*, that are found in an unabridged English dictionary are presented without diacritical marks.

All foreign-language terms, and their Anglicized versions, such as *hadith*, that appear in the glossary are italicized in the text. Definitions are generally provided in the main text upon a term's first appearance only. The glossary is intended to help the reader with later appearances.

CHRONOLOGY

1250–1400	Rise of Islamic kingdoms
1400–1511	Melaka Sultanate
1523	Melaka Digest
1511–1641	Portuguese colonial rule
1641–1824	Dutch colonial rule
1824–1957	British colonial rule
1826	Straits Settlements (Melaka, Singapore, Penang, and Wellesley Province)
1878	Civil Ordinance
1896	Federated Malay States
1906	Unfederated Malay States
1937	Civil Law Enactment
1946	United Malays National Organization (UMNO) formed
1948	Federation of Malaya
1948	Courts Ordinance (excluded sharia courts from federal system)
1952	Alliance Party (later called National Front or Barisan Nasional [BN]) formed
1955	Islamic Party of the Land of Malays (Parti Islam Sa-Tanah Melayu, PAS; later called Parti Islam Se-Malaysia, Islamic Party of Malaysia) established
1956	Civil Law Ordinance
1956	Reid Constitutional Commission
1957	Political independence
1963	Federation of Malaysia
1965	Muslim Courts (Criminal Jurisdiction) Act
1970	Islamic resurgence and *dakwah* (missionary) movements emerge
1970	National Council for Islamic Affairs Fatwa Committee organized
1971	Darul Arqam religious organization established

1982	Kelantan Administration of Muslim Law Enactment (three-tiered system of sharia courts)
1983	Islamic Banking Act
1984	Islamic Insurance (Takaful) Act
1984	Amendment of Muslim Courts Act (1965), raising penalties
1988	Article 121 (1A) amendment to the Federal Constitution
1988	Selangor Non-Islamic Religions (Control of Propagation among Muslims) Enactment
1988	Sisters in Islam (SIS) formed
1990	Islamic Party of Malaysia electoral victory in Kelantan
1993	Kelantan Syariah Criminal Code (II) (Hukum Hudud) passed but not implemented
1994	Amendments to Islamic Family Law Act (Federal Territories)
1998	Kelantan Enactment Controlling Entertainment and Places of Entertainment
2003	People's Justice Party (Parti Keadilan Rakyat) formed
2008	People's Alliance (Pakatan Rakyat) organized
2009	Bank Negara Malaysia gains jurisdiction over Islamic finance sector
2011	Trade Descriptions Act
2015	Conviction of Anwar Ibrahim (leader of opposition) upheld
2015	Islamic Party of Malaysia severs ties with the Democratic Action Party (DAP), a fellow member of opposition alliance (Pakatan Rakyat)

LIVING SHARIA

INTRODUCTION

Sharia and the Anthropology of Knowledge

IN *TRYING TO BE MUSLIM*, NORHAFSAH (2012, 11), A THIRTY-NINE-year-old Malay Muslim woman, shares her ongoing journey searching for more knowledge about her religion, Islam:

> Now I understand that . . . being a Muslim is submitting totally to the Will of God. That includes [abiding] by the teachings of the Quran and our Prophet Muhammad (saw). A Muslim must also love his/her fellow Muslim brothers and sisters and wish for their success, happiness and a place in heaven. A Muslim must adhere to the five pillars of Islam. A Muslim must apply Islamic way of living in everyday life. A Muslim has to balance between this world and the thereafter. A Muslim must prevent evil and encourage good. A Muslim must not let his/her fellow Muslim suffer or go hungry whilst he lives in the ivory tower with plenty of food to last a lifetime. A Muslim should not be too attached to worldly material things. A Muslim must protect Islam and not betray fellow Muslims or their religion.

Although she was born into a Muslim family in 1973, Norhafsah realized she had little understanding of Islam. She describes her personal quest and struggle to be a good person through "following the teachings of Quran and hadith" and wholeheartedly accepting God's "Decrees" (132). The Holy Qur'an, originally an oral text that was later transcribed, is considered by Muslims to be revealed knowledge, which God sent to Prophet Muhammad. *Hadith* are records of Prophet Muhammad's exemplary sayings and actions, his *Sunna*. These are the two main sources for *sharia* (Ar. *sharīʻa*) taken in its theological sense, as Islamic law, norms, and moral values.

Stories like Norhafsah's, of personal growth and transformation through sharia, are often overshadowed by media reports and political rhetoric that paint it as a dangerous religious ideology, a savage penal code, and a threat to civilized secular and democratic life. In September 2010, the Center for Security Policy, a conservative think tank, issued a report titled *Shariah: The*

Threat to America, arguing that it is an "alien and barbaric legal code" and "supremacist and totalitarian" ideology that threatens American freedom and secularism enshrined in the Constitution of the United States. The report's conclusion recommends legally proscribing any promotion of sharia, such as sharia-compliant finance; charging with sedition Islamic figures that support sharia; restricting the immigration of sharia supporters; treating those who espouse sharia as hate groups; and generally striving to make the United States sharia-free (141–44). In the context of the post-9/11 "war on terror," discourses of getting tougher on Islam and Muslims held heightened political currency. Several right-wing preachers and politicians spoke of Islam as a threat, calling for hearings and discriminatory policies. Thirteen US states, embracing this conservative model of sharia as an extremist strategy, considered adopting legislation forbidding sharia (Ali and Duss 2011). Fears motivated by these representations of an ominous "religious ideology" were palpable for many Americans when "confronted" with Muslims praying or wearing modest, Islamic-style attire in airports.

Liberal think tanks and Islamic organizations have responded to these representations. In March 2011, the Center for American Progress, a "progressive" educational institute, published *Understanding Sharia Law*, which criticized and debunked the conservative interpretations of sharia, especially those in the Center for Security Policy's report. The authors described sharia as "personal religious law and moral guidance" and the "ideal law of God as interpreted by Muslim scholars over centuries aimed toward justice, fairness, and mercy" (Ali and Duss 2011, 3). They also contend that most Muslims, as well as academics studying Islam, adopt a broad definition conceiving of sharia as dynamic and multifaceted. Contesting conservative ideas, they argue that it is important to properly target the extremist fringe in Muslim communities and not to cast too wide a net so as to alienate the more moderate majority. Besides, Muslims, like believers in other "faiths," they remind us, are engaging in ongoing conversations about the place of religion in "modernity." The Islamic Circle of North America (ICNA) and other Islamic organizations initiated projects to educate the public about the "proper" understanding of sharia. In May 2011, ICNA mobilized an educational campaign, including seminars in several cities, special editions of its magazine the *Message International*, and distribution of various forms of information on websites and throughout society aiming to correct what they considered "Islamophobic" misrepresentations and intolerance. Saulat Pervez, author of an article in a special edition of the *Message International*, states that "while Shariah provides the legal framework for the foundation and functioning of a society, it also details moral, ethical, social and political codes of conduct for Muslims at an individual and collective level" (2011, 24). Overall, ICNA argued that calls for proscribing sharia violate principles of pluralism and religious freedom in the United States.

Although these pro- and contra-sharia discourses are only a small part of the diverse ways we talk and think about sharia, they demonstrate that discourses about sharia are integral to sociopolitical dynamics in American society. Discourses of sharia are also enmeshed in diachronic processes in other societies with Muslim minorities, such as the United Kingdom, France, China, and the Philippines, as well as Muslim-majority societies such as Egypt, Pakistan, Indonesia, and Malaysia. Sharia dynamics—the roles that discourses and practices of sharia play in sociopolitical processes—is an important topic for anthropological investigation. Scholars of religion, sociology, media studies, and anthropology have often concentrated on deconstructing these discourses and demonstrating that they produce Muslim "others" or represent only a small portion of the multiple interpretations of sharia held by Muslims. Such a task is not difficult in this case. However, it would be more illuminating to direct our anthropological description and analysis on the cultural creativity and knowledge these discourses entail and the ways they articulate with broader sociopolitical processes. Social actors' cultural complexity is routinely elided, given contemporary theoretical conventions, in the haste to provide "thick descriptions" (Geertz 1973) and examine power relations (Foucault 1994). These are definitely important aspects of social and cultural life to explicate; however, a more rigorous description of the cultural knowledge embodied in these discourses will add greater clarity to the subsequent analyses of symbolic action, ideology, and hegemony. For instance, reviewing the discourses about sharia sketched above, we can recognize the need to further explore the conservative think tanks' and ICNA's conceptions of pluralism, secularism, and global politics. Moreover, the manner in which these notions are intertwined with divergent constructions of the "American nation" and "religious freedom" require further examination. Such contrasting perspectives are reflected in their divergent conceptions of sharia. A sustained description of cultural knowledge will shed greater light on symbolic meanings and power relations.

This is the form of study I intend here in examining multiple spoken and written discourses and practices—data collected over the course of ethnographic fieldwork—pertaining to sharia in Malaysian society and inferring cultural complexity and knowledge. My aim is twofold: first, to describe and analyze various conceptions of sharia distributed among Muslims and non-Muslims in Malaysian society and the manner in which these notions articulate with various other forms of cultural knowledge; and second, to discern the ways these discourses and related knowledge and practices are enmeshed in broader sociopolitical processes. This study advances a new approach to the anthropology of Islam.

SHARIA WITHIN THE ANTHROPOLOGY OF ISLAM

The anthropology of Islam, a subfield of the anthropology of religion, has been the venue for opposing approaches that draw an overly sharp dichotomy between "discursive tradition" and "multiple interpretive frameworks." While sharing the disciplinary-wide commitment to relativistic, holistic, and comparative perspectives, anthropologists of Islam have debated how to understand, represent, and study Islam.[1] One approach posits that researchers should study the ideas, feelings, practices, interpretations, and discourses of Muslims as they produce particular *islams*. According to this view, there is no single "real" or "essentialist" Islam based on religious texts, Islamic history, and the practices of exemplary individuals, and therefore theological stances based on these sources should only be considered to the extent they enter into the interpretations and practices of Muslims being studied. Here, "Islam" is considered a "word that identifies varying relations of practice, representation, symbol, concept, and worldview" (Gilsenan 1982, 19) or a "map of discourses on how to 'feel Muslim'" (Marranci 2008, 8). Gabriele Marranci goes so far as to state that "the Qur'an, the hadith, and the arkāna al-islam [pillars of Islam] would remain mute and without meaning if there were no minds, emotions and feelings informing them and making them unique through the individual professing himself Muslim" (29). Thus, this approach underscores the diverse kinds of Islam produced and embodied by various social forces and strata in society (Gilsenan 1982; Marranci 2008).

On the other hand, a major contending approach posits that Islam is a "discursive tradition that includes and relates itself to the founding texts of the Qur'an and the *hadith*" (Asad 1986, 104). This heterogeneous "tradition" has a past that articulates with present conditions, practices, and institutions and teaches Muslims the purposes and proper performance of practices (ibid.; Mahmood 2005; Deeb 2006; Hirschkind 2006). According to Talal Asad, the proper place to begin an anthropological study of Islam is to focus on an "instituted practice into which Muslims are inducted *as* Muslims." People with varying degrees of training and expertise may instruct others in these instituted practices. What is important from this perspective is not the level of the instructor's knowledge, but rather the fact that the practice is "authorized by the discursive traditions of Islam" (Asad 1986, 105). In addition, this approach emphasizes the importance of studying the reasoning and argumentation within the tradition and the connection of particular "orthodox" interpretations with contexts of power relations (ibid.; Mahmood 2005, 116; Grewal 2014, 77). Moreover, Asad argues that the anthropologist of Islam should be concerned with the roles Muslims *and* non-Muslims play in these dynamic processes of power.

I sympathize with both Asad's and Mahmood's effort to focus on contemporary articulations with an Islamic "discursive tradition," and with Michael Gilsenan's and Gabriele Marranci's concern with avoiding essentialism and not designating one particular form of Islam as the "real" or "authentic Islam." This study can be viewed as an attempt to synthesize aspects of both of these perspectives into a new approach to the anthropology of Islam (see also Daniels 2017, 1–27). There are four ways the "discursive tradition" and "multiple interpreted/embodied Islams" contention can be viewed in a new light. First, instead of viewing Islamic texts as mute and meaningless without human interpreters, it would be useful to note that these texts are embodied with knowledge from which particular Muslims and collectivities construct diverse mental representations or cultural models. Semantic study of ethical concepts demonstrates there was a shift in the underlying knowledge associated with key Arabic terms used in the Qur'an (Izutsu 1966). Many of the terms of pre-Islamic Arabic were given new meanings that reflected the transformed monotheistic worldview of the emergent Islamic tradition. The knowledge embedded in the Qur'an and sayings and practices of Prophet Muhammad and in other related texts is *tradition* and *real Islam*, as are the diverse cultural models and embodied practices of contemporary Muslims that stem from knowledge rooted in foundational texts. Rather than attempting to propose a definition of the full range of meanings of human and historical Islam, I use an operational conceptualization of Islam as knowledge implanted in foundational texts, and as varied cultural models and other forms of mental representations and embodied practices that Muslims produce and perform by drawing on knowledge from these texts (cf. Shahab Ahmed 2016). Treating Islamic texts as meaningful in and of themselves, and as an integral part of studying religion in practice, is in accordance with the relativistic perspective that directs anthropologists to try to understand beliefs and practices from local perspectives (Bowen 2014, 8). In contrast to practitioners of some other religious traditions, Muslims generally emphasize religious texts as part of their religion. Moreover, it has been a long-standing characteristic of anthropological theory, including structural functionalism, historical particularism, and structuralism, to consider religious texts as a significant aspect of the study of religion.[2] Recognizing that the Qur'an, *hadith*, and related textual sources embody knowledge is especially relevant to the study of sharia, because Muslims directly or indirectly look to these sources as a basis for their understandings of divine directives. However, studies of other topics, such as Saba Mahmood's of the women's mosque movement in Egypt or Lara Deeb's of the Shi'i piety movement in Lebanon, also demonstrate the productivity of such a tack.

Second, Muslims, drawing on knowledge embedded in religious texts, form diverse mental representations, cultural models, and embodied practices, producing a variety of local Islams. These local versions of Islamic concepts and practices connect, combine, and interpenetrate with other ideas and behavior in local social contexts. Thus, discourses connected to interpretations of foundational texts and exemplary practices, articulate with other discourses and ideas, such as secular, liberal, pluralist, and neoliberal capitalist notions, in a variety of ways. There are multiple Islamic mental representations and combinations within any one society, and these are constructed, reproduced, and transformed through socialization processes. From an anthropological, analytic perspective none of these local varieties of Islam is any more real or truly Islamic than any other. Thus, I try to abstain from prescriptive assertions about how Muslims should conceptualize human and historical Islam (cf. Ahmed 2016, 303). However, we should not be surprised that proponents of particular varieties deem their version to be more Islamic or correct than others. These facts should be an integral part of our analysis.[3] In this study of sharia in Malaysia, diverse conceptions of sharia coalesce and enmesh with other cultural models, such as those pertaining to race, gender, nation, and human rights. Proponents of some of these varieties have considered others to be secular, extremist, less truly Islamic, or even, at times, infidel. Unlike some foreign scholars, I have tried to remain outside the fray of these contentious castigations, and to look instead to the role such denigrating evaluations play in sociopolitical dynamics.

Third, as both perspectives have underscored the importance of power, a new anthropology of Islam must strive to refine the ways we examine the linkage of instituted practices and local Islamic ideologies to power structures and relations. It is vital to examine Muslim and non-Muslim participation in sociopolitical dynamics within Muslim-majority and non-Muslim-majority societies. Contemporary social theories of power have made major contributions to the way we view systems of domination and hegemony, modes of governing, and agency.[4] These theories invite us to examine coercive and discursive means of influencing and governing the actions of others in society as well as agency or the "socioculturally mediated capacity to act" (Ahearn 2012, 278). Furthermore, it is important for anthropologists of Islam to explicate power relations on local, national, and global levels. In this study, I consider the UMNO-led federal government's attempts to convince Malaysians of the correctness of its manner of instituting sharia regulations, as well as the criticism and resistance from those that favor a fuller implementation of sharia laws and those, Muslims and non-Muslims, that favor an elimination of some sharia laws. I also consider the flow of influential concepts of secularism, liberal pluralism, neoliberalism, human rights, and gender equality into Malaysian society. Moreover, I try to sketch some of the ways Malaysians, as active agents, negotiate sharia in their everyday lives.

Fourth, ethnographic methods, advocated by proponents of both perspectives, should be diligently used to collect data investigating each of the three areas discussed above: diverse articulations with knowledge embedded in Islamic texts; multiple models and embodied local Islams and the manner in which they coalesce with other forms of cultural knowledge and practice; and their connections to power structures and relations. After sharply criticizing several ethnographically deficient scholars of Islam, Daniel Varisco (2005, 16) argues that our search "for the idea of an anthropology of Islam should not lead us beyond ideology and theology but rather probe these very powerful discursive traditions through thick description of ethnographic contexts." Indeed, the ethnographic study of Muslims and non-Muslims pertaining to discourses, representations, and practices of Islam is the very heart of our subfield. Conducting fieldwork in which we participate in and observe events and engage local people in discussions about aspects of Islam and various interrelated topics is the source of our major contribution as anthropologists to the study of Islam. Whether we begin by studying the knowledge embedded in the "discursive tradition" or the mental representations of religious experts or less-tutored Muslims, what is most important is that we do either or both in ethnographic contexts (cf. Asad 1986, 104; Marranci 2008, 42). Flexibility and adaptability is essential when using ethnographic methods. If our interlocutors are Muslim participants in a mosque movement and we are observing religious talks referring to Qur'an, *hadith*, and various scholarly commentaries, we would do well to begin to familiarize ourselves with these texts. On the other hand, if our interlocutors are Muslim seekers of healing at a shaman's house, Muslim nightclub enthusiasts, or Muslim activists in secular nationalist political parties, we should begin with their activities and discourses. In this study I have done some of both. I found it useful to reference religious texts as I tried to more deeply understand the religious talks I attended in the mosques; whereas, when I spent time socializing with less-tutored and less-observant Muslims, I began with their ideas and feelings about sharia in society. I was reminded that religious knowledge is distributed unevenly and that Muslims and non-Muslims are diverse and positioned in a variety of ways in society. Moving from data collected and notes written in the field to ethnographic interpretations is a complex process involving micro description and analysis informed by a broader theoretical perspective.

ANTHROPOLOGY OF KNOWLEDGE AND SHARIA

The symbolic and cognitive approaches are the two major anthropological frameworks for the description and analysis of micro details of human behavior and cultural creativity. Clifford Geertz (1973), a pioneer of symbolic anthropology, argued that culture is a public system of symbols and that the main task of anthropologists is to provide a "thick description" or intuitive interpretation of the meanings of symbolic action. In his perspective, symbols are vehicles for conceptions that are outside the boundaries of individuals and located in the "intersubjective world of understandings into which all individuals are born" (92). Symbolic action is "ideational" only in the sense that the meanings of symbols are concepts, but not in any way requiring individual minds that internalize or reproduce them. In fact, Geertz (10–13) severely criticized the ideas of Ward Goodenough and Stephen Tyler, two cognitive anthropologists of the time, claiming that the cognitive perspective confuses the knowledge of how to perform symbolic acts with their actual performance, and further that it commits a "cognitive fallacy" in positing that culture consists of formally analyzable mental phenomena. Moreover, he questioned cognitive anthropological attempts at representing what local people think, suggesting that inferred knowledge structures are only "clever simulations" that are substantively different from what people actually think (11). These charges against cognitive anthropology, regardless of their inaccuracy, have had a lasting impact.

Cognitive anthropologists strive to understand patterns of behavior through inferring mental representations, or knowledge structures, such as taxonomies, scripts, models, schemas, and theories, and psychological processes from social action and discourse. In the cognitive perspective, knowledge structures and cultural logic are public *and* private, distributed in society and internalized in individual minds. Rather than emphasizing intuitive interpretations that aim to render human behavior intelligible, cognitive anthropologists have stressed rigorous data collection and analysis aiming at explanations of behavioral regularities. There has been a strong awareness among cognitive anthropologists that their representations of human thought are just that—representations—and not reflections of actual thought. Roy D'Andrade (1995, 157–58), a prominent cognitive anthropologist, notes that there is "no effective alternative" to cognitive and symbolic anthropologists inferring cultural models from observable forms of behavior, since mental representations do not appear as physical entities in the world. In addition to relying on observable facts, some cognitive anthropologists try to refine their postulated models through eliciting responses about them from local interlocutors and testing them in practice. Cognitive anthropologists have, in turn, criticized symbolic anthropologists for lacking a theory of the mind, inaccurate descriptions of symbolism, and proposing a nonpsychological anthropology while presupposing psychological claims in "describing cultural realities which to a certain extent are acquired, memorized, modified, represented and misrepresented by the actors themselves" (Boyer 1993, 12). Nevertheless, it was the symbolic anthropologists' criticism of the cognitive subdiscipline that stuck and had staying power. Cognitive anthropology became marginalized from the 1980s onward, as symbolic anthropology became a core paradigm, flawed though it may be, of cultural anthropologists—including those studying Islam.

Several cultural anthropologists have argued for a convergence of symbolic and cognitive approaches in order to produce a more powerful social science.[5] Benjamin Colby, James Fernandez, and David Kronenberg (1981), pointing out the strengths and weaknesses of each of these subdisciplines, tried to project the way forward for a substantive merging of them, thereby forming a more rigorous and contextual approach. In their afterword to two special issues of the *American Ethnologist* on symbolism and cognition, Janet Dougherty and Fernandez (1982, 820) noted that "no total synthesis" emerged in any of the papers, but that there was a "convergence" in the sense of several "emergent foci of inquiry." My detailed ethnographic study (Daniels 2009) of Islamic diversity in Java went a long way toward synthesizing these approaches. Nevertheless, there is little interest in contemporary anthropology for incorporating the strengths of the cognitive perspective into social theory. Mainstream cultural anthropology has combined the symbolic or interpretative approach with the new focus on practice and the ambiguities of power. Anthropologists of Islam, including those working on Islam in Malaysia, have followed this post-structuralist trend in anthropology.[6]

There are three major negative repercussions of integrating a defective symbolic/interpretative approach with post-structuralist foci of inquiry in studies of Islam in Malaysia and beyond. First, many researchers continue to describe Islamic symbols and concepts as if they were the same as signs such as words or lexical items with particular referents. For instance, some researchers conflate the signs and symbols of Islamic revival in Malaysian society. While the words *tudung* (headscarf), *kopiah* (skullcap), and *janggut* (beard) are linguistic signs or signifiers with particular meanings, these articles of clothing and forms of bodily appearance are symbols that *evoke* potentially unlimited meanings. Similarly, the word *flag* has a definite dictionary meaning, but the familiar American red, white, and blue flag is a symbol that evokes many, and at times contradictory, meanings. The popular, Geertzian-style approach treats symbols as if they were linguistic signs, eliding the polysemy or multiple meanings of symbols in favor of singular, conventional meanings. Likewise, many researchers describe performance of rituals and complex religious concepts as if they were linguistic signs or icons with a definite referent.

Second, intuitive interpretations researchers make based on these faulty descriptions of symbols and concepts tend to overestimate consensus and downplay variation. Thus, Malays are assumed to share meanings for headscarves, skullcaps, beards, and acts of worship that are associated with Malay or Muslim identity. Malays also are interpreted to share a conceptual framework that conceives of Islamic narratives, greetings, and practices as icons. However, meanings of these symbols and Islamic conceptual frameworks are diverse and vary across society and even over the course of the life of an individual, as they become part of different social networks and change in their subjectivities. In addition, other levels of hermeneutic interpretations built on these bases are unreliable, such as Hoffstaedter's intuitive spin that elite Malays are committing "politicide" on lower-class Malays by promoting exclusionary Malay and Muslim identities (2011, 219).[7]

Third, many researchers, striving to situate their studies within the macro perspective or broader sociopolitical processes and power relations, produce interpretations based on linking these defective descriptions of symbolic meanings, concepts, and/or embodied practices to particular projects or organized social usage of knowledge. Such presumed linkages are also misleading or, even worse, mistaken. One common faux pas in this regard is the assumption that the state's projects are more dominant or powerful than the data indicate. For instance, Fischer (2008), disregarding his own ethnographic reporting that *dakwah* groups' discourses are influential among many of his interlocutors, concludes that the Malaysian state's "nationalization of Islam" and control of *halal* certification exert control over the everyday lives of Malay Muslims, who are depicted as "shopping for the state." A related error is to tacitly or explicitly treat one project, usually the state's, as the only project. This often stems directly from the presumption of a shared public code and totalizing state hegemony. For instance, Peletz (2002, 278) argued, "the Islamic courts in Malaysia, and local institutions of Islam as a whole, have encouraged a certain type of modernity and civil society that is characteristically Asian and distinctively Malaysian." Moreover, he argues that the prevalence of *sulh* (M. *suluh*; mediation) and *nusyuz* (disobedience) in sharia courts is "an entailment of bureaucratic rationality" within the Malaysian state's modernity project (Peletz 2013, 624). My study demonstrates that many of the government religious scholars, officials, and civil servants operate with ideas and visions that contrast with those of Malay political elites. The UMNO political leaders' approach to sharia and modernity is one of several projects that, even if they are not analyzed fully in any particular study, should at least be acknowledged. Furthermore, analysis of the dynamic interplay between these various projects, under the auspices of state and non-state actors, is vital to understanding broader sociopolitical processes at work in Malaysia.

I strive to resolve these problems by adopting a revised anthropology of knowledge approach that incorporates the intuitive, contextual-based, and translation-oriented strengths of the symbolic/interpretative perspective, and connecting it with social theories of power. Within an anthropology of knowledge, "we envision human agents with the cognitive capacities and predispositions that constitute the common architecture of the mind. Using these abilities, actors construct mental models from experience. These models in turn facilitate and are potentially modified in future activities. The human cognitive architecture simultaneously constrains and provides the potential for knowledge representation. Yet specific representational structures are derived from and applied in the everyday contexts of human behavior" (Keller and Keller 1996, 171). From this theoretical perspective, I consider symbols evocative rather than semiotic (Sperber 1974; Lehman 1997). Rather than signifying specific meanings, like the word *headscarf*, symbolical materials—flags, headscarves, beards, ritual objects and actions— trigger associations that remind people of other concepts. Lehman (1997) distinguishes two broad kinds of symbols: ones that "stand for" something specific, thereby holding conventional meaning, through evoking many encyclopedic lines of association, and ones that do not "stand for" any particular referent at all or hold conventional meaning, although some of the wide variety of referents evoked may share some features. This helps differentiate between arbitrary linguistic signs and open-ended symbols with conventional meanings based on the distinct ways they are associated with referents. Likewise, instead of reducing concepts to signs and icons, I will seek to discern and represent various forms of cultural knowledge associated and interconnected with relevant concepts. Complex religious concepts often constitute or are embedded within culturally particular theories of a domain (Keller and Lehman 1991). In this study of sharia in Malaysia, I attempt to infer and explicate cultural models from written and spoken discourse.

Such a description and analysis of symbolical and conceptual representations informs interpretations about the distribution and flow of knowledge in society. Attention to micro-descriptive details of discourse collected across many segments of society allows interpretation of the variation and social placement of ideas about sharia—those in favor and opposed to varying degrees to the implementation of sharia family and criminal laws. Further interpretations can be made about the interplay between social actors, socially distributed cultural models, and sociopolitical contexts. Subsequently, these interpretations facilitate movement to even broader levels of analysis, including the ways these forms of knowledge articulate with structures of power and power relations, drawing on some of Antonio Gramsci's and Michel Foucault's ideas about power. Here, I attempt to describe and evaluate the social struggles for influence and hegemony over whose ideas about, and projects pertaining to, sharia and interconnected issues will hold sway. The interpretation that certain discourses of sharia may hold greater or lesser influence informs more extensive interpretations about agency and subject formation, sociopolitical dynamics, and the interplay of projects. Thus, haphazard intuitive interpretations are avoided by aiming to situate each level of interpretation on sound description and analysis.

Finally, I situate my treatment of "discourse" and "practice" within this revised anthropology of knowledge. Foucault and Bourdieu, two influential social theorists, have proposed overly broad conceptions of "discourse" and "practice." In Foucault's theory, "discourses" are frameworks that organize and produce talk, writing, thought, understanding, and conduct. They define and construct ways for talking and thinking about topics, such as sharia, and influence "how ideas are put into practice and used to regulate the conduct of others" (Hall 2001, 72). Similarly, in Bourdieu's theory of practice, he uses *habitus* to refer to "predispositions that produce practices and representations conditioned by the structures from which they emerge" (Ahearn 2012, 23). Foucault (1972) collapses talk, thought, and understanding into "discourses," and Bourdieu (1977) does the same with practice and thought in *habitus*. They thereby suggest overly broad and blunt tools of social analysis, when sharper and finer ones are needed. I use the term *discourse* to refer to "all the varieties of talk and text," including the "invitations and clues, the silences, [and] the inferences that the literal content of a text or an utterance invites" (Hill 2008, 32–33). From an analysis of spoken and written discourse, I infer diverse and socially distributed cultural models. Likewise, I treat "practice" as observable behaviors, performed in social contexts, that "emerge from the mental, material, and social structures in which they are situated and, in turn, reproduce or lead to transformations of those structures" (Keller and Keller 1996, 16). Rather than collapsing thought into practice, I consider practice, including cultivated techniques of the body, to be embodied with knowledge (Mauss 1973; cf. Asad 1993, 2003). Furthermore, I conceive of *knowledge* and *practice* within a dynamic perspective that recognizes that "ideas acquired through prior experiences are at risk as subsequent experiences unfold and practices are at risk in reflected thought" (Keller and Keller 1996, 205). That is, changes in mental representations and knowledge structures can emerge in practices and changes in practices can arise through interpretation and reasoning.

METHODS

I returned to a society where I have been working on field projects as an anthropologist for the last seventeen years to study how Malaysians think and talk about, and practice, sharia. My initial fieldwork experience in Malaysia covered 1998–2000, during which time I lived in Malaysia, primarily Melaka, for twenty months. Ever since, I have continued to visit Malaysia, staying for shorter periods, ranging from one to five months. I have lived in the various states of East and West Malaysia for three and a half years. For this book, I draw on experiences and data collected over the course of this time in Malaysia; however, most of the data on which this text is based were collected during eleven months of ethnographic fieldwork conducted from August 2010 to August 2012.

This is a multisited and reflexive ethnographic study. I lived among and participated in some social activities and observed many others during this period of fieldwork in several states of Malaysia, including Penang, Kedah, Kelantan, Selangor, Melaka, and Negeri Sembilan. I observed, interacted with, and engaged in discussions with Malaysian Muslims and non-Muslims from various "racial" backgrounds in restaurants, food stalls, homes, offices, mosques (*masjids*), sharia courts, and venues of public transportation. During the six months of research funded by the Wenner-Gren Foundation, spanning from August 2010 to January 2011, I was based in Penang, Kedah, Kelantan, and Kuala Lumpur; whereas during the summers of 2011 and 2012 I traveled to Melaka and Negeri Sembilan and other places in Selangor from a base in Greater Kuala Lumpur. At the time, as a result of the landmark twelfth Malaysian general election, Penang, Kedah, Kelantan, and Selangor were under the administration of opposition parties, and Melaka and Negeri Sembilan remained under the control of the UMNO/BN, the ruling federal coalition. In these multiple sites, I negotiated, developed, and strove to maintain relationships with my interlocutors. Some of them became friends with whom I continue relations, and many others were helpful respondents who kindly shared their views and experiences with me. This book has emerged from a wide range of complex, intersubjective processes, especially those involving my relations with actors and interlocutors in Malaysian society and my interpretations, at times coproduced in collaboration with Malaysians, of various forms of data. The description, analysis, and stories constituting this ethnography are representations of sharia in Malaysia. Moreover, I am present throughout this text as a positioned observer, participant, reporter, analyst, and storyteller.

In order to begin to ascertain how various conceptions of sharia are distributed among Muslims and non-Muslims in Malaysian society and how they articulate with other forms of cultural knowledge, I visited several organizations and institutions and interviewed members and officials. I conducted these open-ended, semi-structured interviews, in Malay and English, with representatives of Islamic and secular, nongovernmental organizations; members and supporters of the Islamic Party of Malaysia and the United Malays National Organization; students and teachers at Sufi brotherhoods (*tarekat*); and mosque officials. Since I have high proficiency in Malay, I gave my interlocutors the choice or followed their leads in speaking in Malay or English. Many of my Malay contacts felt more confident responding to questions in Malay or otherwise preferred communicating in Malay. Some Indian and Chinese contacts also preferred speaking with me in Malay while others gravitated toward English. I present direct quotes from spoken and written discourse in English and my translations of discourse in

Malay. Through these interviews I became aware of the range of pro- and contra-sharia positions pertaining to the implementation of sharia in Malaysian society.

I also interviewed and engaged in discussions with sharia court officials—chief justices, judges, lawyers, and administrators—and government civil servants in the Department of Islamic Development Malaysia (JAKIM; Jabatan Kemajuan Islam Malaysia) and scholars in the Institute of Islamic Understanding Malaysia (IKIM; Institut Kefahaman Islam Malaysia), a government think tank in the Prime Minister's Department. These dialogues provided me with important information about the government's pro-sharia posture and the logic of court officials overseeing the implementation of sharia in Malaysia. I also collected copies of the sharia enactments, banking acts, family and criminal law cases, law journals, and scholarly articles as sources of information on the details of sharia regulations and as additional evidence of the reasoning styles of sharia court judges as they implement sharia.

There are potentially contrasting ideas about sharia distributed across the axes of gender, age, and rural/urban locality. In order to gauge this dimension of cultural diversity, I conducted a structured survey, in Malay and English, with Malaysian Muslims that elicited their ideas about the implementation of sharia—for instance, whether they thought the current laws needed to strengthened or weakened. Some of these short surveys later turned into longer, semi-structured interviews and life histories focusing on the shifting role of sharia in participants' everyday lives.

Throughout the main period of research for this fieldwork project, I collected "naturally occurring" language data—that is, discourse I did not elicit but which occurred over the course of speech and literacy events within various social contexts. I recorded Friday prayer sermons (*khutbah*), religious talks in mosques (*kuliah masjid*), and political speeches. In addition, I gathered written discourse in bulletins, newsletters, newspapers, human rights reports, books, and magazines. Unlike the interview data—in which I tried to prompt my interlocutors to express their views and frameworks for interpretation, thereby utilizing their models (D'Andrade 2005, 90)— these spoken and written discourses are integral to ongoing sociopolitical processes in which the speakers and authors have different aims and audiences. Both of these forms of data are important. Although these discourses are situated in the dynamic processes and are essential to my interpretations of the roles sharia discourses play in the broader sociopolitical dynamics in Malaysian society, they may contain gaps and silences and thereby do not express certain ideas openly. Interviews can be used to elicit more direct expression of these ideas. Therefore, I tried to use my semi-structured and open-ended discussions as sources to complement situated speech and literacy events.

I subject these forms of data—interviews, speech events, literacy events, and observations—to discourse and context analysis. I adopt the approach of many cognitive and linguistic anthropologists who use various linguistic cues to infer underlying cultural knowledge.[8] Examining interview data and other discourse events, I construct representations of cultural models or schemas that embed, and are combined with, other knowledge and shared, negotiated, and contested across and within social groups (cf. D'Andrade 1989, 809).[9] Similarly, I build representations of the reasoning style of sharia court officials from subjecting interview data and written court records to discourse analysis, inferring patterns of cultural logic from these forms of data. As noted above, in this redrawn anthropology of knowledge it is important to not only produce rigorous descriptions and analysis of conceptual phenomena, but also to build insightful and well-founded interpretations of the immediate and broader contexts. While the contextual component of analysis has recently been recognized and emphasized by cognitive anthropologists (Keller and Keller 1996), concentrating on contextual phenomena has in the past been stronger among symbolic/interpretative anthropologists. Moving to produce a more unified and potent anthropology of knowledge, I pay careful attention to the particular social contexts as well as the broader national and global contexts pertinent to discourses and practices of sharia in Malaysia.

1 SHARIA IN MALAYSIA

The Historical Background

SHARIA HAS GONE THROUGH MANY TWISTS AND TURNS OVER THE
course of Malay history. Muslim merchants, traders, and mystics brought
Islam to Island Southeast Asia at least as early as the thirteenth century.
They sailed along the monsoon winds that delivered Hinduism and Buddhism throughout much of the region during preceding centuries. Islam
took root in the coastal maritime kingdoms joining Hinduism, Buddhism,
and other beliefs and customs in local cultural tapestries. These Islamic
kingdoms, part of political and economic networks in China, India, Persia,
and Arabia, spread Islam to their subjects and throughout the region. During the era of European expansion and colonization, this process was disrupted in some respects and spurred on in others. Eventually, Island Southeast
Asia was divided between areas under British, Dutch, and Spanish control. The
Malay Peninsula and Singapore—an island at its southern tip—and Brunei,
Sabah, and Sarawak—territories on the island of Borneo (Kalimantan)—fell
under British colonial administration (see map on following page). Malaya,
later Malaysia, attained a negotiated political independence in 1957; and
in 1963 Singapore and the two Borneo states of Sabah and Sarawak joined
the federation, but Singapore seceded from it in 1965. Brunei refused to join
the Federation of Malaysia and regained independence in 1984. Postcolonial
Malaysia appeared in a modern world characterized by nation-states and
the dominance of global capitalism. The new nation-state was confronted
with the challenges of constructing a sense of nationality for its diverse population and coping with the transformations of urbanization and globalization. Conceptions of sharia connected and combined with a variety of other
notions during these precolonial, colonial, and postcolonial eras.

Sharīʿa is an Arabic term referring to "the revealed law of Islam" and "the
right Way of Religion" (Wehr [1960] 1979, 544; Abdullah Yusuf 1992, 1536).
Muslim scholars and everyday Muslims interact with revealed knowledge,
making a variety of interpretations about what are the divine rules and
proper prescriptions for conduct. By the time Islam reached the shores of

PHILIPPINES

Sulu Sea

Celebes Sea

SABAH

Kota Kinabalu ⊙

LABUAN ✱
Victoria •

BRUNEI

Miri •

SARAWAK

Borneo

Sibu •

Kuching ⊙

INDONESIA

National capital ✱
State capital ⊙
City •

International boundary ─ ∙ ─
State boundary ─ ∙ ∙ ─
Federal territory ✱

N

0   100   200 Miles
0   100   200 Kilometers

CAMBODIA

VIETNAM

South China Sea

M A L A Y S I A

Natuna Besar

Kepulauan Natuna

INDONESIA

Kepulauan Anambas

Kepulauan Lingga

THAILAND

Gulf of Thailand

PERLIS

Kangar ⊙
Alor Setar ⊙
KEDAH

Butterworth
George Town ⊙
PULAU PINANG

Ipoh ⊙
PERAK

Teluk Intan •

Kota Bharu ⊙
KELANTAN

Kuala Terengganu ⊙
TERENGGANU

Kuantan ⊙
PAHANG

Kuala Lumpur ★
Shah Alam ⊙
SELANGOR
Kelang •
WILAYAH PERSEKUTUAN ✱

Seremban ⊙
NEGERI SEMBILAN

Muar •
MELAKA

JOHOR

Johor Bahru ⊙

★ Singapore
SINGAPORE

Kepulauan Riau

INDONESIA

Strait of Malacca

Island Southeast Asia, Muslim scholars had already consolidated the four main schools of jurisprudence (*fiqh*) in Sunni Islam. The Shāfi'ī school came to predominate in Malaysia, as it did in Indonesia, Lower Egypt, Hijaz, South Arabia, East Africa, and coastal parts of India (Riddell 2001, 55). Southeast Asian Muslims localized ideas about sharia, including them within cultural models used to interpret and shape behavior in various domains of life.

Furthermore, this history is not divorced from the dynamics of sharia and other sociopolitical projects in contemporary Malaysian society. Across the diverse ethnic and religious tapestry of Malaysia, people negotiate the meanings of Malaysian history, imagining and framing it within their ideological perspectives. Although their discourses are, in many instances, about ethnicity, race, gender, or nationality, sharia and the place and character of Islam in society figure prominently within them. Both the broad contours of the history of sharia and the voices of Malaysians inform this narrative.

ISLAMIC KINGDOMS, SYNCRETISM, AND LOCAL CUSTOMS

Hindu, Buddhist, and Hindu-Buddhist kingdoms arose and fell ruling over the largely agricultural populations of tropical Island Southeast Asia for several centuries prior to the arrival of Islam. These kingdoms, often located in lowland and coastal environments, were centers for trade and cosmopolitan populations. Upland cultivators of the mountain ranges that zigzag across the region and foragers of the tropical rainforests also exchanged their produce, which then entered trade circuits extending overseas. Variants of Hinduism and Buddhism, including Saivite and Tantric forms, blended with local beliefs and practices influencing cosmologies, rituals, literature, art, and forms of statecraft. From the thirteenth through the fifteenth centuries, these kingdoms were gradually overtaken and replaced by Islamic kingdoms or sultanates. Pasai, Perlak, and Aceh appeared in northern Sumatra and Melaka on the other side of the straits, an important node for trade through the region. Kelantan, Terengganu, and Pahang rose in the east, and Kedah, Perak, and Johor in other parts of the Malay Peninsula.

The diffusion and localization of variants of Islam added another dimension to the complex mixtures of beliefs and practices. Sharia and legalistic varieties of Islam flowed in with mystical and ascetic varieties as well as other fields of Islamic knowledge. Many of the Sufi brotherhoods found in other Muslim societies took root in the fertile, mystic-oriented soil of the Malayo-Indonesian world. As in the Middle East and South and Central Asia, conceptions of sharia and *taṣawwuf* (Sufism) fluctuated between relations of tension and harmony. Some Sufi scholars claimed that sharia was a lower stage in the spiritual path that could be disregarded once one reached the higher stages, while others asserted that sharia and mystical pursuits must go hand and hand for practitioners to experience the sweet taste of deep conviction and closeness to Allah.[1] Royal elites also synthesized Hindu, Buddhist, and Islamic forms of statecraft, presenting themselves as spiritually elevated or sacerdotal figures with special natures, abilities, and relationships with divinity. Islamic and Hindu forms of mysticism became intimately intertwined in a broad range of syncretism. In some cases Hindu and Buddhist elements persisted or were only partially "Islamized," and in others they were more fully incorporated into an Islamic worldview.[2] Sharia-oriented scholars and believers were persistent catalysts for altering local cultures as they strove to bring them more in accord with their models of revealed knowledge.

In addition to Hinduism, Buddhism, local religious traditions, and Sufi mystical ideas, conceptions of sharia came into close association with local customary law and principles (*adat*) for social life. Unlike the Middle East and South Asia, kinship in Island Southeast Asia was primarily organized according to bilateral or matrilineal principles. In the Malay world, these organizational principles came to be known as *adat temenggong* and *adat perpatih*. *Adat temenggong* organized society according to territorial units under the authority of the ruler, prime minister, chief of police, ministers, and governors. *Temenggong* laws covered constitutional, criminal, civil, and maritime laws, and in cases of criminal law they prescribed the death penalty or lesser penalties based on principles of compensatory justice (Mackeen 1969, 111–14). According to the generally unwritten constitutions, the territorial chiefs possessed the most effective power over their districts and checked the authority of the raja and his central government (Harding 1996, 7–9). On the other hand, *adat perpatih* organized society into matrilineal clans that constituted territorial units or districts of the state. Legal authority rested in matrilineal-based units from the heads of subclans, clan and territorial chiefs, and ultimately the ruler. Unwritten *perpatih* laws contained within customary aphorisms covered all aspects of law and tended to lean toward principles of restitution and compensation more than the retribution-oriented *temenggong* laws. The four constitutional heads of states in eighteenth-century Negeri Sembilan elected and assisted the ruler (10). *Adat perpatih* extended over West Sumatra (Minangkabau) and Negeri Sembilan and parts of contemporary Melaka but also influenced the laws of other precolonial Islamic kingdoms, while all the other states stressed *adat temenggong* intertwined with Hindu customs. *Adat* also covered many other areas of social life such as ceremonies, rituals, and healing practices. Sharia gradually merged with both of these customary patterns as Islamic states established legal codes.

The legal codes of several Islamic kingdoms, such as the Melaka Digest of 1523, the Pahang Digest of 1596, the Kedah Digest of 1606, and the Johor Digest of 1789, indicate the influence of Islamic law (Abdullah Alwi 1996, xlvii). A substantial part of these digests reproduced rules of Islamic jurisprudence and reflected sophisticated knowledge of the standard texts of the Shāfiʿī school (Hooker 1983, 161–62). Malay states, to varying degrees, applied sharia in family laws, land laws, law of sales, criminal law, and maritime laws (Abdul Samat 2003, 96; Abdullah Alwi 1996; Yusoff 1977–78). The laws of Melaka were also strongly influenced by Indic Hindu-Buddhist ideas and customary principles in many of these areas. For instance, the inclusion of laws for forced marriage (*kahwin paksa*)[3] and discrimination in criminal punishment for low- and high-ranking strata (castes) in the Melaka code are reminiscent of Indic Hindu-Buddhist notions (Yusoff 1977–78). However, family laws, laws for religious worship (Ar. *ʿibādāh*, M. *ibadah*), and several areas of criminal law, such as adultery, fornication, and theft, demonstrated the application of sharia (ibid.). Severe *hudud* (penalties set by the Qurʾan and *hadith*) punishments for some crimes were implemented by several Malay states. In Terengganu, Kelantan, Kedah, and Perlis, Islamic law was more firmly entrenched and adhered to, but still combined with local customary principles. By the middle to late nineteenth century, Terengganu and Kelantan implemented criminal law enactments that were "clearly Islamic and in conformity with the *hukum syarak* (Islamic law)" and only applied customary principles that did not conflict with the principles of sharia (Abdullah Alwi 1996, 5). In the early twentieth century, a translation of the Ottoman Al-Madjella (Turkish Islamic Civil Code) was adopted in Johor (Kamali 2000, 18; Abdul Samat 2003, 96).[4] According to the oft-quoted R. J. Wilkinson (1908, 49), a British observer, "There can be no doubt the Moslem law would have ended by becoming the law of Malaya had not the British law stepped in to check it." Although it is impossible to predict the course Islamic law would have taken, it is clear that the process of precolonial Malay states applying increasingly less customary and more Islamic laws over time was disrupted by the intrusion of British colonialism (Ahmad Ibrahim and Ahilemah 1987, 53; Kamali 2000, 17; Abdul Samat 2003, 97).

New constructions of Melayu (or Malay) identity began to take shape within the contexts of these maritime Islamic kingdoms. For some time,

Malay identity had been associated with indigenous participants in coastal trade empires, such as the Buddhist South Sumatran–based kingdom Sriwijaya, and with speakers of Malay language and practitioners of prestigious customs and mannerisms (Daniels 2005, 21–22). This prestigious culture and Malay identity spread among inland foragers, upland cultivators, and seagoing folks as they were incorporated into economic and political relationships with the cosmopolitan centers located downstream and on the coasts. The diverse residents of these coastal trade centers, such as Chinese, Indians, and Arabs, began to adopt many elements of the prestigious cultures of Malay elites. As Islamic kingdoms spread across the region and became active forces spreading the faith, Islam began to constitute an important component of Malay identity. Now, conceptions of sharia—disseminated by Muslim traders, missionaries, and Sufis, and institutionalized by rulers—came into intimate contact with constructions of Malay identity.

The history of precolonial Islamic kingdoms holds multiple meanings, as it is selectively filtered and framed within Malaysians' varying cultural models. Most Malaysian Muslims, operating with strong or moderate pro-sharia perspectives, underscore the significance of Malay sultans and states embracing Islam and implementing sharia. However, secular nationalist elites have formulated and promulgated a hegemonic discourse that connects the glorious history of Malay states, especially the Sultanate of Melaka, to the model of a harmonious Malaysian nation led by sovereign Malays with diverse groups of assimilating citizens. In my interview with Tan Sri Rahim Thamby Chik, chief minister of Melaka from 1982 to 1994, he describes how his state administration used an image of historical Melaka and multiculturalism to develop the state's tourist industry.[5] His discourse presented their selection of Melaka as the "mother history" of Malaysia and conveyed their project of embodying this representation in numerous museums (see Daniels 2005, 137–54):

> I decided to look at a different angle: what can be done . . . to boost up, rejuvenate [the] Melaka economy. Other than the very small industrialization that had taken place in Melaka at that time, I perceived that Melaka should be moving toward the development of tourism products. And being the oldest state in Malaysia and the capital of ancient Malaya or Malaysia at that time, we have a lot of historical culture . . . to be capitalized on as the tourism product for the state. . . . From there, we cooperated with some investors to look into the possibility of developing the tourism potential in Melaka . . . and created a lot of projects to restore the glory of Melaka, with

one slogan . . . "Melaka where it all began." Six hundred years of Malaysian history actually started in Melaka, and of course it is the mother history of Malaysia. . . . With that slogan, first of all we created museums. Our plan was to create 101 museums of all kinds . . . a state of museums.[6]

Here, Melaka is selected as the place where Malaysian history began. It was not with the other Islamic kingdoms across the peninsula or the pre-Islamic Malay states of the region where Rahim Thamby Chik and other UMNO ideologues sought to locate the origins of the Malaysian nation. Rather, it was a Malay Islamic kingdom with a diverse population, which can readily accommodate notions of Malay and Islamic supremacy/sovereignty residing at the pinnacle of a multicultural society. Rahim Thamby Chik described the way they invented, appropriated, and utilized material and immaterial urban resources as tourist products:

We explored deeply into tourism development because we have products that other states don't have—for example, the historical buildings and ruins in Melaka you can't find in other states in Malaysia. . . . One hundred years of the Melaka Malay Sultanate, . . . the Portuguese administration for a hundred years, the Dutch one hundred years, the British over one hundred years, the Japanese four years, the British [again] for a few years, and [then] we attain independence. It is a very glorious chronological history of Malaysia, through Melaka history, where you experience different kinds of colonialists. . . . Melaka became a real melting pot, a potpourri of multicultural, multireligious, and so forth. We have learned how to live together for six hundred years or more. We have become very tolerant, very moderate, and very wise. . . . This adds to our spirited heart to see that Melaka rise as one of the most successful tourism destinations in Malaysia, based on the historical and cultural products. . . . This gave us the opportunity to really contribute to the cultures of the Malays, Chinese, and Indians, together with the Portuguese, the Babas and Nyonyas and Chitties. The administrations of Ali Rustam and previous chief ministers have been able to consolidate and strengthen this position, and that has made Melaka, in terms of the development of tourism, . . . one of the most successful destinations in the country.

Malay political elites created "replicas" of places and objects, such as the Melaka sultan's palace and a Portuguese ship, and renovated and packaged old buildings and a fort embodying their narrative of a Malaysian history that began with the Melaka Sultanate, sailed through successive colonial eras, and culminated with political independence and the postcolonial nation-state. This historical imaginary, which erased the pre-Islamic Malay states, multiple Islamic kingdoms, and various colonial histories across the Malay Peninsula, featured "rejuvenated" ethnic groups that index the diversity of contemporary Malaysian society. Rahim Thamby Chik informs us that special attention was paid to the Melaka Portugis, Chitty, and Baba/Nyonya minorities who are conventionally thought to be hybrid categories of descendants of Portuguese, Indians, and Chinese that intermarried with local Malays. Malay officials use representations of these minority hybrid ethnicities together with larger Malay, Indian, and Chinese categories to construct a multicultural model of the Malaysian nation.

Datuk bandar (mayor) of Melaka Yusof bin Jantan, who was appointed by chief minister Mohamad Ali bin Rustam, filled in more details of this elite Malay model:

> We have a long history, from the year 1400 until today . . . more than six hundred years, but we can note in this case [that] the origination of the port of Melaka has been determined over two hundred years, there is the history of the Sultanate of Melaka, there is the history of the Portuguese, then enter the Dutch, the British, and . . . [the] Japanese. . . . Then there was an evolution with Chinese from early on until today. . . . There was assimilation of the group of traders that came to Melaka; many of them did this. Chinese married with local people. Indians traders married local people. So, most of them practiced the culture and language of local people, but without leaving behind their understandings of religion and beliefs. This is something that is unique about Melaka. . . . There are several outstanding values; in other countries there are only one or two. But if you look at Melaka there is the group of Malays, the original people, then . . . Chinese, Indians, Baba/Nyonya, and Chitty. There is the group of *orang asli*, forest people, but now they are rural people. This is also our heritage. . . . We can note that these groups have various kinds of cultures. If we look at the Baba and Nyonya group . . . half of them . . . follow Malay culture and half of them follow Chinese culture. The same with Chitties— half of them follow Malay culture and half follow Indian culture; in language, all of them speak Malay. Their mother tongue is Malay because they intermarried with Malays. They married Malay women or men. If you go to a Baba and Nyonya house over on Jonker or Heeren Street you can

find interracial people who descend from someone that long ago had married . . . a Malay woman. . . . There is also assimilation with clothing and food. . . . We received recognition from UNESCO because of the outstanding values here, first because of our monuments, and second because of the "living heritage" that still continues . . . including traditions of these people, of Baba/Nyonya and Chitties. . . . The old-time crafts are still done, still live, within the heritage zone.[7]

The mayor's discourse entails a model of partial assimilation of the culture of Malays, designated as the "original people," by Chinese and Indian immigrants. Indigenous *orang asli* are recognized as part of the "heritage" of Melaka, but as distinct from the carriers of prestigious Malay culture. Immigrant traders are constructed as intermarrying with Malays and subsequently assimilating Malay clothing and food styles and becoming speakers of Malay language while maintaining their religious identity and beliefs. However, instead of continuing to develop this image of cultural hybridity, he shifts to the awkward formulation of "halving" Baba/Nyonyas and Chitties into those that follow Malay culture and those that follow Chinese or Indian culture. That is, the Melaka mayor avoided wholeheartedly embracing hybridity—the complex blending and synthesizing of cultures—in favor of preserving the representation of Malay, Chinese, and Indian cultures as distinct things. Moreover, this sort of reification of cultural diversity appears to have fit with the criteria and expectations of UNESCO for recognizing World Heritage Sites with "living cultures."[8] The mayor then melded the values of interethnic and interreligious tolerance and harmony into the constructed elite Malay historical imaginary:

There was also a development of mutual understanding between Eastern and Western cultures, like an interlocking of them . . . If you go to Harmony Street you can see the . . . [Hindu] temple, the Chinese temple, and [the] mosque all along the road, and not far from there is a church. . . . Then, if you say, "The way these people perform their prayers will disturb other people or bring about the sanctions of other people or other religions," [this] does not happen in Melaka, since the early period until today. They still can have tolerance, because . . . next to them there is a masjid or a *kuil* [Hindu temple]. [Nowadays] if there are Malay people you can't have a church nearby because they are scared. . . . But long ago in the early period there was no fear because they believed in each other's places.

If you consider Baba and Nyonyas they would say that . . . [we] pray to Buddha in the temple but we recite our prayers in Malay language. And we Malays pray and recite our prayers in Arabic, and there are half who recite in [the] Malaysian language, Malay, but to understand, that is why religion is meaningless. What we mutually understand . . . can be said to be the heritage values we have, what knowledge we share that is our roots. Where we don't think we have our own separate culture, then we don't feel that we need to apply sanctions to different cultures. All cultures are going in the direction of goodness and not in the direction of badness. This also goes for religion. All religions teach good things and not bad.

He interprets the proximity of diverse religious institutions in the built environment of the city to represent the harmony and tolerance among different groups in Melaka. These religious institutions, actually built during the colonial period, and friendly relations among believers of different faiths, are viewed as demonstrating values that go back to the earlier period of the Melaka Sultanate. Whereas he notes that Malays today may be disturbed or even fearful of the religious worship of others, he imagines a cosmopolitan Melaka in which people from various religious backgrounds use the Malay

Jalan Tokong or Harmony Street, Melaka

language in their respective religious activities, believe in one another's right-ful place in society, and emphasize the culture they share rather than their differences. Moreover, the mayor considers this cosmopolitan perspective—which deems all cultures and religions as inclined toward goodness and allows them all to flourish freely, without sanctions—to be part of the heri-tage values of Melaka.

Secular nationalist Malay elites have widely institutionalized and distrib-uted this model of the early history of Melaka. Though many Malaysians have internalized and reproduced these models, they are also often con-tested and subverted as subalterns negotiate meanings of history and their positions in contemporary society. For instance, Mohamad Suhaimi, a young Malay professional, told me in a disgruntled fashion that "[i]t is hard to talk to Chinese about Islam because they usually respond by saying that if they become Muslims then they will have to become Malay. But what is wrong with becoming Malay? Malays have never oppressed them and have treated them well, so why do they have this objection with becoming Malay?"[9] In contrast, Rajan, an Indian factory worker in his early thirties, rejects the assimilation model and subverts the historical imaginary that locates the origins of Malaysian history with Malays and Islam:

> Malay people will accept Indians into their families and eventually these Indians become Malays, they *masuk Melayu*. . . . But the history of Melaka started with a Hindu, Parameswara, who fled from Palembang to escape Majapahit rulers and killed someone in Singapore . . . and then came to Melaka, where only his son became a Muslim. . . . But it [Sriwijaya] was under Majapahit control for a time, and he tried to rebel against Majapahit, which was a Hindu state . . . and Hinduism and Buddhism are almost the same anyway. . . . They came to Melaka, and many Indian traders came from Gujerat, bringing Islam and trade to Melaka. These Gujerati traders were the first ones to bring Islam to Melaka . . . and then the Malays began to become Muslims.[10]

In his discourse, Melaka history begins with the flight of a Hindu or Bud-dhist prince from Palembang to Melaka, after which Indian Muslims con-verted Malays from Hinduism and Buddhism. From this perspective, it makes no sense to have to become Malay as a result of converting from Hinduism to Islam, since Malays themselves were originally Hindus before Indians brought them into the fold of Islam. Several Indian Muslims I have spoken with underscored the role Indians played in transporting and teaching Islam to Malays. Abdul, a young university student at Universiti Sains Malaysia in Penang, proudly told me, "My family have been Muslims for hundreds of years. My great great-grandfather came to Malaysia as a *mubaligh* [Muslim missionary] making *dakwah* . . . and one of my fore-fathers opened a sundry shop in Seremban and then moved to Perak, where my family is from now."[11] Similarly, Mohideen, an Indian Muslim from Negeri Sembilan, told me, "Melaka is where the first Indian Muslims came, bringing Islam to Malaysia. They stayed in Tanjung Keling originally, and were called *orang keling* because the Malays did not understand Tamil and heard the bangles on the Indian women's ankles going 'kling, kling, kling' and so called them *orang keling* [*keling* people]."[12]

Another subaltern interpretation of precolonial history takes off from the representation in the elite Malay model of Chinese and Indian traders intermarrying with local Malays without being required to convert to Islam. Robert Seet, the secretary of the Peranakan Association of Melaka, stated:

> Baba and Nyonya were Hokkien originally . . . and we follow all the traditions strictly, even more than the other clan groups. . . . We follow the traditions on each day before the New Year, like last night, the gods went up to have a conference in the sky . . . [and] on the Fourth of the New Year they come back down. . . . On the eighth and ninth we pray to Cheng Kong. . . . They [Hokkien and Hakka] do not follow these traditions as strictly. . . . We make the *kue bakul* [*bakul* cake] as offerings for the gods, a very special cake. . . . Baba are more Chinese than the Chinese; we follow all the significance of each day. . . . No doubt we had intermarried, but we are more Chinese than the Chinese. In the earlier days Islam was not as strict, and they [Malays] may not have converted yet, so they followed Chinese customs.[13]

While elite Malay discourse constructs all Babas/Nyonyas as assimilating Malay culture in early history and "half" of them in contemporary society, Robert Seet and many other Babas and Nyonyas I interviewed stress that they are more "Chinese" in their cultural practices than are Chinese of other sub-ethnic categories. Intermarriage did not lead to assimilation because either Malays were not Muslims yet or they did not follow sharia as strictly as they do today. From this subaltern perspective that promotes liberal pluralism and the loosening of sharia norms, early history provides a model for facilitating greater integration of non-Muslims into the Malaysian nation.

COLONIALISM, BRITISH LAW, AND THE SECULAR FORMAT

Beginning in the sixteenth century, a succession of European colonial powers seized control of the Straits of Melaka and parts of the Malay Peninsula. Galvanized by a combination of religious and commercial zeal, Portuguese attacked and captured the city of Melaka in 1511, driving the Malay rulers to flee inland. Their defeat at the hands of Portuguese invaders marked the end of the Melaka Sultanate. Dutch forces, mercantilist competitors of the Portuguese, took control of Melaka in 1641 following several months of fierce fighting. Finally, the British gained temporary control of Melaka through negotiations with the Dutch, who were embroiled in the Napoleonic Wars in Europe (1795–1815). Dutch officials regained control for a short period, before the Anglo-Dutch Treaty of 1824 transferred Melaka to the British in return for possessions in Island Southeast Asia. Unlike the British, Portuguese and Dutch colonial administrations disrupted sharia minimally throughout the Malay Peninsula. It was under expanding British control that sharia laws were displaced and demoted while English law gained dominance.

British colonial rule was extended in a gradual, piecemeal fashion across the Malay Peninsula and in the territories of North Borneo (Sabah), Sarawak, and Brunei in Borneo. Soon after obtaining Melaka, the British organized Singapore, Penang, Wellesley Province (located on the mainland across from the island of Penang), and Melaka into a colony called the Straits Settlement. Over the course of the next six decades, the British extended direct control over three protectorates in Borneo and indirect colonial control over the Malay states of the peninsula. The four Malay states of Perak, Selangor, Negeri Sembilan, and Pahang were organized into the Federated Malay States (FMS) in 1896. Meanwhile, Johor and the four northern states—Kedah, Perlis, Kelantan, and Terengganu—formerly under Siam's suzerainty, were loosely organized into the Unfederated Malay States (UMS) following a treaty between the British and Siam in 1909. British governors and residents administered the Straits Settlements, territories in Borneo, and the FMS, and these colonial units were brought under Western rule and influence. However, the northern UMS, given more latitude for sharia and Malay *adat* under Siamese suzerainty, experienced the intrusion of British "advisors" or "agents" differently (Andaya and Andaya [1982] 2001, 160–209). In particular, these states had a later encounter with British notions of dividing the secular from the religious and the public from the private (197; Kamali 2000, 22–24).

English law was introduced into the various units of "British Malaya" through several charters and civil law ordinances. The Royal Charters of Justice of 1807, 1826, and 1855 implemented English law and the court system in the Straits Settlements. In addition, the Civil Ordinance of 1878 in the Straits Settlements, the Civil Law Enactment of 1937 for the FMS, and the Civil Law (Extension) Ordinance of 1951 for the UMS consolidated the application of English law. Both of the latter enactments were subsequently replaced by the Civil Law Ordinance of 1956 that was applied to all the states of the Federation of Malaya (formed in 1948). These enactments continued after political independence and were extended to Sabah and Sarawak of postcolonial Malaysia through their incorporation in the Civil Law Act of 1956 (revised in 1972) (Abdul Samat 2003, 98; Kamali 2000, 24–25).

However, the process of displacing and narrowing the application of sharia varied across British Malaya. In the Straits Settlements colony, English law became the general and governing law. Here, British governors directly controlled the *kadis* (or *qaḍis*; Muslim judges), appointing and dismissing them and limiting their power. Similarly, in the Borneo protectorates, English law was established as the general public law, with Islamic law considered as one of the native customary laws of indigenous ethnic groups. The Federated Malay States, also legally obligated to receive English law under the "advice" of residents, underwent a gradual process of adopting a system of courts in which religious courts were separated and placed into a lower position within a *single* hierarchy of courts. In contrast to the direct colonies, the Sultan in Council with the British Resident and secular State Council appointed and dismissed all *kadis* and administered justice, including religious matters, in the FMS. However, the process was even more varied and indirect for the UMS: "In the Unfederated Malay States . . . the system of the administration of justice varied somewhat from one State to another, except Johore as it was more aligned to the Federated Malay States. The rules of the syariah in the Unfederated Malay States were observed so strictly that the British found it difficult, for example in Terengganu, to introduce English law" (Abdul Samat 2003, 98–99). There are reports from Terengganu of Muslim judges sitting together and sharing equal powers with British agents administering Islamic and state laws, and from Kedah of sharia experts advising appeals in the High Court (99). Indeed, in Terengganu and Kelantan, "legal administration was brought more closely under the supervision of Muslim law courts, presided over by experts in Islamic law" who tried to enforce sharia statutes regulating mosque attendance, correct dress, and observance of the fasting month (Andaya and Andaya [1982] 2001,

197–98). Islamic scholars, trained in the numerous traditional religious schools in Kelantan, were a driving force for the centralization of the religious bureaucracy and the introduction of the Islamic legal system in the state. However, "the aspiration of the *ulama* [Islamic scholars] to incorporate Islamic law as the law of the state was greatly diminished with the establishment of the British advisory system" (Abdullah Alwi 1996, lii). Across the Malay States, British authorities strove to reorganize and standardize the administration of sharia courts according to their own ideas about modernity (cf. Peletz 2002, 47–59). While the British introduced a systematic methodology for administering the sharia courts and pushed to formalize substantive rules of colonial "Muhammadan" law in statutes, they also minimized their jurisdiction (Hooker 1983, 173; Abdullah Alwi 1996, 205).

One of the main results of the dominance of English law, even in the east coast states, was the reduction of the scope of sharia laws to Islamic family and personal laws. This reduction stemmed from the British separation of the "public" aspect of sharia from the "private" aspect. The public aspect, covering fields such as criminal law, commercial law, and contract, evidence, procedural, and land law, was replaced by English law. Meanwhile, the private aspect, embracing fields such as matrimonial, divorce, and inheritance laws, was viewed as falling under Islamic law (Kamali 2000, 22–25). Likewise, in reference to Kelantan, "The newly established administration headed by W. A. Graham in 1904 superseded the former system. This resulted in the enforcement of Islamic law within a limited sphere only, namely those concerning personal matrimonial and succession matters. These matters were to [be] dealt with by the *Syariah* Court. The *Syariah* Court was later separated from the secular courts, and was soon neglected by the government" (Abdullah Alwi 1996, 15). Within the British secular format, sharia laws were reduced to matters considered "private" or "personal" and subordinated in the court system below the governing English laws. Moreover, British discourse expressed their hegemonic view that their judicial practice was far superior to that of Malay *kadis* (Peletz 2002, 38–47). Although Islamic law and Muslim jurists were marginalized in the colonial system, Malay sultans continued to play an important role in governance as "heads" of religious and ethnic affairs, including the limited domain of Islamic law (Hussin 2016).

There was Muslim resistance to British colonial rule. Before the emergence of Malay nationalism, some Muslim resistance involved calls for a holy war and evoked the Ottoman Caliphate centered in Istanbul (Andaya and Andaya [1982] 2001, 166, 172; Malhi 2014). Uprisings in Sungai Ujong, Pahang, Kelantan, and Terengganu deployed symbolism conventionally associated with the caliphate, including the Ottoman flag. These uprisings entailed "counter-colonial place-making" that imagined local Muslims as part of an *umma* (religious community) "with Ottoman Istanbul as its exemplary center," far beyond the constructed colonial boundaries (Malhi 2014, 4). In the Terengganu uprising of 1928, the last of this series of revolts, Malay cultivators contested colonial land reform and claimed ownership of forest plots using narratives that combined notions of sharia and Malay *adat*. From this subversive perspective colored by their Islamic jurisprudence–inflected model, Malay cultivators' actions were construed as pious and the claims of the colonial state for the enclosure of land as impious (6). British rulers, increasingly challenged by Malay nationalists and Malayan Communists, held onto power for two more decades before beginning to negotiate political independence.

Prior to the end of the colonial period, British administrators established a secular format situating the sharia courts outside the federal court system, a pattern that continued in postcolonial Malaysia. Previously, as the court system evolved across British Malaya, the sharia courts were included within a single hierarchy of courts. They were delegated to a lower status and reduced jurisdiction, but still not excluded from the overall court system: "Until 1948 the Courts of the Kathis [*kadis*] and Assistant Kathis were part of the structure of the courts. However, the Courts Ordinance 1948 established a judicial system for the Federation of Malaya and excluded the syariah courts from the federal court system" (Abdul Samat 2003, 99). This format became a significant feature of the form of secularism institutionalized in postcolonial Malaysia.

Contemporary Malaysians interpret and negotiate the meanings of the colonial era from a variety of perspectives. For instance, Chandra Muzaffar, a scholar in the Islamic human rights network of Sisters in Islam, emphasizes the relationship between colonialism and Muslim religious conservatism:

> By challenging Muslim identity and integrity, as it had never been challenged before, Western colonial domination from the 16th century CE onwards also reinforced religious conservatism and habitual political support for any prevailing *status quo*. If anything, continuing Western control over Muslim lands and resources, and Muslim helplessness *vis-à-vis* Palestine and other traumas, have persuaded sections of the Muslim *umma* that their survival depends upon their ability to preserve Muslim identity through rigid adherence to dogma and doctrine. . . . It is this conservatism, particularly pronounced in the case of theological matters, which the

present-day Muslim world has inherited from the past. The *ulama* reflect
this conservatism. Indeed, more than any other group within the *umma*, it
is the *ulama* who are largely responsible for impeding all attempts at
reconstructing aspects of the *sharīʿa*. (Chandra Muzaffar 1994, 22–23)

Here, Chandra Muzaffar focuses on the responses of Muslims to colonial
domination rather than the devastating impact of colonialism in transform-
ing Muslim societies, including the position of sharia. According to this
interpretive framework, Muslim conservatives, especially religious scholars,
embrace traditional theological and jurisprudential positions in order to
bolster a Muslim identity undermined by colonial domination. These traditional religious scholars are major opponents of the Sisters in Islam project
of reforming sharia family laws.

On the other hand, Haji Hassan, an Indian Muslim activist in a network
of Islamic NGOs, takes exception to narratives that express nostalgia for a
past in which Muslims were less observant of sharia laws and norms:

A lot of people here in this country think that Muslims are becoming more
Arabized. They are wrong. . . . [If a] person . . . says that, I will see [that he
is] wearing some sort of Western dress, invariably. . . . And I say if they
are going on about Arabization, can I go on about Europeanization? But
they don't see it . . . because it is coming so smoothly and slowly; they
evolved into it so they can't tell. . . . Please understand what happened in
this country. In 1511, the Portuguese came, and whatever this society was
evolving stopped, and then they . . . instituted certain measures and we
evolved [on] a different track. . . . The only courts operating in 1511 would
have been sharia courts. They would have stopped those sharia courts
from operating. Those sharia courts would have evolved. We have lost
over six hundred years of sharia court evolution in Malaysia because of
something not of our making. You guys [Chinese and Indian non-Muslim
immigrants] came in, and I also came in at a time when they were in
control. Who are we to talk about when they became more Arab or
we became more European? Point number one: [upon] independence,
on this street . . . at Christmas there would be large lights celebrating
Christmas. . . . I saw that up to 1965–66, and then slowly it faded. . . . So
that was the big festival—why? What was the big presence of Christians
here, only ten or eleven percent? . . . But the culture, the commercialization,
all the activities, [were] centered around whites. . . . The Muslims drank.
The Muslim girls wore *kebaya* [long traditional skirts] with slits up to their

thighs. Everybody was, haha hehe, friendly. . . . The Muslims were not observant, but now they have become more observant. Wouldn't you, if you had a certain faith tradition, want to be observant about that faith tradition? Why . . . deny the Muslims what is natural for them? They were not supposed to have slit skirts up to their thighs. The men were not supposed to be topless and in Bermuda shorts and drinking and eating non-*halal* [permitted] food. They were not supposed to be doing this. You cannot sell integration as the way we were . . . the good 'ole days. The good ole days from a religious perspective were the bad ole days.[14]

Hassan interprets colonialism as an interruption in the evolution of sharia courts and the beginning of a gradual process of Europeanization. He stresses that colonialism places greater value on the culture and activities of whites, a condition made evident by the way Christian celebrations dominated public spaces. In this colonial context, many Muslims were not observant of sharia. From his pro-sharia perspective, increased observance of sharia laws and norms in contemporary Malaysia are a welcome reversal of the negative influences of colonial domination.

FEDERAL CONSTITUTION, *DAKWAH* MOVEMENTS, AND *HUDUD*

In 1956, the Reid Constitutional Commission, consisting of members from the United Kingdom, Australia, India, and Pakistan, drafted a constitution modeled on the American and Indian constitutions and submitted it to a review party appointed by the British government, the Conference of Rulers, and the Government of the Federation (Ahmad Ibrahim 1992, 508, 510). The Alliance Party (later named Barisan Nasional; BN), with a mandate from its overwhelming victory in the federal elections of 1955, influenced the recommendations made to the Reid Commission. However, it is important to note that the Alliance was dominated by the race-based parties—UMNO (United Malays National Organization), MCA (Malaysian Chinese Association), and MIC (Malaysian Indian Congress)—which negotiated and reached a compromise on a number of contentious issues (Andaya and Andaya [1982] 2001; Daniels 2005, 34–44; Ahmad Fauzi 1999, 31–32).[15] The Federation of Malaya (named Malaysia in 1963) adopted and promulgated the Federal Constitution when it attained independence on August 31, 1957. This constitution embodies the bargain reached by these allied but skirmishing parties over matters such as the priority of Islam, freedom of religion, Malay special rights, political preeminence of Malays, equality before the law, and common citizenship.

The Federal Constitution simultaneously embraces the priority of Islam and the freedom of religion. Article 3(1) declares that "Islam is the religion of the Federation; but other religions may be practiced in peace and harmony in any part of the Federation." It goes on to state in Article 3(2):

> In every State other than States not having a Ruler the position of the Ruler as the Head of the religion of Islam in his State in the manner and to extent acknowledged and declared by the Constitution of that State; and, subject to that Constitution, all rights, privileges and powers enjoyed by him as Head of that religion, are unaffected and unimpaired; but in any acts, observances or ceremonies with respect to which the Conference of Rulers has agreed that they should extend to the Federation as a whole each of the other Rulers shall in his capacity of Head of religion of Islam authorize the Yang di-Pertuan Agong to represent him.

Thus, this key article establishes "Islam as the religion of the Federation" and the Rulers or Yang di-Pertuan Agong (King) to be the "Head of the religion of Islam" in each state and for the federation overall, together with religious freedom for "other religions." What does this mean? Is it calling for a theocratic state and for sharia to be the general law of society? In contemporary Malaysia, divergent interpretations of this article have ignited firestorms of controversy. Nevertheless, according to the Reid Commission Report and the White Paper, the framers of the constitution expressed concerns about the potential impact of this article on the religious freedom of non-Muslims. However, the Alliance submitted a memorandum stating that "the religion of Malaysia shall be Islam. The observance of this principle shall not . . . imply that the State is not a secular State" (Abdul Aziz and Farid 2009, 5). Mr. Justice Abdul Hamid, a Pakistani member of the Commission, added a note of dissent arguing that many countries have such a provision in their constitutions that has not caused harm to anyone. Moreover, the White Paper in the report recommended that this declaration "will not in no [sic] way affect the present position of the Federation as a secular state" and the freedom of non-Muslims to practice and propagate their religions, except for restrictions imposed by state law on the propagation of their religions to Muslims (6). Furthermore, the constitution enshrines the notion of a secular state in the way it locates the highest political authority in each state and the nation in the hands of the state constitutions (Article 71) and the Cabinet or its authorized ministers (Article 39) rather than the "heads of religion"; and, as we will see below, in the way it continues the pre-independence format of limiting the scope of sharia laws and excluding them from the Federal List. Nevertheless, many contemporary Malaysians interpret Article 3 in ways contrary to the expressed intentions of those who drafted the constitution.

It is also important to note that the idea of religious freedom was further inscribed in Article 11(1), which states, "Every person has the right to profess and practice his religion and, subject to Clause (4), to propagate it." This article does not appear to have been intended to apply to Malays, who are Muslims by definition elsewhere in the constitution, or Muslims in general, although some contemporary proponents of liberal rights would extend it to Muslims who want to convert to other religions. Article 11(4), the caveat to this provision the Commission White Paper pointed to, clarifies that "State law and in respect to the Federal Territories of Kuala Lumpur, Labuan and Putrajaya, the federal law may control or restrict the propagation of any religious doctrine or belief among persons professing the religion of Islam." Most Malaysian states have issued such enactments specifying restrictions on the propagation of non-Islamic religions to Muslims.

The compromise over the primacy of Islam and religious freedom for non-Muslims was part of a broader bargain. In Article 153, Malays were bestowed recognition as natives or *Bumiputera*, together with the indigenous groups of Sabah and Sarawak, and accorded a "special position" and "legitimate interests" to be safeguarded by the king of Malaysia. Article 152(1) recognizes the Malay language as the national language. On the other hand, Article 8(1) declares that "all persons are equal before the law and entitled to the equal protection of the law." In addition, non-Malays attained a broad and inclusive form of legal citizenship as specified in Article 14(1). Representations of these sorts of compromises, inscribed in the Federal Constitution, were widely distributed throughout society and came to be known by many as "the social contract": "Representations of diverse social groups and their horizontal inter-relations as equal citizen-members and representations of Malay privilege and special status on top of vertical re-arrangements of diverse social groups are closely related to dominant and alternative senses of cultural citizenship" (Daniels 2005, 263). These representations of Malaysian society and the notions of ethnicity, citizenship, and the nation-state they entail have become intertwined in various ways with conceptions of sharia.

The marginalization of sharia laws is perpetuated in the Malaysian court system as structured according to the Federal Constitution. Sharia laws are omitted from the Federal List, List 1 of the Ninth Schedule, which includes civil and criminal law and procedure and the administration of justice. Sharia laws appear as Item 1 on List II, the State Legislative List, which reads as follows:

> Except with respect to the Federal Territories of Kuala Lumpur, Labuan and Putrajaya, Islamic law and personal and family law of persons professing the religion of Islam, including the Islamic law relating to succession, testate, intestate, betrothal, marriage, divorce, dower, maintenance, adoption, legitimacy, guardianship, gifts, partitions and non-charitable trusts; Wakafs and the definition and regulation of charitable and religious trusts, the appointment of trustees and the incorporation of persons in respect of Islamic religious and charitable endowments, institutions, trusts, charities and charitable institutions operating wholly within the State; Malay customs; Zakat, Fitrah and Baitulmal or similar Islamic religious revenue; mosques or any Islamic public places of worship, creation and punishment of offences by persons professing the religion of Islam against precepts of that religion, except in regard to matters included in the Federal List; the constitution, organization and procedure of Syariah courts, which shall have jurisdiction only over persons professing the religion of Islam and in respect only of any of the matters included in this paragraph, but shall not have jurisdiction in respect of offences except in so far as conferred by federal law, the control of propagating doctrines and beliefs among persons professing the religion of Islam; the determination of matters of Islamic law and doctrine and Malay custom.

Civil laws based on English law are generally applied across postcolonial Malaysia. The various levels of civil courts—High Courts, Court of Appeal, and Federal Court—are part of the federal system and hear a wide range of cases for Muslims and non-Muslims, including all criminal cases except for those committed by Muslims against the "precepts of Islam." Moreover, several of the kinds of cases on the state-level sharia list overlap with those on the federal-level civil court list, and many of these are in fact heard in local civil courts rather than sharia courts. The Federal Constitution and the Acts of Parliament determine the jurisdiction of sharia courts. Even in the case of gross violations of the "precepts of Islam" that transgress the limits of religious norms (*hudud*), offenses with fixed punishments in the Qur'an and

Prophetic Traditions (*hadith*), the sharia courts are restricted from imposing penalties beyond those set by federal law. From 1965 to 1984, federal law limited penalties meted out by the sharia courts to RM 1,000 and six months of imprisonment. The Syariah Courts (Criminal Jurisdiction) Act of 1965 as amended in 1984 provides that sharia criminal jurisdiction should not be exercised for any punishment exceeding three years or with a fine exceeding RM 5,000 or whipping exceeding six strokes, or any combination of these penalties (Abdul Samat 2003, 104). This restriction has come be known as the three-five-six limits in the Malaysian judicial community, and is under consideration for another increase in the level of *ta'zir* (discretionary punishment) a Muslim judge can award. In the 1950s and 1960s these punishments existed only in the form of imprisonment and fines but were heightened in the 1980s and 1990s under the influence of the ongoing Islamic resurgence, in some cases including caning penalties.

Islamic resurgence, including a variety of *dakwah* movements, has spread across Malaysian society since the 1970s. Initially, student activists, several Islamic nongovernmental organizations, and the Islamic Party of Malaysia (PAS) actively struggled for a more public presence and observance of Islam in society. However, by the 1980s, the UMNO-led federal government under the leadership of prime minister Mahathir Mohamad initiated its own *dakwah* movement and tried to get out in front of the growing Islamic turn of the Muslim community. UMNO, PAS, and a variety of Islamic missionary, Sufi, and activist organizations mobilized and motivated the Muslim grass roots to participate in Islamic education, study groups, and religious revival meetings, and to implement more sharia in their personal and family lives. Campaigns were waged promoting Islamic attire and covering the female body according to Islamic norms, and for expressing Muslim identity and values in media. The federal government set up the International Islamic University and several Islamic think tanks. Expanding corps of *ulama* (Ar. *'ulamā'*) were developed and established in increasingly public roles in society. The National Council for Islamic Affairs Fatwa Committee (Jawatankuasa Fatwa Majlis Kebangsaan Bagi Hal Ehwal Ugama Islam Malaysia), which was first organized in 1970 to issue fatwas or legal opinions on a national level, shifted the label for its meetings from *persidangan* (M. conference) to *muzakarah* (Ar. *mudhākara*; consultation, deliberation) in 1981. This council comprises all the state-level and Federal Territories' muftis, nine *ulama*, a Muslim legal professional selected and appointed by the Council of Rulers, and a director appointed by the National Council for Islamic Affairs (Majlis Kebangsaan Bagi Hal Ehwal Ugama Islam Malaysia; MKI). The state and national fatwa councils issue rulings covering all categories of Islamic law, including *akidah* (Ar. *'aqidah*; religious belief), *ibadah* (worship), *munakahat* (marriage and family), *jenayah* (criminal), and *muamalat* (economics). Looked at from a broad perspective, the affiliations of these increasingly public and influential Muslim scholars and jurists are varied, with some more or less attached to UMNO or the UMNO-led government and others with PAS or PAS-affiliated NGOs, while other *ulama* are more independent. These *dakwah* movements also explored making the economy more sharia-compliant, including *halal* certification and expansion of companies producing *halal* products and the development of Islamic banking, insurance, and investment vehicles. The Islamic Banking Act was passed in 1983 and the Islamic Insurance (Takaful) Act in 1984. Malaysia developed one of the most regulated Islamic finance sectors in the world and eventually shifted the jurisdiction of these institutions and products from civil courts to Bank Negara Malaysia (Malaysian Central Bank) in 2009 (Kamali 2000, 328–30; Fischer 2008; Sloane-White 2011).

In this historical context of resurgent Islam and the growing emphasis on Muslim identity for Malay "natives," several states passed laws on non-Islamic religion and made amendments to family and criminal law enactments, and the federal government pushed through an amendment of the Federal Constitution raising the status of sharia courts. In the 1980s, the peninsular states of Kelantan, Terengganu, Kedah, Melaka, Pahang, Perak, and Selangor passed enactments restricting non-Muslim usage of several words and phrases deemed to be uniquely Islamic. The Selangor Non-Islamic Religions (Control of Propagation Among Muslims) Enactment of 1988 bans non-Muslims from using twenty-five words, including *Allah*, *ulama*, *ibadah*, *syariah*, *dakwah*, *wali*, and *nabi*, and ten phrases, such as *Subhanallah*, *Alhamdulillah*, *Lailahaillallah*, and *Allahu Akbar*, in reference to non-Islamic religion. All the peninsular states, except for Penang, passed similar enactments. Malay leaders considered these laws consistent with Article 11(4) of the Federal Constitution. However, the Christian Federation of Malaysia argues that these enactments are too broad and infringe on their rights of religious freedom, which is upheld in "the supreme law of the land," the Federal Constitution (see chapter 3). The federal government passed amendments to the Islamic Family Law (Federal Territories) Act of 1984 in 1992 and 1994 that altered some of the reforms concerning polygamy and divorce. Sisters in Islam and many of their supporters consider these amendments a step backward for gender equality. In 1982, in Kelantan, and after 1993 in other states and jurisdictions, revised Administration of Muslim Law enactments were passed providing for a three-tiered system of courts—Sharia Subordinate Court, Sharia High Court, and Sharia Appeal Court—independent of the state religious councils and with enhanced status for sharia judges (Roff 1998, 224). Subsequently, many peninsular states also passed new enactments or amendments to family laws: Kelantan in 2002 (under a PAS-led administration), Melaka in 2003, Negeri Sembilan and Selangor in 2003, and Kedah in 2008. Similarly, Malay leaders passed new sharia criminal enactments in the direction of strengthening the punishment of crimes that violate Islamic precepts. Kelantan passed the Syariah Criminal Code in 1985, Kedah the Kanun Jenayah Syariah in 1988, Melaka the Enakmen Kesalahan Syariah in 1991, Negeri Sembilan the Enakmen Jenayah Syariah in 1992, Selangor the Syariah Criminal Enactment in 1995, and the federal government the Syariah Criminal Offences (Federal Territories) Act in 1997. In several cases, these enactments repealed more lenient laws from the 1960s.

Meanwhile, with a more than two-thirds majority in Parliament in 1988, the Mahathir-led BN government was able to make an important amendment to the Federal Constitution for raising the status and jurisdiction of the state-level sharia courts. This new provision was intended to address the overlapping and conflicting jurisdictions of the civil and sharia courts that saw many cases falling within the purview of sharia courts being heard and decided on by civil courts. This condition was carried over from the colonial period. Article 121(1A) states, "The courts referred to in Clause (1) [two High Courts] shall have no jurisdiction in respect of any matter within the jurisdiction of the Syariah courts." Although this provision was supposed to establish an exclusive jurisdiction for the sharia courts, it appears that the power of the civil courts to hear cases in the fields of succession, testate, intestate, legitimacy of a child, interpretation of wills, guardianship and conversion, Islamic religious endowments (*wakaf*), and divisions of joint marital assets (*harta sepencarian*) upon divorce has not been eliminated (Abdul Samat 2003, 105–6).[16] This provision raises the authority of the sharia courts to handle matters that fall under its jurisdiction and is a powerful symbolic gesture for reducing the perceived marginalization of many in the Muslim community. Although it is only a slight tweaking of the secular format established prior to political independence and not a transformation of the subordinate position of sharia courts, this provision has become a principal target of liberal rights organizations protesting the unwelcome authority of sharia courts in conversion and child custody cases involving Muslims and non-Muslims (see Martinez 2008; Moustafa 2013).

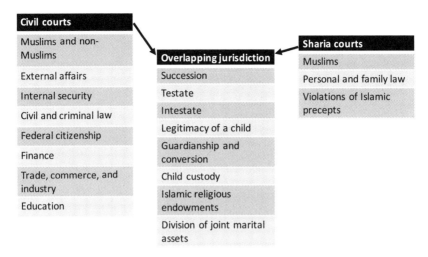

Civil courts	Overlapping jurisdiction	Sharia courts
Muslims and non-Muslims	Succession	Muslims
External affairs	Testate	Personal and family law
Internal security	Intestate	Violations of Islamic precepts
Civil and criminal law	Legitimacy of a child	
Federal citizenship	Guardianship and conversion	
Finance	Child custody	
Trade, commerce, and industry	Islamic religious endowments	
Education	Division of joint marital assets	

Civil courts and sharia courts jurisdiction

On the other hand, PAS, reorganized under the leadership of *ulama* in the 1980s, waged a strong campaign for a more thoroughgoing transformation of Malaysian society and the establishment of an Islamic system. After its electoral victory in 1990, it regained control of the state of Kelantan and began trying to manifest its notion of an Islamic state. In 1991, the Kelantan state government banned performances of *mak yong* and *wayang*, traditional dance and shadow puppet arts, which they interpreted as entailing elements of "superstition" and "un-Islamic beliefs" as well as inappropriate attire and the mixing of genders. The official Enactment Controlling Entertainment and Places of Entertainment of 1998 (Enakmen Kawalan Hiburan dan Tempat-tempat Hiburan) codified restrictions on traditional arts and entertainment venues deemed to be flouting Islamic values and norms.[17] PAS also tried to deliver on its criticism of the secularism of UMNO and their own arguments for a full implementation of sharia laws by having the state governments of Kelantan and Terengganu pass sharia criminal laws that included *hudud*. The Kelantan state government issued the Syariah Criminal Code (II) in 1993 (Hukum Hudud) and the Terengganu state government the Syariah Criminal Offences Bill in 2002. These enactments, though of powerful discursive value, were unable to be implemented in practice due to federal-level legal and structural constraints. Nevertheless, PAS leaders have maintained a commitment to replacing the reduced *ta'zir* punishments with the *hudud* code. Tuan Guru Nik Abdul Aziz, the spiritual leader of PAS and chief minister of Kelantan, in the Kelantan House in Kuala Lumpur, told me emphatically:

> In Malaysia, there are two courts. There is the civil court and the sharia court. Who said it is supposed to be this way? In the time of Prophet Muhammad, in the time of the caliphs, there was only one court. Why is there two? In Malaysia, there is a mufti and a chief justice. Why is there two? The chief justice is different from the Mufti. In terms of knowledge, they are the same. If I speak about it, if I had the power, I would make the chief justice a mufti and the mufti a chief justice; there must be only one. The knowledge of both of them is the same; they all study in universities. Why is there two of them? They divide and rule.[18]

In Nik Aziz's vision of an Islamic state, there would be only one court system: the sharia system. Many Malaysian Muslims have been swayed by PAS leaders' arguments for Islamic sovereignty. Nevertheless, there are also many committed to the more moderate, secular format of UMNO. For instance, Halim, a middle-aged Malayali Muslim from Kerala, remarked:

> Malays are becoming more fanatic. They have to realize that Malaysia is a cosmopolitan society. You can't force non-Muslims to follow Islamic law. If a person steals, then you cut off a finger and if they steal again, you cut off a hand. What if a Chinese person steals, what will you do, cut off his finger or hand, too? No, you cannot do that; they are not Muslims. Islamic law does not apply to them. . . . But this is not Allah's law. Allah is merciful and forgiving. How can you just punish people like this? People should be forgiven if they ask for it and [be] given a chance to change and be good people. This is what Allah wants because Allah has all the power, and if he wanted to punish us for all the wrong things we do each day he could do it right away.[19]

Most non-Muslims I spoke with also expressed similar anti-*hudud* sentiments and fears about the rising tide of Islamic resurgence.

Indeed, many non-Muslim interlocutors described their experiences with the changes that took place in their everyday relations with Malay Muslims after the Islamic resurgence. Ching, a middle-aged Chinese Buddhist woman, explained that things were different when she grew up on the east coast of peninsular Malaysia:

I grew up in Terengganu and I used to have lots of Malay friends, and we used to mix with each other, and they came over to eat with us. But it has all changed after the Islamic movement. Now we do not mix because they are restricted from mixing with us. They cannot come into a temple or church. . . . It was the Muslim extremists that started all this. . . . They say they cannot marry a Christian or Jew, but this is not what Islam teaches. . . . But they do not allow it here.[20] A Muslim man or woman must marry a Muslim, so a non-Muslim has to convert. They are following Malay customs and call everything they do Islam, but they don't realize that there are many Muslims in the world. Malays are not the only Muslims.[21]

Ching now lives in the more ethnically diverse west coast city of Melaka, but she found that social relations had changed there, too. She laments the distance she felt grow between non-Muslims and Malay Muslims. In addition, the separation she experienced appears to be hardened by the way race and religion were intertwined. Malay custom and identity took on more of an Islamic aura, while Islam, the prestigious religion of the federation, was claimed as an essential Malay attribute.

CONCLUSION

Sharia and legalistic varieties of Islam entered the Malayo-Indonesian world in the thirteenth century, and various forces directed it along a curving path through the precolonial period to the present. From the earliest period, conceptions of sharia traveled together or alongside mystical and ascetic varieties of Islam and were localized in Island Southeast Asia, where they came into contact with Hinduism, Buddhism, and local religious traditions and customary principles of social organization. A spectrum of syncretistic cultural models and practices emerged and were distributed throughout the region. Even some of the legal codes implemented by Islamic kingdoms reflected this blending of multiple cultural streams. Nevertheless, a process of placing more emphasis on sharia in legal codes was underway when European invaders, especially the British, began to dominate the Malay states.

British forces gradually extended their control over different portions of the Malay Peninsula and some territories in northwest Borneo. They infused English law and their notions about secular/religious and public/private dichotomies into the directly and indirectly ruled components of British Malaya. Sharia laws were not eliminated from legal venues under British colonialism. Instead, they were limited in scope to personal and private matters beneath English law, which was institutionalized as the general and governing public law. Moreover, sharia laws were considered part of the overall court system until 1948, near the end of British colonial rule, when they were excluded from the federal system. The secular format of relegating state-level sharia courts and religious authorities to subordinate positions under the authority of civil forces was carried into the postcolonial period.

With political independence and modern constitutionalism, sharia came into close contact with notions of the nation-state, citizenship, and civil rights such as equality and religious freedom. Therefore, conceptions of sharia were amalgamated, to some extent, with representations of Malaysian society and notions of ethnicity. In the midst of the Islamic resurgence, from the 1970s to the present, constructions of Malay identity became increasingly politicized and intertwined with Islamic identity. More conservative family and criminal laws were enacted in the 1980s and 1990s, and notions of sharia were infused into the economy. In addition, the Mahathir-led federal government amended the Federal Constitution, raising the status and jurisdiction of the state-level sharia courts. Despite the UMNO-led federal government's multifaceted *dakwah* movement, their measures were not going far enough to "Islamize" Malaysian society for some quarters. Calls for *hudud* penal codes, rather than the reduced *ta'zir* punishments, and the establishment of an Islamic state were made from PAS and some Islamic nongovernmental organizations.

Malaysians interpret the history of sharia from various contrasting and competing perspectives. Malay secular nationalist elites imagine a linear continuity from the precolonial Islamic kingdom of Melaka to the postcolonial nation-state. In their vision, the polity has been and should be led by sovereign Malays and Muslims utilizing a "moderate" approach. While PAS supporters and some other Malaysian Muslims appreciate this elite model's emphasis on Muslim rule, they contest the "moderate" approach, stressing that all of Allah's directives must be implemented, including the controversial *hudud* penal code. Members of the Muslim feminist organization Sisters in Islam contest the conservatism they perceive in both of these pro-sharia perspectives and argue that this religious orientation is based on the rupture in Muslim identity caused by colonial domination and the influence of Islamic movements from abroad. Moreover, from some subaltern perspectives, Hindu, Buddhist, and non-Muslim origins are found for Malaysia rather the Malay Muslim origins of the dominant imaginary. Many non-Muslims interpret the Islamic resurgence as an "extremist" movement that has led to less mixing and more distance between non-Muslims and Muslims. Subalterns also appropriate the "tolerant" and "cosmopolitan" elements of elite Malay representations calling for a "return" to more friendly intergroup relations. These contrasting perspectives have increasingly challenged the hegemony of the elite Malay viewpoint over the last two decades. Nevertheless, the influential framework of the Malay political elites remains widely distributed and institutionalized in society.

2 FAMILY LAW

Religious Officials, Reasoning Style, and Controversies

STATE AND FEDERAL RELIGIOUS COUNCILS AND DEPARTMENTS
have institutionalized sharia family and criminal laws. The implementation
of these laws remains somewhat variable across the states of Malaysia, given
that they are directly under the administration of state-level religious councils. However, the Department of Islamic Development Malaysia (JAKIM;
Jabatan Kemajuan Islam Malaysia) has been striving to make sharia family
and criminal laws more standardized across the states of Malaysia and in
the Federal Territories. JAKIM, established in 1997, assumed the role of its
predecessor, the Secretariat of the National Council of Islamic Affairs, formed
in 1968. These centralized institutions located in the Prime Minister's
Department discussed and managed Islamic religious affairs and made recommendations to state governments and religious councils and the Council of
Rulers. State and federal religious councils and courts, despite being situated within an overarching secular format, have rendered controversial
decisions and policies at odds with some sectors of civil society that are pushing for greater secularization. Although these institutions exhibit an outward drive for bureaucratic efficiency, corporatization, and the continued
influence of civil law procedures, they appear to also be drawing on a logic
based in a traditional Islamic worldview (cf. Peletz 2013).

I made a visit to JAKIM during October 2010 hoping to interview an
official from the religious law department. From Kuala Lumpur International Airport I caught the local train to the Putrajaya/Cyberjaya stop, a
remote station surrounded by a patchwork of roads and open fields, from
which buses and taxis head to federal government buildings in Putrajaya
and private universities and high-tech firms in Cyberjaya. My taxi driver, a
young Indian man, sped around the winding paved roads traversing the
fields beneath the pulsating subtropical heat. I could tell from the religious
symbols on his dashboard that he was Hindu.

"When is the Thaipusam festival this year?" I asked him, trying to break
the chilly silence.

"I think it begins in late January this year," he answered with a softening demeanor.

When we arrived at the enormous campus of administrative buildings, my driver asked the Malay security guards where the JAKIM office was located. Before dropping me off, he passed me his card and suggested I call him later if I needed a ride back to the station. I thanked him, figuring I probably would, there being no convenient mass transit out there. Inside, one of the guards at the information counter, a Malay woman, directed me to the religious law department of JAKIM, where I was to ask for Ustazah Hamidah. After exchanging my New York State driver's license for a visitor's pass, I took the elevator to the eighth floor.

Hamidah's receptionist invited me to take a seat, and after a few minutes, a young Malay woman wearing a light tan and orange *baju kurung* (long skirt and matching tunic) with matching *tudung* (headscarf) emerged from an adjoining office space and sat down on the couch across from me. She was Hamidah. She asked me politely in English how she could help me. I presented her my letter of introduction from USM (Universiti Sains Malaysia), my Malaysian academic sponsor, and explained that I was conducting a research project on sharia in Malaysia. Hamidah took me inside the large human resources area to an internal reception area, having realized that I was a professor from the United States and not a student working on a thesis. She called one of their officials to speak to me, and while we waited for him, she gave me information about JAKIM in order to determine which departments would be most appropriate to assist with my research topic. Hamidah thought sharing the JAKIM reports with me would not be of much help, since they are written in Malay.

"Actually our report books are not in English so it is difficult for us to show for you," she said apologetically.

"You mean they are in *bahasa Malaysia*?" I queried using the Malay term for Malaysian language.

"Yes, in *bahasa Malaysia*."

"I can also read *bahasa Malaysia*," I said in Malay.

"You can?" she said excitedly.

"Yes, I can. I read lots of books in Malay."

"Okay, wait for awhile, and I will get them for you."

She returned in a few minutes with three telephone-book-size JAKIM annual reports covering the years 2007–9. Hamidah was curious about how an American anthropologist could be so competent in Malay. Malay language is an important symbol of Malay-ness and is recognized as the official national language, which reinforces Malay identity as the preferred racial category. I explained that I had learned the Malay language in small university classes in the United States led by Indonesian graduate students.

"So these are all our annual reports. You can have a look at this. This is from 2009."

She paused for moment while I looked through the most recent report, and then asked about the title of my research project. I explained that my research proposal, titled "Sharia Discourses in Malaysia," encompassed sharia enactments as well as the way sharia is implemented, forms of *dakwah*, and so forth. Hamidah went to speak to some of her coworkers about my research project while I examined their annual reports. After about five minutes she set up a computer on the small table in the reception area and started a video overview of JAKIM for me to watch. A Malay man speaking English narrated this presentation with easy-listening jazz occasionally playing in the background. It described the history of JAKIM, its objectives, and various divisions and sections. Near the end of the video, Hamidah brought an official from the *halal* certification section to speak with me. He was a Malay man in his late thirties wearing a white Islamic cap (*kopiah*) and a bright smile that exuded strong religious convictions.

"*Assalamu'alaikum*," he said greeting me.

"*Wa 'alaikumsalaam*," I replied.

"*Kayfa halak*, how are you?" he asked, saying the same thing in Arabic and English.

"I'm doing fine, thank you."

"I'm Zainul."

"I'm Professor Daniels from Hofstra University in Long Island, New York."

"My friend said you can speak Malay," he stated with a tone of excitement in his voice.

"Yes, I can speak Malay," I said, responding in Malay language.

He chuckled with delight. "*Subhaanallah* [Glory is to Allah]."

"I took several classes with Indonesian students who were studying for their graduate degrees in the US."

"Somebody from UKM [the Malaysian National University] called me and said they had a friend coming to visit from the US."

"I'm affiliated with USM and Dr. Farid from the Islamic Studies Department—"

Hamidah interjected, providing information about her coworker, "Actually, he has already done his master's degree in Islamic studies on *murtad* [apostates]."

"I'm quite interested in the issue of *murtad* and the variety of laws dealing with them in various states in Malaysia," I said, hoping for some information on what he found in his thesis.

Chuckling and smiling confidently, he asked, "So what can I help you with?"

"I'd like to ask [you] about the implementation of sharia in Malaysia."

"I can answer questions about this topic, but if you use my name in your research, they will ask who is this giving these views. . . . I work with certification of *halal* and investment in Islamic businesses."

"Actually, he is also an expert in sharia law, but I think he does not want to talk . . . about it," Hamidah interjected, acknowledging his broad background in Islamic studies. "Let me bring you to the Islamic law department." Hamidah went to call downstairs on the seventh floor to make sure some officials in the Islamic law department were available to meet with me today. After confirming the appointment, she returned with a JAKIM souvenir bag, helping me to place the three annual reports inside. Zainul and I continued our discussion for a short time on the couch in the reception area.

"Islamic law in Malaysia is on the state level and is not federal, that is the problem," Zainul stated.

"Yes, that's what I noticed looking in the different states. I went to Negeri Sembilan . . . to the sharia court, and they had different enactments and laws. There are some similarities, which I want to ask someone about, but there were also differences."

"This is our problem. It comes from the British colonial system, *warisan daripada sistem penjajahan*." Zainul repeated this apparently disturbing historical fact in Malay, adding emphasis. His comments imply a cultural model of sharia that envisions a broader scope for Islamic law beyond the confines of the secular format inherited from the British colonial era.

Hamidah informed us it was time to go downstairs for my appointment. Zainul and I made a few polite parting comments and I followed Hamidah. We arrived in the Law Division (Bahagian Undang-undang), a wide rectangular space with several cubicles for office clerks situated in the interior and large offices for upper-level civil servants around the sides. Hamidah took me to the office of Zawati binti Yusuf, a federal counselor. Two other women, Aisha and Haryaty, who are lawyers in the legal division, also joined us. They were all wearing *baju kurung* and *tudung* of various hues. Hamidah and another office intern, a young man studying communications at an Islamic university, attended this interview and group discussion as well. Zawati informed me that the head of their department was not there today

JAKIM's offices in the Putrajaya government complex

because he was making a presentation at the Parliament. I introduced myself to the group and began asking questions.

"How does sharia fit into the aims and general goals of JAKIM?"

"Actually sharia law in Malaysia is a state matter, and in Malaysia we have fourteen states. Every state has its own enactment, and all the laws that we drafted for sharia we make sure are in line with *hukum syarak*. Our Federal Constitution is the supreme law of the federation. So, all the sharia laws [that] pass by the Parliament or state legislative assembly must fulfill the *hukum syarak* and also the federal law," Zawati responded.[1]

The relationship between Islamic law and the constitution has been at the center of many charged debates and sociopolitical struggles. Liberal pluralist and human rights activists argue that the constitutional principles of religious freedom, equality before the law, and the federal authority of civil courts severely constrain the scope of sharia laws. They believe that sharia laws only apply to Muslims so long as they don't contradict civil laws and liberal rights. On the other hand, political Islamic activists argue for a sharia-based constitution that would in effect scrap the current constitution. For them, the supreme law of the land is the Holy Qur'an. Recently there has been a rising chorus asserting that there are no constitutional obstacles to the extensive implementation of sharia laws, including the con-troversial *hudud* penal code. This JAKIM federal counselor expressed the moderate position of passing sharia codes that fit within the prevailing sec-ular format.

"But even with that sort of restriction, there's still a lot of variation in the laws of each state, because it is not very tight. There is still some leeway for the laws to be different. For instance, I went to Negeri Sembilan and picked up their book of laws for Islamic family law and also for criminal law. There were lots of similarities but also some differences from state to state. And, then, from what people tell me, there is *adat perpatih* in Negeri Sembilan, so I don't know to what extent the *hakim* [judge] would also take into account ideas of local Malay *adat perpati*," I continued.

"For Negeri Sembilan, it might be different, because they have their own *adat* and the laws that pass . . . the state legislative assembly also . . . must be assented by their ruler. But in the *wilayah* [Federal Territories], all the laws must be passed by Parliament through the Cabinet instead of in the state assembly. It is only a little different in Negeri Sembilan because they have their own *adat* and their ruler has a certain level of power."

"But, then, one of the objectives of JAKIM is to standardize the laws from the different states. How is that process working?" I asked.

"In JAKIM we try to uniform all sharia laws that are practiced in the states. We try to make one modern law. After we discuss [it] at a federal level, we also invite states to join the discussion, before we draft a law; and after we . . . draft the complete law, we circulate it to all the states and it is up to [them] to decide to adopt the law or not. As the federal government, we did not interfere at all to force the states to implement the law. . . . We just circulate and it depends on them, because the Islamic matter is under the state power, so we have no power to force them to adopt the federal law in their state."

Islamic jurists and legal counselors working in the Prime Minister's Department of the federal government strive to formulate one modern law through deliberation and consultation. Such processes of standardization, bureaucratic rationalization, and corporatization have been seen as features of Malaysian modernity in which "symbols and idioms of Islam" are com-monly invoked for legitimacy and dealing with various kinds of change (Peletz 2013, 624). However, concepts such as *nusyuz* (disobedience) and *murtad* are not just symbols and idioms, but complex notions partially con-stitutive of diverse cultural models of sharia. Moreover, some of the discourse from Zainul, Hamidah, and other civil servants of the Islamic bureaucracy who were socialized during the ongoing religious resurgence, suggests they are committed to models of sharia that contrast with the moderate models of the secular political elites. Thus, processes of standardizing and managing Islamic laws, as well as productions of Malaysian modernity, are fraught with internal cultural tensions and possibilities. Islamic tradition and modernity as well as processes of Islamic resurgence and bureaucratic rationalization are intimately intertwined (cf. Peletz 2002, 2013).

I went on to say, "But the federal laws that are passed in the Federal Territories like Kuala Lumpur, are they like a model for the laws to be implemented in the other states? I noticed that the general outlines of the sharia laws are largely consistent and the same across the states. But there are some variations in Islamic family law? Can you speak about the progress in the way Islamic family laws are being standardized across the states?"

Zawati looked to the other two lawyers in her department to address this question. One of them, Aisha, said, "Actually all the provisions in the sharia law, the substantive, the general content of the laws, are the same, but the differences are more in terms of the procedural matters, some differences in how they want to implement the procedure and enforce the provision in their state. The content of the provision is quite similar across the states."

Changing the topic, I said, "I spoke to a professor who is affiliated with Sisters in Islam (SIS), and she told me that group is trying to change some of the implementation of sharia laws. They think that some of them are unfair for the rights of *Muslima* [Muslim women]. How has JAKIM been working on dealing with some of their concerns in family and even in criminal law, considering that they apparently supported Lina Joy and her right of religious freedom?"

The Lina Joy case is one of the most highly publicized conversion (or apostasy) cases. It involved a Malay woman, born into a Muslim family and given the name Azalina binti Jailani, who later applied to the National Registration Department (NRD) to change her name and religion. She said she had renounced Islam for Christianity and intended to marry a Christian. Eventually she was allowed to change her name in the official government registration, but the NRD informed her that in order to change her religion they required an order from the sharia court. In 2001 the High Court Malaya, Kuala Lumpur decided that because she is Malay and Malays are Muslims according to Article 160 of the Federal Constitution, she cannot renounce her Islamic religion. Subsequently the Court of Appeal, in 2005, dismissed her appeal on the grounds that "her renunciation of Islam was

not confirmed by the Syariah Court or any other Islamic religious authority" (Abdul Aziz Mohamad 2007, 141), a decision the Federal Court upheld
in 2007. This case received so much media attention in Malaysia and around
the world that mere mention of her name evokes strong emotions and opinions. In Malaysia the "Lina Joy case" has become a polysemous symbol,
given various meanings within divergent cultural models of sharia.

Haryaty, the other lawyer sitting on the side, remarked, "Well, the first
thing we know is that Sisters in Islam is a feminist movement. So, basically,
most of what they are fighting for is based on feminism. Yes, they do believe
that some sharia laws discriminate against women, but [those sharia laws]
actually don't. And the way we counter the Sisters in Islam is that sometimes
we have a discussion and we do invite them, in terms of when we want to
regulate some laws, and we do have a discussion with them. . . . They are
basically a feminist movement, and we hardly take a suggestion from them
to insert into the sharia law."

"Apparently they were the only Muslim organization that supported the
Lina Joy sort of argument," I replied. "They joined with several mostly non-
Muslim NGOs like Aliran and Suara Rakyat, but they do argue . . . that they
are a feminist organization, but they are Muslim women, and they want to
have total equality between men and women. They argue that the Qur'an
and Sunna needs to be reinterpreted in line with their goals and they find
some support . . . in their reinterpretations of Qur'an. They have a feminist
orientation, but they're saying they are *Muslima* struggling for equality and
fairness, and surely Islam is a fair and just religion. . . . There is definitely a
basis in many respects for equality between men and women in the Qur'an,
in my view, but I don't understand exactly what they're talking about in
terms of total equality, and is that consistent with the revelation we have
received from Allah *Subhaana wa Ta'ala* [the Glorified and Most High]?
What are some of your views about that?"

Zawati, beaming across her large wooden desk, responded, "Actually,
when you talk about equality in Islam it is not like if a man got one that a
woman should also get one. The terminology of equality in that context must
not be treated like that. As an example, we can look at the issue of inheritance, and we can say that the man should get two and the woman should
get only one. Islam makes it like that; we cannot say that it is unequal for
women. But we have to see why the Qur'an put it this way. . . . Men have the
responsibility to maintain their families, and that is why Allah revealed in
matters of inheritance that men should get two and the women should get
one. But the Sisters in Islam, as an example, put it in another way."

Gender equality means something different for these women than for the Sisters in Islam. They don't believe that equality implies symmetrical allocations or that what goes for men goes for women. Instead, they look to what Allah has decreed in terms of rights and responsibilities to men and women and try to understand them as an overall system that organizes this domain of social life. Their concept of *equality* stems from a cultural schema of sharia that includes the notion that Allah has sent down *hukum* (laws) in the Qur'an for people to apply in the world.

"Yes, they do," I said, agreeing with Zawati's statement about SIS. "They argue that historically that was based on a context in which men were providing most of the *nafkah* [economic support] and women were not working the way women are working now. They're saying that there are changed conditions. Many more women now are able to provide support for the family . . . or at least to help . . . and so they're arguing that can be reinterpreted now within the new context. I think that is their . . . methodology, that we have to consider the different context. But, of course, then that relates to the issue of the division of property when couples are divorced. They argue that from their research in some of the states there are some *hakim* who are actually dividing the property and calculating the wealth that women have provided . . . when they divide the property. They say this is not fair if it is the man's responsibility to provide the *nafkah* but the women's wealth she produced from her own work is included in the property to be divided."

"So far I don't think we have cases in which . . . men get the property of the wife unless the property is a joint property," Aisha said. "The judge only divides the property if it is joint property . . . but if the property is from what the wife worked for, the judges will not give it to the husband upon divorce. There are no cases in which the judge does this."

"Let's say they bought the house together, then the judge will calculate how much the wife contributed to it. . . . The joint property is divided according to sharia family laws. . . . The wife does not get to take the husband's retirement savings, and it is the same the other way around."

I considered how this contrasts with the way family courts handle divisions of marital property in the United States. In New York State, for instance, the funds accrued in both spouses' retirement accounts over the course of the marriage are divided fifty-fifty upon divorce. Shifting the topic to international human rights, I asked the government sharia experts about some of the human rights concerns of NGOs about women and Muslims in general, particularly in regard to Article 11, and the argument that the implementation of Islamic laws contradicts the universal standards of human rights that have been agreed on at an international level.

Aisha responded directly, saying, "Internationally, the freedom of religion can only be practiced by those who are non-Muslims. For Muslims there is no such thing as freedom of religion. . . . The intention of the Parliament when they regulate such laws is to give the non-Muslims freedom to practice whatever religion they want, but not for the Muslims. And we, in every state, [are restricted from promoting] other religion to Muslims. It is a crime to persuade Muslims to commit . . . apostasy. Yes, we have the Article 11 movement, which is led by Professor Shad Faruqi, but he is actually . . . In Malaysia we practice the Shāfiʿī school of law, but some of those who join this movement follow the Ḥanafī school of law or Shia."

I was taken aback by the claim that Muslim supporters of the Article 11 movement were deviating from norms of Shāfiʿī jurisprudence in Malaysia, but I did not want to interrupt her. Aisha didn't complete the sentence about Dr. Shad Saleem Faruqi, a professor of law and supporter of SIS, but it appears she wanted to say that he is a Ḥanafite or Shiite. While Ḥanafites are considered followers of one of the four schools of jurisprudence within the fold of Sunni Islam, Malaysian religious officials have deemed Shiites to be a deviant sect and followers are occasionally arrested for offenses related to ʿaqidah (proper religious beliefs).

Elaborating further on their position, Zawati stated, "I think that Article 11 gives freedom of religion to all persons, but it is not absolute freedom. Because we have to follow laws that guide us, as cited in the Lina Joy case, if she intends to convert out of Islam she must follow the procedures. She must go to the sharia court and get a declaration that she is no longer a Muslim. So, in that case, the judge can perform an ijtihād [religious interpretation based on scriptures] whether to give her counseling or to take her back to Islam. But if there is no other way, and we fail to take her back as a Muslim, then maybe the judge can decide after that that she is no longer a Muslim. But we have to follow the laws. If you want to convert out, you have to go to the court. We cannot simply declare that we are no longer a Muslim, because it will cause a more chaotic situation in Malaysia."

"But from the non-Muslim point of view . . . they often complain that if they want to marry a Muslim, they have to convert under the law," I interjected. Then there are issues of conversion that happen in the midst of marriages. Apparently there was an Indian mountaineer who converted to Islam and his wife did not know. He passed away, and of course he had to get a proper Islamic burial, [but] I think his family was Hindu. These are some of the issues that many . . . non-Muslims are concerned about, that violate what they perceive to be their rights."

Moorthy Maniam alias Mohammad Abdullah, a former mountaineer, had converted to Islam before his death in 2005. His widow, Kaliammal, wanting to provide Hindu last rites for him, challenged the conversion. Before the civil court heard her plea, the Federal Territory religious department obtained an order from the sharia court giving them the right to provide Islamic last rites for her deceased husband (Netto 2007). Cases like this, contested and labeled "bodysnatching" by liberal rights activists, occur frequently in Malaysia. On the other hand, there are cases in which sharia courts have decided that Malaysians "born as Muslims" were not Muslims at the time of their death.[2]

Zawati responded right away to this issue: "As you said a problem arises when, as an example, a party has a civil marriage and then one of the couple converts to Islam. From here a lot of problems [arise], and we also have not been able to settle them in terms of the legality of marriage, because we have two laws governing the marriage of these persons. One [law is that] according to civil marriage, the non-Muslim party has the capacity to make a petition for divorce [but the Muslim party does not]. Although, in Islam, we know when one of the parties converts to Islam automatically the marriage will be dissolved. . . . But in the civil law it's stated like that. It can't be like that, where only the non-Muslim party has the capacity to petition for divorce. In our Islamic family law, we have a different provision, that the sharia court has the power to certify that the marriage has been dissolved."

I asked about what law takes precedence in a case where one party converts to Islam and the other remains non-Muslim.

Aisha interjected, "The current law is that in three months after the conversion a non-Muslim wife can apply for divorce. . . . It is up to the wife to apply for the divorce. But according to sharia law, after one pronounces Islam automatically the marriage is dissolved."[3]

"But what if she doesn't? Can the husband go to the sharia court and get a declaration?" I asked, expressing confusion at how this can be worked out.

"That is the problem that arises now in Malaysia," Zawati said with a brief chuckle expressing frustration. "Because of the dual system, we [have] a problem. The civil law says like this and the sharia law says like this." She explained that they are conducting research and working to amend the laws to make these conversion cases easier to resolve.

Haryaty added, "If the [non-Muslim] wife does not apply for the divorce, then the marriage would go on."

"So the civil marriage would go on? If the man wanted to marry a *Muslima*, wouldn't they have to get a formal order from the sharia court [confirming] that the former marriage was dissolved?"

"The sharia court can't produce the proper order to say that the civil marriage is dissolved or not, because the sharia court has no power to declare that the civil marriage is dissolved when a person converts to Islam."

"So then they could issue a new marriage agreement for that Muslim man to marry a *Muslima*, right?"

"Yes, that is correct. That is the problem now because of the dual system, and each law states it in a different way. We try to harmonize between the civil and the sharia to settle the problem because there are lots of persons that convert to Islam, but we cannot cater for their past marriages because the sharia court has no jurisdiction over the non-Muslims," Zawati said, summing up the current impasse and ongoing effort to work things out between the two court systems.

Continuing on this topic, I stated, "So it seems . . . that the civil court used to be considered the higher court . . . and you have people like Karpal Singh saying that it should always be the 'high court' and that Malaysia should never be an Islamic state. But what do you think now? Are the sharia court and the civil court on the same level now in terms of the procedure and the kind of power that the different courts have?"

Zawati chuckled again, expressing her discontent, and stated, "I think the civil and sharia courts actually have their total independence as courts. But because all the laws [were] drafted in Malaysia, we are bound to follow the Federal Constitution. The Federal Constitution converts the power to state [and] federal [levels], and [specifies] what laws they can regulate. It is hard to say. But I don't think the sharia court is not independent, still bound to follow the civil court . . . they have their own jurisdiction."

Aisha added, "In my own personal opinion, there is no such thing that the sharia court is higher or lower from the civil court. I believe that both stand on their own and both have their own powers. As it states in the Federal Constitution, in Article 121(1A), the civil court and the sharia court shall have separate jurisdiction and both stand on their own. Maybe in terms of management we will say that the civil court has a higher style as compared to the sharia court, because the sharia court covers most of the Muslims, and every state in Malaysia has their own standing and same rank with the civil court. They both issue binding decisions in Malaysia."

Given the extant overlapping jurisdictions of civil and sharia court cases involving non-Muslim and Muslim parties, political and police forces are faced with resolving situations in which both legal systems issue competing decisions. When a civil law marriage dissolves due to the conversion of one spouse to Islam, both court systems are implicated in resolving an interfaith child custody battle. In addition, the new Muslim convert may unilaterally convert the children to Islam or at least change the official registration of their religious status. Therefore, whether the offspring are Muslims or non-Muslims is a further complication. The civil court is involved because the marriage was originally between two non-Muslims, but the sharia court also becomes involved due to one spouse's conversion to Islam. For instance, S. Deepa, a Hindu woman, and Izwan Abdullah, a Muslim convert, disputed the custody of their two children, a nine-year-old girl and a six-year-old boy, whom Izwan converted to Islam. In 2013 Izwan received an order from the Shariah High Court of Seremban, Negeri Sembilan, awarding him custody of their son, whom he took from his mother to live with him. However, in April 2014 Deepa received an order from the Seremban High Court awarding her custody of both children, which was subsequently upheld in the Court of Appeal. Although the civil court ordered the police to return the six-year-old son to Deepa, the inspector general of the police refused to side with either the civil or the sharia court, claiming to be caught between the two legal systems (*Malay Mail Online* 2014a). Amid growing public attention and controversy, prime minister Najib Razak called on the parties in child custody cases with competing civil and sharia orders to seek judgments from the Federal Court and to accept the decision rendered by the highest civil court (*Malaysiakini* 2014). It is telling that the prime minister did not direct the parties to seek a binding decision from the highest sharia court in the state of Negeri Sembilan, the Shariah Court of Appeal. While the apparent stalemate between the civil and sharia court orders indicates that Malay authorities were interpreting Article 121 of the constitution to mean that the sharia courts and the *lower* civil courts have an equivalent level of jurisdiction when Muslims and non-Muslims are involved in family law cases, the prime minister's practice of pointing the parties toward the Federal Court suggests that it has authority not only over the *lower* civil courts but also over the state-level sharia courts. His practice embodies a cultural model of sharia in Malaysian society.

"How about the variations in the polygamy laws? Have they been standardized across the states?" I asked, shifting the topic again.

"Yes, in terms of polygamous marriage, we have standardized all the provisions and the states have adopted the provisions in their enactments. I don't think there is much difference in terms of polygamous marriage. The provision clearly states that if a man wants a second marriage, he must come to court with his current wife, future wife, and the parents-in-law, and in this forum the judge will decide whether the man has the capability to get married to another wife. . . . The content of the provision is similar with all the states because they have adopted the provisions from federal law."

Aisha clarified, "Most of the states have the same provisions. Out of all the states in Malaysia, eleven states adopted the provision from federal [law]."

They asked me about the topic of my previous research in Malaysia. I described my earlier project in Melaka, focusing on ethnic and religious diversity, and some of my work in Indonesia. I thanked them for their time and their responses to my questions, and they gave me a copy of the 1999 enactment on *wakaf* (religious endowments) and *wasiat* (Muslim wills) in Selangor.

MARRIAGE, MALE GUARDIANSHIP, AND RIGHTS AND DUTIES

Religious officials, like those I met with at JAKIM, IKIM, and in the sharia courts, are involved in debates with people from several other segments of society—such as liberal rights activists, Muslim feminist reformers, and nongovernmental, conservative *ulama* and worshipers—about the manner of implementing sharia family laws. Many perspectives wrangling over approaches to sharia are circulated in spoken and written discourse in mass media, bulletins, books, and conversations. These engagements in the public sphere are often also about matters intertwined with Islamic law and ethics, such as the position and rights of ethnic and religious minorities in the Malaysian nation-state, the condition and status of Muslim women in contemporary society, and the proper stance on universal human rights in a secular but Malay Muslim–dominated polity. Government religious officials and political leaders adjust their policies in response to discourses pushing them in different directions.

Malaysia, like many other Muslim societies, has enacted a sharia family law provision prohibiting the marriage of Muslims to non-Muslims. This provision standardized across the states of Malaysia states that "no [Muslim] man shall marry a non-Muslim except a *Kitabiyah*, and no [Muslim] woman shall marry a non-Muslim." In the Islamic family law acts, *Kitabiyah* is defined as a "woman whose ancestors were from the *Bani Ya'qub* [People of Ya'qub]; or a Christian woman whose ancestors were Christians before the prophethood of the Prophet Muhammad; or a Jewess whose ancestors were Jews before the prophethood of the Prophet Isa." Because of the

difficulty of demonstrating such unbroken descent from these early communities of "People of the Book," it is commonly understood in Malaysia, by
Muslims and non-Muslims alike, that Muslim men and women can only
form valid marriages with fellow Muslims. This sharia provision is based on
the Qur'an, Sūra Al-Baqarah 2:221—"Nor marry (your girls) to unbelievers
until they believe"—and Sūra Al-Mā'ida 5:5—"(Lawful unto you in marriage) are (not only) chaste women who are believers, but chaste women
among the People of the Book, revealed before your time" (Abdullah Yusuf
1992). In some plural societies, arguments have been made to reinterpret
these verses in the direction of expanding the category of "believers" to
include Christians, Jews, and others who believe in God (Black, Esmaeili,
and Hosen 2013, 113). As it stands in Malaysia, conversion of the non-Muslim
party is required before he or she can marry a Muslim, and his or her family
members often view such religious conversions as acts of leaving behind
one's own ethnic identity and becoming Malay (*masuk Melayu*). In addition, if one party of a non-Muslim civil marriage converts to Islam, the marriage is dissolved once the sharia court confirms the conversion. This leads
to volatile contests over unilateral conversions of children, child custody,
and overlapping court jurisdictions. For many years, Buddhist, Hindu, and
Christian minorities have been arguing for relaxing these regulations requiring conversion in favor of facilitating greater national integration.[4] Religious
officials and Malay political elites show no signs of changing this provision.
However, highly publicized legal disputes over child custody in these conversion cases have garnered a limited but significant response from the
fatwa council in one northern state (discussed below).

The Sisters in Islam, non-Muslim women's organizations, and Democratic Action Party members of Parliament have been openly critical of
underage marriage in Malaysia. The Islamic family law enactments set the
minimum age for marriage at eighteen for men and sixteen for women,
"except where the Syariah Judge has granted his permission in writing in
certain circumstances."[5] Several publicized cases of sharia courts allowing
underage Muslim girls to marry drew strong reactions and calls for reform
from several sectors. One such case that appeared in the media while I was
in Malaysia in 2010 was the marriage of Siti Marham Mahmod, a fourteen-
year-old girl, to Abdul Manan Othman, a twenty-three-year-old man. This
case even elicited a public statement from Datuk Seri Shahrizat Abdul Jalil,
the minister of Women, Family, and Community Development, who said,
"At 14, one is too young to understand what marriage is all about. There
is responsibility and a lifetime of commitment, as a wife and later on, as a

parent. The syariah court must be more cautious when granting approvals in such cases" (Masami 2010). In the same *New Straits Times* article, Maria Chin Abdullah, the executive director of Empower Malaysia, criticized the government for permitting "child marriages" and thereby not upholding the Convention on the Rights of the Child (CRC) and the Convention on the Elimination of All Forms of Discrimination against Women (CEDAW).[6] Many calls have been made for setting the minimum age of marriage for both men and women at eighteen.

Shariah Lower Court judge Hakim Suhaily told me he was disturbed that the minister of Women, Family, and Community Development had made this public statement without first consulting with him as the judge on the case. He explained that he was also concerned about education and the rights of children, but that judges in sharia courts must also consider other criteria before reaching a decision. In this case, he said, both sets of parents were in favor of the marriage, and the prospective husband was capable of providing financial support for his family. The young man also exhibited strong Islamic knowledge and was willing to allow his wife to continue her education in the Islamic school where she was studying. The judge was also concerned about the possibility of these youth committing a sin if they were denied permission to marry. Speaking in his office in the Federal Territories Shariah Court in Kuala Lumpur, Hakim Suhaily explained:

> The Hindus, Christians, and Buddhists say . . . if these children are underage they cannot get married. But we have to think is it fair enough? Is it perfect? In the US, they allow the underage children to have sexual intercourse but . . . the underage children cannot get married. In Islam, the worst thing in human life is actually adultery, the *zina*. And the best way to . . . overcome the *zina* is marriage, with the *halal* way. . . . We as sharia judges definitely have our own *ijtihād*, our own approach about how to make a judgment.[7]

Criticism of the sharia courts and religious officials continued to mount from both Muslim and non-Muslim segments of society, raising questions about the impact of such marriages on the well-being of children. The Fatwa Committee of the National Council for Islamic Affairs, the national body of jurists that issues authoritative sharia legal rulings (fatwa), which become law and guide the practice of judges, deliberated on the issue of child marriage. In October 2014 it issued a fatwa titled "Child Marriage: Investigation from the Aspect of Religion, Health, and Psychology," which was later published in a gazette and on its website.[8] Based on the findings of a Universiti Teknologi Malaysia research team, the *muzakarah* (consultation) of the National Fatwa Committee decided that the "marriage of children is not a new issue in Malaysia and that it can't continue to be viewed as a healthy practice in these times"; it continued to say that "although there are laws that solemnize the marriage of children in Malaysia, it does not mean that it can be done easily without considering the interests of children that desire to be married."[9] They proceeded to note that many of these underage marriages are caused by emotions that cannot be controlled by the couple and the desire of families to hide the shame of children being born out of wedlock. Furthermore, these marriages have been found to bring more harm than benefit, especially for young girls who develop many physical and mental health problems.

The *ulama* of the National Fatwa Committee integrated the scientific findings of the research team into their application of traditional legal methodology of the Shāfiʿī school. They stress that there is no *hadith* that promotes or advises the marriage of children, and that the marriage of Prophet Muhammad to the underage ʿĀisha does not make such marriages obligatory or recommended. To the contrary, they state that the *ijmaʿ* (consensus) of the Companions[10] during the time of the Messenger of Allah was to watch out for the *maṣlaḥah* (benefit, welfare) of children, which includes rulings tied to certain "*Maqasid Shariah* [objectives of Sharia] and *Qaedah Fiqhiyyah* [principles of jurisprudence] such as 'Avoiding Harm' (Darʾ al-Mafasid) and 'Grasping Benefit' (Jalb al-Masalih)." Moreover, they mention that the *ulama* of the Shāfiʿī school placed several conditions that have to be met before the marriage of children can be permitted. Finally, the council of jurists agreed that the criteria for approving underage marriage must be tightened and that sharia courts must carefully attend to the *maṣlaḥah* in the following manner before any such approval is granted: the *wali hakim* or judge representing the children has to fulfill the condition of justice; the marriage must not damage the life and future of the children in regard to education, psychology, health, and finances; and the couple being married must be of the same age group. This fatwa did not state any specific age limits, but it does suggest that marriages of elder men to underage girls would no longer be allowed.

Along with underage marriage, the Sisters in Islam has been critical of several other areas of family law, including marriage guardians (*wali*), polygamy, marital rights and duties, and domestic violence. They strive to push sharia family laws away from patriarchal gender hierarchies and toward gender equality and universal human rights. The standard sharia legal provision, Section 13 of the Islamic Family Law (Federal Territories) Act of 1984 as amended in 1992 and 1994, on the consent required for marriage, states that "a marriage should not be recognized and shall not be registered under this Act unless both parties to the marriage have consented thereto, and either the *wali* of the woman has consented thereto in accordance with Hukum Syara'; or the Syariah Judge . . . has . . . granted his consent thereto as *wali Raja*." Nik Noriani Nik Badlishah (2003, 19), an SIS activist, condemned the provision in the state of Kelantan's Islamic Family Law Enactment of 1983 that provided the *wali mujbir* (father, paternal grandfather, and above) of a virgin woman with the right of solemnizing a marriage without her consent. She noted that the traditional Shāfiʿī doctrine of *ijbar* (compulsion), which the jurists in Kelantan were following, which granted the *wali mujbir* this right under certain conditions, did not fit the local customs of economic self-reliance and independence of women and the direction of legal change in most Muslim countries. The Kelantan Islamic Family Law Enactment of 2002 repealed and replaced the 1983 enactment and included the standard provision above that required the consent of both the prospective husband and wife. Nevertheless, a male *wali* is still required to consent to the marriage of the bride. Among the four Sunni schools of jurisprudence, only the Ḥanafis validate marriages without a *wali*. However, the Federal Territories Shariah Court chief justice Datuk Haji Mohamad bin Haji Abdullah informed me that marriages performed according to this Ḥanafi position would not be valid in Malaysia.

SIS efforts to address gender discrimination and patriarchy in sharia family laws continue to come up against stiff opposition from traditional jurists. Nik Noriani (2003, 126–27) and an affiliated working group of scholars recommended that "responsibility for the property of a minor child should be granted to a trustee appointed by the court, and not become an automatic legal right of the father." One of the cofounders of SIS, Zainah Anwar, told me emphatically, "Women are heads of household; women are protectors and providers of families; families cannot survive on one salary. We do not live in an extended family system; we live in a nuclear family system." The group argues that the laws must be reformed in the direction of reflecting these changing social realities. However, many Malaysian jurists and other conservative social forces are committed to a more traditional Islamic worldview that understands the family and household sphere as one properly under male leadership. When I mentioned some SIS ideas about gender equality to Dato' Wira Sheikh Yahaya bin Hj. Jusoh, chief justice of

The Federal Territory Shariah Court, 2010

the Kedah Shariah Court, he stated, "In Islam . . . [the] goal in marriage . . . is for extensive harmony in the family. . . . The reason for the requirement of having a *wali* in a marriage is that he acts as the head of the family. His children can come and ask him questions. It is better to have a *wali* to keep things under control. The family can follow him. If there are grandchildren and they don't know who is in control, there is no harmony in the family."[11] These contrasting ideas about guardianship and leadership in households are part of different cultural models of social relations in families.

After the marriage is solemnized, the sharia registrar enters the prescribed particulars, including the value of the *mas kahwin* and *pemberian*[12] and the *ta'liq* (promises expressed by the husband in accordance with Hukum Syara'), and both parties to the marriage, the *wali*, and two witnesses attest to these recorded details. The law requires that each marriage be officially registered, and each party to the marriage receives a marriage certificate and a *ta'liq* certificate. If the husband violates these promises during the course of the marriage, this can be considered grounds for divorce once verified by the sharia court. SIS argues that the standard *ta'liq*—promises not to fail in providing *nafkah* to his wife for more than four months and not to cause her bodily harm—should be expanded to include other stipulations, such as a promise that the husband will not practice polygamy during the marriage (Nik Noriani 2003, 21). However, there is opposition even to these limited standard contractual stipulations. Dato' Dr. Zaleha binti Kamarudin, the deputy director of the Institute of Islamic Understanding Malaysia (IKIM) and professor at the International Islamic University Malaysia, told me, "Those guys trained in the Middle East say this is not pure sharia: 'I just got married to her, and you have me recite all these *ta'liq.'* . . . When I was teaching, [my students, who] were trained in Medina and Jordan, said they recited them [these stipulations] to save the face of their family and the bride's family. . . . They said these were never practiced in Saudi [Arabia]."[13] Dr. Zaleha informed me that *ta'liq*, first introduced in the state of Negeri Sembilan and later across the states of colonial Malaya in the 1940s, were found to be "good because you don't have to bring the husband to court. . . . If the men have breached this [stipulation] one, two, three, or four . . . you don't have to get the man to pronounce the *talaq* [repudiation]. The wife is already divorced after the breach of one of these conditions." Thus it is easier for a woman to divorce a man that has broken a stipulation he agreed to as part of the marriage contract.

As the sharia lawyers from JAKIM informed me, the provisions for polygamy have been adopted by the various states based on the Federal Territories Family Law Act of 1984, in which Section 23, from the amendment in 1994, states, "No man, during the subsistence of a marriage, shall, except with the prior permission in writing of the Court, contract another marriage with another woman nor shall such marriage contracted without such permission be registered under this Act: Provided that the Court may if it is shown that such marriage is valid according to Hukum Syara' order it to be registered subject to section 123 [polygamy without the court's permission]." This latter section states that the penalty for contracting a polygamous marriage without the court's permission is a fine of up to RM 1,000 and/or up to six months in prison. Other subsections of Section 23 describe the process for a man to legally apply to contract an additional marriage and the hearing of his application in court, in which he and his existing wife or wives are summoned to appear. The provision calls for the sharia court judges to evaluate the applicant's grounds for the proposed marriage, his ability to support all his wives and dependents, and his ability to accord equal treatment to all his wives. SIS and their supporters contend that Muslims need to rethink the Qur'an, Sūra An-Nisā 4:3: "Marry women of your choice, two, or three, or four; but if ye fear that ye shall not be able to deal justly (with them), then only one . . . that will be more suitable, to prevent you from doing injustice" (Abdullah Yusuf 1992). In my discussion with Zainah Anwar, she queried why the final part of this verse could not be the basis of the law: "For me, I'm not happy with polygamy, I read 4:3 and I read the whole verse and it says, 'If you feel you cannot do justice, marry only one.' Now, why can't that be the source of the law? Why should marry two, three, or four be a source of law? Who decides that marry two, three, or four shall be the Islamic position and marry only one is not Islamic?"[14] Contemporary religious officials have taken a contrasting stance in responding to SIS concerns about women's rights. Following traditional Sunni jurisprudence that looks to the Qur'an and *hadith* as the major sources of law, they uphold husbands' rights to marry up to four wives, but under conditions controlled by the sharia courts intended to also protect the rights of women.[15] Another cofounder of SIS, Norani Othman, a sociologist and professor at UKM, told me that the Sisters in Islam responded to the pressure from conservative forces of the Islamic resurgence of the 1970s and 1980s: "The pressure to change came first from the Islamists. They did not like the law that was in existence prior to 1984, because the law we had until that time was one of the best, a good model law for all the Muslim countries. For example, for polygamy it [placed] five conditions, [including] the explicit permission of the first wife; [and the right of] the judge to inquire from the first wife whether she thinks this will affect her happiness and her standard of living."[16] In response to resurgent Islamic movements and scholars, religious and government officials removed conditions, such as permission of the first wife, that were considered contrary to traditional understandings of Islamic principles. Current family laws defend the husband's prerogative to practice polygyny without direct restraints from his wife or wives, but under judicial control designed to curb abuse of the practice by men who are financially and morally unqualified.

However, as SIS and some sharia lawyers point out, there is a significant gap between the provisions in theory and the actual practice of implementation concerning many areas of sharia law, including polygamy. Norani Othman informed me that SIS organized a nationwide study of polygamy to "collect the data of the lived experiences of women, men, and children in polygamous situations" to show conservative Islamic groups the harm this practice brings. They found that the courts allow men to marry additional wives although they are financially incapable of supporting their families, and that women are forced to provide *nafkah* for themselves and their children. In addition, courts tended to penalize men who contract additional marriages without permission of the court with fines far below the maximum allowed under the law. Norani asked emphatically, "If he cannot afford to pay the fine of five hundred ringgit, how in the hell can he afford to support another wife?"

Disputes over conceptions of marital rights and duties between SIS and religious officials illustrate contrasting cultural models organizing the domain of social relations. In standard sharia family law enactments and in Malaysian Muslim society, a man is required to pay *mas kahwin* and present *pemberian* (or bride wealth) to the bride, and to provide *nafkah* to his wife or wives and children. In addition, fathers, paternal males, or male judges have the right to be marriage guardians, and in Section 88 fathers are considered the "first and primary natural guardian of the person and property of his minor child," and if he dies, the right devolves to his father. On the other hand, women, mothers, and grandmothers are expected to be primary caregivers for children, and wives are obligated to be obedient to their husbands. Section 129 states, "Any woman who willfully disobeys any order lawfully given by her husband according to Hukum Syara' commits an offence and shall be punished with a fine not exceeding one hundred ringgit [approximately US$33] or, in the case of a second or subsequent offence, with a fine not exceeding five hundred ringgit [US$166]." In addition, if the court finds that the wife has been *nusyuz* "without valid reason according to Hukum Syara'," then she is not entitled to maintenance from her husband or former husband (Sections 59 and 65). Taken together, these and other provisions suggest a cultural model of male providers, protectors, and guardians of the family and female caregivers and obedient wives.

The Sisters in Islam advocated a modernist model that they argue better fits with contemporary times. Zainah Anwar argued:

> Women now are playing the roles that men played traditionally, so should women then stop being educated, and stop working? They say that your money is your money, but of course if your kids are starving, your house is leaking, and your car has broken down, and your husband does not pay for all that and does not have the means to pay, then of course you will pay. And anyway, we think that today's marriage should be a marriage of partnership and not a marriage of domination. We don't want the man to be the sole provider, because women are working. Just as women's roles have changed, men's roles should change, and in some situations they have changed. Many men are helping in the house and sharing toward more of a partnership of marriage. Therefore, legal rights and the law have to reflect

reality, because if the law doesn't reflect reality, then that is why we have all these social problems.

She maintains that the laws (*hukum*) should be made to fit the times (*zaman*), rather than the other way around. The SIS methodology is to move from the lived realities and experiences of women to reinterpretations of the sacred texts that resonate with these contemporary realities. Her discourse suggests a cultural model in which men and women are marriage partners, both providers and caretakers in the household.[17]

Dato' Dr. Zaleha binti Kamarudin told me that IKIM, similar to JAKIM, invites SIS members to their conferences and engages them in discussions on several issues pertaining to gender and sharia laws, although IKIM officials acknowledge that they have a different perspective and approach. In contrast to SIS, she asserted that in the *muzakara* of traditional Muslim scholars in Malaysia "you don't change the law, you change the society to follow the law." She expressed the view that Muslim men should be the *khalifah* (or caliph) of the family, but as good leaders they should engage in consultation (*mushawarah*), participate in discussion with other family members, and be reliable and trustworthy (*amanah*). From her research and experience with divorce in Muslim families, she learned that most problems stem from issues related to the rights and duties of husbands and wives. In her opinion, the solution is to promote Qur'anic governance of the family through implementing sharia laws:

> When you just talk about the concept of *khalifah* without all these *necessary* things, there goes everything that is going to be wrong. But we realize that because the society today is not a God-fearing society, what we should do—this is from my humble opinion—is the Qur'anic governance of the family should be supported by the legal requirements in terms of Islamic family law. . . . For example, we make it a regulation that for a man and woman to marry, it must be with their consent. They must have a certain age, the age of majority, although in Islam there is no such thing as age of majority before you marry. . . . But we say, okay, we realize that the concept of *taklif*, of pro-responsibility, is important because to become a *khalifah* you must understand the responsibilities. Based on . . . what we call the *maqāṣid sharīʿah*, then you must have a certain age for marriage because it is related to pro-responsibility, which is part of *khalifah*-ship. But you cannot realize that in a society which is not God-fearing—therefore you make it a law, because you know that people will follow the law.

SIS has also been critical of domestic violence in Malaysian society. Norani Othman stated that there was a rise in the rates of domestic violence from the 1960s to the 1980s in all social classes, and she felt it was explained, at least partially, by the influence of the "more Arabized, the more fundamentalist view of what Islam means, that you have to practice Islam in your personal life, in your family life."[18] She noted that many conservative Muslims of the Islamic resurgence were opposed to a domestic violence act that applied to non-Muslims and Muslims alike. In response, SIS and other women's rights groups lobbied, charging that there was "really no gender equality" unless such an act were passed. Religious and government officials have integrated women's concerns about domestic violence into sharia family laws. Standard marriage contracts include a stipulation that if the husband beats his wife, it is grounds for a *ta'liq*-mediated divorce or a *fasakh* (at-fault) application for divorce. SIS complained about the onerous burden of proof placed on battered wives, which required them to provide two male witnesses. They called for use of medical reports as documentary evidence. Subsequently, Malaysian jurists have adopted the Mālikī school's position on evidence in these cases rather than the strict Shāfiʿī requirement of two male witnesses. Their use of Mālikī rulings on evidence allows abused wives to present medical evidence and thereby facilitates judgments in their favor in sharia courts. Many in the sharia judiciary have informed me that although Shāfiʿī school is their foundation, they also follow the opinions of the other three Sunni schools of jurisprudence in order to attain goodness and to seek out the *maṣlaḥah*. Ahmed Fekry Ibrahim (2015) argues that this practice of *takhayyur*, selecting the less stringent juristic position within and across schools, is one of the principles of pragmatic eclecticism that introduced more flexibility into Islamic law.

DIVORCE, CUSTODY, AND SUPPORT
OF CHILDREN AND EX-SPOUSES

The Sisters in Islam, liberal rights activists, and conservative Islamic forces also wrangle over several aspects of sharia law provisions pertaining to divorce, custody, and financial support. As noted above, violations of *ta'liq* in the marriage contract or change of religion may lead to dissolution of the marriage. In addition to conversion to Islam within a marriage of a non-Muslim couple, renunciation of Islam in a marriage between two Muslims may also dissolve the marriage once confirmed by the sharia court. Section 130 states that any spouse who "by deception makes himself or herself an apostate in order to annul his or her marriage commits an offence and shall be punished with imprisonment not exceeding six months." Much of the controversy surrounding divorce is related to husband-initiated unilateral pronouncement of divorce or *talaq*. There are seventeen subsections to the standard provision on divorce by *talaq* in which the religious officials and sharia courts attempt to control and supervise pronouncements of divorce by husbands. They initially attempt to organize *suluh* or mediation with conciliatory committees to effect reconciliation between the husband and wife. However, if this fails the sharia court will direct the husband to pronounce a *talaq* before the court. A husband can also apply for divorce by *li'an*, in which he claims under oath that his wife committed adultery; even if she denies it in her oaths, the court accepts the husband's oath after "he invokes the wrath of God should he be lying" (Black, Esmaeili, and Hosen 2013, 138). A woman can apply for a *khul'* divorce or *cerai tebus talaq*, in which she pays an agreed-on amount to her husband and in turn the court orders him to pronounce a divorce by redemption. The court can appoint a conciliatory committee that may draw out the process of the wife attaining this form of no-fault divorce. Women more commonly apply for at-fault divorce (*fasakh*) based on Mālikī opinions that extend the valid grounds beyond the more limited position of the Shāfi'ī school. Moreover, one of the subsections of Section 52 opens up the women's application of *fasakh* "to any other ground that is recognized as valid for dissolution of marriages or *fasakh* under Hukum Syara." SIS and some other women's groups have complained about both long processes when women apply for divorces and "unfair bargaining pressures" during negotiations aimed at compelling women to forfeit some of their interests in *mut'ah* (obligatory divorce gifts from the husband), *'iddah* maintenance (paid for three months after divorce), and joint marital property (Nik Noriani 2003, 37).

According to the sharia family law enactments, a husband is required to pay *nafkah* to his ex-wife for the three-month *'iddah* period and for all children of the marriage until they reach eighteen years of age. The amount of maintenance the man is required to pay is based primarily on an assessment of the means and needs of the parties involved, and the courts have the power to vary the amount of maintenance as circumstances change. Maintenance for the divorced woman includes entitlement to stay in the home where she lived when she was married or another suitable accommodation during the period of *'iddah*. The sharia court may extend financial support for children beyond the age of eighteen to enable them to pursue higher education or training. A man willfully failing to comply with the court order for maintenance may be fined or imprisoned. However, Zainah Anwar told me that a high percentage of fathers do not pay maintenance despite having the money, and the sharia courts rarely punish them for being in contempt of court. She argues that the fact that men are not performing their traditional duty as providers—and, instead, women are often playing this role nowadays—necessitates a change in the traditional conception of marriage and the framework of sharia family laws.

Finally, the standard sharia family law enactments give custody (*hadhanah*) of an infant to the mother until a male child reaches the age of seven and a female child reaches the age of nine. If a mother applies to extend this period of custody, the court may allow her to retain custody until a male child reaches nine and a female child eleven. After this time custody shifts to the father until the child has reached the age of *mumaiyiz*, or discernment of right and wrong, which can be as early as seven for boys and nine for girls.[19] At the age of *mumaiyiz*, the provision entitles the child to make his or her choice of living with either of the parents, unless the court orders otherwise. The sharia court judges I interviewed tell me that they try to allow the children to make their own decisions without any unfair interference from the parents. According to Federal Territories Shariah Lower Court judge Hakim Suhaily, "There is no right of the father or mother to go against the children's decision. . . . If the children choose the father, we just go with what the children prefer to do. We cannot reject . . . because in Islam everyone has their own rights. It is *haram* [forbidden] if other parties try to ignore the other's rights. . . . After the age of *mumaiyiz* the children have their own rights." In Alor Setar, Kedah Shariah Higher Court judge Syeikh Mohd Roze bin Abdul Wahab shared a few of his recent files from child custody cases. In one case, three children beyond the age of *mumaiyiz* chose to stay with their mother and the court arranged visitation for the father; in another case, with two children, one selected the mother and the other selected the father.

Many liberal rights organizations and activists are clamoring over several highly publicized cases of child custody, such as that of S. Deepa and Izwan Abdullah described above, that involve the conversion of one of the parties to Islam. The standard sharia family law provision states that one of the main qualifications necessary for a mother to be entitled to child custody and for a father to be the guardian is that she or he be a Muslim. Most religious officials in sharia courts tend to favor giving custody to the Muslim parent in these cases of conversion to Islam within civil law marriages. Sharia courts recognize that the marriage has been dissolved and give custody of the converted, or registered as Muslim, children to the parent that has become Muslim. This appears to be consistent with the primary necessity of sharia (*maqṣid al-sharī'a*), which according to the well-known Shāfi'ī scholar Abū Ḥāmid Muḥammad al-Ghazālī (d. 1111 CE) is preservation of religion. However, the Conference of the Perlis State Fatwa Committee issued a fatwa in April 2015 on the issue of "The Right of Child Custody for Parents of Different Religion" that conflicts with the standard provision across the states of Malaysia.[20] They decided that in these cases the right of custody should not be based on the religion of the mother or father, but rather on guaranteeing the *maslahah* of the child in terms of "moral and emotional growth and development." The Muslim parent has the right and is obligated to introduce Islam to the child regardless of whether he or she has custody. Thus, the mother has custody of any breastfed child, and then custody belongs to whichever parent can best nurture the growth of the child. Just as in the standard provision, after the age of *mumaiyiz*, the child is given the right to select the parent to have custody. It is yet to be seen whether any other state fatwa committees or the National Fatwa Committee will rule on this specific kind of custody case.

CONCLUSION

From my excursions to JAKIM, IKIM, and sharia courts, I was able to glean several important points about discourses of sharia in Malaysian society. First, civil servants educated under the ongoing Islamic resurgence fill the ranks of the religious bureaucracy. Their efforts to rationalize, modernize, and standardize the administration of Islamic law are intertwined with processes of raising the prominence and influence of Islam. Second, while many of these children of the Islamic resurgence express commitment to the Federal Constitution as the supreme law of the country, they also consider the secular format inherited from the colonial era as increasingly problematic. Third, their cultural models of sharia appear to differ both from those of the Sisters in Islam that entail ideas of gender equality familiar to many from Western societies and from those of the Malay Muslim political authorities that involve a stronger commitment to positioning sharia within an overarching secular format. While working within the common law and civil law structures inherited from the British colonial period, their legal provisions and reasoning style indicate a basis in a traditional Islamic worldview. Fourth, these civil servants of the religious bureaucracy combine their traditional Islamic ideas with notions of making Malaysia a well-organized, modern nation. Their perspectives represent a merging of ideas of the paradigmatic modern nation-state with those of the paradigmatic Islamic moral-legal system (cf. Hallaq 2013). In some ways they converge and diverge from perspectives of the Islamic Party of Malaysia and UMNO government officials. Fifth, there appears to be a tug-of-war over the shape of sharia family laws between Muslim conservative forces, liberal rights activists, and Muslim feminist reformers. The Malaysian state has sought to navigate a middle position between these forces in the dynamic context of the ongoing Islamic revival and an upsurge of opposition electoral politics. Finally, the current sharia family laws indicate reform within a traditional jurisprudential framework that has been more responsive to discourses from Muslim feminists than from liberal rights activists.

3 CRIMINAL LAW

Taking the Middle Road

IN CONTEMPORARY MALAYSIA, SHARIA CRIMINAL LAWS ARE IMPLE-
mented within the secular format inherited from the British colonial period.
The distinction between "public" secular laws and "private" Islamic laws
persists in postcolonial legal structures. Civil courts are federal and have
jurisdiction over most "public" aspects of criminal law for all Malaysians,
whereas the sharia courts operate at the state level and only have jurisdiction over "private" or "personal" violations of Islamic ethical norms and the
regulation of proselytization of non-Islamic religion to Muslims. The Federal
Constitution declares that state-level sharia courts have jurisdiction over
the following elements:

> [the] creation and punishment of offences by persons professing the
> religion of Islam against precepts of that religion, except in regard to
> matters included in the Federal List . . . the constitution, organisation and
> procedure of Syariah courts, which shall have jurisdiction only over
> persons professing the religion of Islam and in respect only of any of the
> matters included in this paragraph, but shall not have jurisdiction in
> respect of offences except in so far as conferred by federal law, the control
> of propagating doctrines and beliefs among persons professing the religion
> of Islam; the determination of matters of Islamic law and doctrine and
> Malay custom. (Abdul Aziz and Farid [2004] 2009, 405–6)

Sharia criminal laws are to be applied solely to Muslims, and only in areas
not included on the Federal List. Killing or causing bodily harm to others
without sufficient cause is against the precepts of Islam, but since these offenses
are on the Federal List for civil courts they are outside the purview of sharia
law. The Federal Constitution also provides for restrictions on non-Muslims
propagating religion to Muslims, as an exception to the broad religious freedom it extends to non-Muslims. Moreover, the level of punishment of Muslims transgressing Islamic norms is limited to that allowed by federal law.

The Syariah Courts (Criminal Jurisdiction) Act of 1965 as amended in 1984 states that such punishment cannot exceed three years of imprisonment, a RM 5,000 fine, a whipping of six strokes, or any combination of these penalties (Abdul Samat 2003, 104). Thus, the constitution and this federal law, as they stand, shut off the possibility of implementing ḥudūd and qiṣāṣ laws and the concomitant death penalty, amputations, retaliatory bodily harm, and more severe beatings that classical Islamic law—sharia codes canonized by early medieval times—imposed under certain conditions.

Taking a cue from Foucault, Wael Hallaq (2009, 308), a scholar of Islamic law, notes the epistemological difference between modern European conceptions of "criminal law" or "penal law" and premodern Muslim jurists' notions of "offenses against life, body, morality, public conduct and property," and asserts that it is imprecise to use the terms "criminal" and "penal" in reference to sharia "offenses." However, the epistemic transformation that overtook non-European legal and political structures and the inability to restore or institutionalize sharia laws under altered structural conditions are not as thoroughgoing as he contends (cf. Hallaq 2004, 2013). In fact, in Muslim-majority contexts, such as northern Nigeria, Pakistan, and Iran, "modern" concepts of the nation-state, citizenry, and criminal law articulate with traditional Islamic notions of an omniscient God, public morality, and an Islamic community (umma). In Malaysia, there is also a comparable articulation of these and related epistemes. Not only is the limited, state-level sharia criminal law structurally subordinate to the extensive, federal-level civil criminal law, but English common and civil law codification and procedures have also had a strong impact on sharia law. Nevertheless, the Malaysian judiciary and much of the Malaysian Muslim community consider the "substance" of sharia family and criminal laws to be Islamic. Malaysian jurists do use the term "criminal" along with jenayah and kesalahan (offense, wrong) for sharia offenses, and state religious agencies are involved in surveillance of citizens and enforcement of these laws. Even a non-Malaysian outsider glancing at the provisions of the sharia criminal law enactments and tables of offenses would recognize that the content of these laws is rooted in the traditional norms and values of an Islamic worldview. Yet the linking of concepts of international human rights, liberal rights of citizens, and secular-pluralism to concepts of the rights of Allah, the imperative to preserve Islam, and the centrality of the Muslim and/or Malay majority in a sharia-oriented polity are not so easily fused.

As with sharia family laws, JAKIM, IKIM, and other government ulama and officials have been working to modernize and standardize sharia criminal laws. However, while some states have adopted many of the Federal Territories' provisions, there remains more variation in sharia criminal laws across the states than in family laws. There are also heated debates and skirmishes between social forces—such as Muslim conservatives, reformers, and liberal rights activists—over the implementation of sharia criminal laws. These clashes are propelling a drive toward strengthening sharia laws; nonetheless, dominant Malay Muslims continue to grapple with notions of the nation and plural citizens within a worldview, constituted by sharia models, symbols, and metaphors, that increasingly challenges the secular format.

SHARIA CRIMINAL LAW OFFENSES

The Malaysian Islamic judiciary strives to uphold Islamic ethical norms and public morality through extending discretionary punishments (Ar. *ta'zīr*; M. *takzir*) to cover offenses that faced more severe *ḥudūd* penalties in classical jurisprudence. In classical *fiqh* texts, there were three main categories of criminal law, each with separate chapters: provisions regarding offenses against persons that included retaliation (*qiṣāṣ*) and financial compensation (*diya*), provisions regarding offenses mentioned in the Qur'an and considered violations of the claims of Allah (*ḥuqūq Allah*) with mandatory fixed punishments (*ḥudūd*), and provisions regarding discretionary punishment of forbidden acts that endanger public order or state security (*ta'zīr* and *siyāsa*) (Peters 2005, 7; Hallaq 2009, 311). The *ḥudūd* offenses were theft (*sariqa*), highway robbery or banditry (*qaṭ' al-ṭariq, ḥirāba*), unlawful sexual intercourse (*zinā*), slanderous accusation of unlawful sexual intercourse (*qadhf*), drinking alcohol (*shurb khamr*), and apostasy (*ridda*) (according to Shāfi'īs and some other schools of jurisprudence). These all had fixed punishments based on the Qur'an or *hadith*. Depending on fulfillment of the strict rules of evidence of classical jurisprudence, thieves could be penalized with amputation of a hand or foot, bandits with amputation of the right hand and left foot, fornicators with one hundred lashes, adulterers with capital punishment, slanderers with eighty lashes, alcohol drinkers with forty lashes, and apostates with the death penalty. Currently in Malaysia, theft and robbery are under the jurisdiction of civil courts and the offenses of drinking alcohol, *zinā*, *qadhf*, and apostasy face less strict discretionary punishments. There are three different kinds of laws for apostasy across the states of Malaysia, which will be discussed below. Malay government officials and religious leaders are criticized from both sides for institutionalizing these discretionary punishments—from secular and Muslim human rights activists who claim that these laws violate individual freedoms, and from political Islamic activists who call for full *ḥudūd* penalties. UMNO leaders, who often present a posture of *wasaṭiyyah* (moderation), have taken the middle path between the "extremes" of secular liberalism and radical political Islam. Hakim Shukri, a judge in the Melaka Shariah Court, pointed out that institutionalizing limited penalties when it is not possible to implement *ḥudūd* is based on a principle of Islamic jurisprudence:

> This is based on a *fiqh* principle . . . that states that if you can't fulfill something completely you still can't leave it altogether. Even though we can't implement *ḥudūd*, we still can't leave punishing these acts altogether. . . . Like Prophet Muhammad *sallallahu 'alaihi wassalam*, when he performed *akikah*[1] for his grandsons, Hassan and Hussein, for both of them he slaughtered one lamb each. . . . Prophet Muhammad also did one lamb for other *akikah* ceremonies. . . . His regulation [reported in *hadith*] states that for each son two lambs should be slaughtered for the *akikah*, but he did one in these cases. Based on the spirit of sharia, that is the authority of the court. With the permission of Allah, in the future, we will be able to get it. Now, everything is *ta'zīr*. Whatever we can get we implement it.[2]

The Syariah Criminal Offences (Federal Territories) Act of 1997 contains a preliminary section and two latter sections addressing general matters and exceptions, and core parts covering offenses relating to *'aqidah* (M. *akidah*; Islamic belief), the sanctity of the religion of Islam and its institutions, decency, miscellaneous offenses, and abetment and attempt. Offenses relating to *'aqidah* include provisions restricting wrongful belief, false doctrine, propagation of deviant religious doctrines, and false religious claims. Muslim government officials and religious leaders use these provisions to regulate religious belief within the Muslim community striving to maintain a normative Sunni orthodoxy. Muslims performing syncretistic rites at grave sites or shrines (*keramat*), and Muslims professing Sufi (*taṣawwuf*) or Shi'i beliefs may be disciplined and brought into line with dominant notions of orthodoxy. Darul Arqam, a popular Sufi organization founded by Ustaz Ashaari Muhammad in 1971, was subject to intense pressure from Malay elites that casted it as deviating from and threatening proper Islamic belief (Kamarulnizam 2003; Ahmad Fauzi 2005). In 1994, the National Fatwa Council issued a fatwa declaring this movement deviant, banning it, and prohibiting its many economic enterprises from using any words connected with Islam.

Ustaz Ashaari Muhammad was held in detention for ten years under the Internal Security Act, and the group's members were forced to undergo special classes at the State Islamic Centre (later renamed Jabatan Kemajuan Islam Malaysia; JAKIM). Ahmad Fauzi notes that during the ten years of Ashaari's detention neither he nor former group members were ever officially charged by, or put on trial in, any sharia court for offenses violating 'aqidah, although other individuals were. He suggests that this different treatment was due to the fact that Ustaz Ashaari Muhammad's Darul Arqam had a mass following that challenged authoritarian Malay elites (113).

On the other hand, individuals and small groups of Shia Muslims have been arrested and officially charged with helping to spread Shia doctrines in Malaysian society. In 1996, the Fatwa Committee of the National Council for Islamic Religious Affairs Malaysia decided to abolish the previous ruling of the Fatwa Committee Conference issued in 1984, which declared that "only the Zaidiyyah and Jaafariyyah Shi'ite sects are accepted to be practiced in Malaysia."[3] They decided in this new ruling that "Muslims in Malaysia must only follow the teachings of Islam based on the doctrine of Ahl al-Sunnah wa al-Jama'ah [People of the Tradition of Muhammad and the Consensus of the Umma, Sunni Islam] on creed, religious laws, and ethics," and that the propagation of any other teachings would be prohibited. Moreover, every state and the Federal Territory of Kuala Lumpur fatwa council have issued a similar fatwa restricting the propagation of Shia doctrines in their jurisdictions. Shortly after the Selangor Department of Islamic Religion (Jabatan Agama Islam Selangor; JAIS) arrested around 128 people in a raid of a storefront believed to be a center of Shia activities in Taman Sri Gombak, four representatives of the group met with the Human Rights Commission of Malaysia and submitted a memorandum requesting that their human rights be defended by those with authority. They stated, "If the right of freedom of religion and belief are given to minorities that are Hindus, Buddhists, Christians, Sikhs or other religions, why are we abused, despised, slandered, and now threatened apparently because we practice our beliefs?" (Riswandi 2010).[4] According to the sharia criminal law codes in the Federal Territories and Selangor, a person found to be guilty of teaching any doctrine or performing any acts contrary to Islamic law or any fatwa in force in the Federal Territories (Section 2[4]) or Selangor (Section 2[7]) could face the strictest punishment currently allowed under sharia jurisdictions: a fine of RM 5,000, three years imprisonment, six strokes, or any combination of these penalties.

The part of the Federal Territories act relating to "the sanctity of the religion of Islam and its institutions" includes the offenses of insulting or bringing into contempt the religion of Islam, deriding Qur'anic verses or *hadith*, contempt or defiance of religious authorities, defiance of a court order, religious teaching without *tauliah* (authorization), opinion contrary to a fatwa, religious publication contrary to Islamic law, failure to perform Friday prayers (for males beyond puberty), disrespect for Ramadan (month of fasting), nonpayment of *zakat* or *fitrah* (obligatory tithes), instigating neglect of religious duty, gambling, and the consumption of intoxicating drinks. These offenses reinforce traditional values of holding Islam, sacred texts, normative practices, and religious authorities in high esteem and are punishable by fines ranging from RM 1,000 to RM 5,000 and/or prison terms from six months to three years.

Likewise, the following part relating to "decency" sanctions violations of public morality and proper sexual behavior. It includes the offenses of incest, prostitution, *muncikari* (the procurement of unlawful sexual behavior), sexual intercourse out of wedlock (*zina*), an act preparatory to sexual intercourse out of wedlock, *liwat* (sexual relations between men), *musahaqah* (sexual relations between women), *khalwat* (people of opposite sex found in any secluded place), a man posing as a woman (*pondan*), and indecent acts

The Federal Territory
Shariah Court
(new location), 2012

in a public place. All of these offenses, except for the last three and acts preparatory to *zina*, are punishable up to the three-five-six limits under sharia
jurisdiction. Provisions in sharia criminal procedure acts describe how sentences of whipping are to be carried out. Hakim Suhaily, a Federal Territories Lower Court judge, informed me that the whippings in sharia courts
are less severe than are those in civil courts, and complained about misper-
ceptions and obstacles from the public and politicians when they want to
perform such penalties:

> The *sebat* [caning] in our Mahkamah Shariah [sharia court] and the civil,
> the practice is different because we definitely follow 100 percent the
> sharia. . . . The *sebat* in the civil court is much different . . . because here in
> the sharia court we still consider the person a human. But in the civil court
> they will *sebat* very hard, very strong. . . . If they are hit once in the civil
> court definitely they will bleed. I had an experience one time . . . we had a
> visit to the Sungai Bulong prison. . . . [They showed] all the judges how
> they perform the *sebat*. It was very scary. . . . It is a rattan . . . the person will
> be bleeding. But in the sharia court there will [only] be a scar [bruise]. So it
> is different. But the acceptance of the people, the public, is still not clear
> about it. Because once we want to perform it there will be an obstacle from
> the politicians, the powerful people. They will come and try to get involved
> in this kind of thing. They should give us an opportunity. Once we inform
> the people about it . . . they still do not respect our way to do this.[5]

During one of my interviews with Judge Suhaily we discussed the procedures for arresting and charging a male person wearing woman's clothing
(*pondan*) in public. This offense and several others were left out of the figures his court provided me (see figure 3.1). For these cross-dressing cases, he
told me, there is a special unit from the Department of Islamic Religion for
the Federal Territories. This unit goes out and investigates, and once they
find a person committing this offense they will arrest him and bring him to
court and state the charge within twenty-four hours. Then the sharia court
will hear the case and proceed with the punishment.

After he provided this general description, I asked, "Have you had a
recent case like this?"

"Yes, usually there is no objection with these transsexual people[6] . . . they
don't contest. The punishment is usually based on the type of act. Here we
have consideration. If it is [a] first-time offense, we can consider [that] and
give a lower penalty. Actually for the lower penalty . . . we can consider the

TABLE 3.1. Criminal cases of the Federal Territory of Kuala Lumpur Shariah Court, 2000–2010

Violation	'00	'01	'02	'03	'04	'05	'06	'07	'08	'09	'10
Gambling	1	5	31	63	18	8	5	52	17	42	56
Khalwat	212	290	366	202	88	192	142	194	188	423	452
Drinking	1	6	3	3	5	4	1	2	10	14	7
Zina	0	0	0	2	0	4	0	2	7	56	161

Source: Federal Territory Shariah Judicial Department.

money. . . . It would be [RM] 1000 normally or one month [in] jail. If he cannot afford to pay . . . the penalty, then he will be in jail for one month. That is for the [first-time] case. If for the second time there is no change, and [it is] the same transsexual person, then there is no more consideration in terms of how much they pay or how long they go to jail. But it depends. We will study it and make an investigation."

His response was rather general, so I continued to probe for more details about his recent cases. "So how old was this 'transsexual' in your recent case?"

"There are many levels of transsexuals. The youngest so far is around eighteen or nineteen. My recent case was thirty-four. . . . He was from another state but living in Kuala Lumpur. The oldest case is fifty or over. . . . This case was after a few times, so there was no consideration. . . . Based on the chronology of the case and the statement from the prosecutor and based on the statement from the transsexual person, the offender . . . if I am still not satisfied, I will have him take an oath. . . . But he agreed with everything. . . . He was dressed like a woman and offering sexual service to the guys. It is very embarrassing. . . . I gave him a conditional judgment that he had to pay an amount or he would have to go to jail. . . . But the amount for more than one time, it will be higher than [for] the first timer. If it is for the first time, I will advise him not to do the same thing and for him to repent."

The part on "miscellaneous offences" in the Federal Territories act includes the offenses of giving false evidence, *takfir* (alleging that a person professing the religion of Islam is an infidel), destroying or defiling a place of worship, the collection of *zakat* or *fitrah* without authority, illegal payment of *zakat* or *fitrah*, encouraging vice, enticing a married woman, preventing married couple from cohabiting, enticing a woman, instigating husband or wife to divorce or neglect duties, selling or giving away a child to a non-Muslim, a slanderous accusation of unlawful sexual intercourse (*qazaf*, Ar., *qadhf*), and abuses of the *halal* sign. The provision on *takfir* applies to an unauthorized person who alleges that any person professing the religion of Islam is a *kafir* (infidel) or has ceased to profess the religion of Islam. Anyone proven guilty of this offense could be fined up to RM 5,000 and/or imprisoned for three years. The provision on *qazaf* states that if a person accuses another person of committing an unlawful sexual act without presenting four witnesses or a confession of the accused, then the person would be guilty and punishable upon conviction of a fine up to RM 5,000 and/or imprisonment up to three years. A sharia court judge told me he thought Anwar Ibrahim, the former deputy prime minister and leader of the opposition coalition, should have had his accusers put on trial for *qazaf* in the sharia court, where they would have been required to present four witnesses to substantiate their accusation.[7] He also opined that Anwar Ibrahim should have taken an Islamic oath swearing that he did not commit the act of *liwat*. However, Anwar's application for having his *qazaf* case heard in the sharia court was rejected, and a civil court subsequently found him guilty of *liwat* for the second time in 2015. The civil courts inherited their laws against *liwat* from British common law.

The final core part of the Federal Territories act covers "abetment" and "attempt." Abetment involves the instigating, aiding, and conspiracy to commit an illegal act, and any person found guilty would be punished with the penalty for the offense they were abetting. The provision on "attempt" provides that any person who attempts to commit an offense or cause an offense to be committed could face the full punishment for the offense or half of the maximum prison term for the offense.

The Syariah Criminal (State of Selangor) Enactment of 1995 contains the same provisions as the Federal Territories act, but some of them are placed in different parts. Sharia criminal enactments for Melaka (Enakmen Kesalahan Syariah, 1991), Negeri Sembilan (Enakmen Jenayah Syariah, 1992), Kedah (Kanun Jenayah Syariah, 1988), and Kelantan (Syariah Criminal Code, 1985) have substantial differences from the Selangor and Federal Territories criminal codes. Nevertheless, there are significant overlaps as they all strive to uphold normative Islamic beliefs and practices, public morality, and the authority of religious institutions. Some of the sharia court officials in these states informed me that they were in the process of having updated enactments passed through the state legislatures and presented before the sultans. Not surprisingly, *khalwat* or attempted *zina* is one of the offenses with the highest frequency in figures of sharia criminal offenses reported across the

TABLE 3.2. Criminal cases of the Negeri Selangor State Shariah Court, 2003–2010

Violation	'03	'04	'05	'06	'07	'08	'09	'10
Gambling	67	48	89	64	73	51	119	129
Khalwat (male)	457	466	528	414	504	590	650	491
Khalwat (female)	478	463	513	409	513	602	665	464
Drinking	7	3	1	0	0	4	4	31
Zina	47	26	44	15	8	12	25	9
Request to leave Islam	0	0	10	13	10	9	18	23

Source: Negeri Selangor Shariah Judicial Department.

states (see tables 3.1–3.6). Scandalous cases of religious department units discovering and arresting unmarried couples, some of them cheating on their spouses, in hotel rooms or apartments appear often in the mass media.

Melaka, Kedah, and Kelantan have provisions for "abetment" or *bersubahat* of the commission of an act of unlawful sexual intercourse, although they still have separate provisions for abetment and attempted *zina* or actions preparatory to *zina*. Hakim Shukri from Melaka told me that this additional *bersubahat* provision is especially designed for cases where there is not sufficient evidence to prove that the culprits were attempting to perform unlawful sexual acts, but enough to support the lesser charge of abetment to engage in such immoral behavior. In the many cases where unmarried couples are caught in various states of undress in a secluded place, he stated there is sufficient evidence for the charge of attempted *zina*. These offenders may have actually committed *zina*, but they cannot be charged without four witnesses. Yet, if there are fewer witnesses, the court can charge the couple with attempted *zina* and the witnesses would not be liable to any charge of *qazaf* because they are witnesses and not accusers. Unlike other states, Melaka does not have a provision for *khalwat*, but Hakim Shukri informed me that they use their corresponding provision for *bersekediaman* (Section 53) or their special provision for *takzir* (Section 92) for cases when unmarried students are alone in a room for many hours, sometimes into the middle of the night, and people in the vicinity are often aware of it. This sort of behavior is wrong according to Islamic values, he asserted, and must be punished. They process a relatively large number of *zina* and *bersekediaman* cases (see table 3.3). In Melaka, a person found guilty of attempted *zina* faces a fine up to RM 5,000 and/or up to three years in prison; those found guilty of *bersekediaman* face a fine of RM 3,000 and/or up to two years in prison.

TABLE 3.3. Criminal cases of the Melaka State Shariah Court, 2000–2010

Violation	'00	'01	'02	'03	'04	'05	'06	'07	'08	'09	'10
Gambling	0	4	47	65	115	69	77	43	113	94	36
Drinking	0	0	0	0	2	0	9	2	7	0	0
Zina	0	1	0	1	0	0	136	130	170	47	45
Attempted Zina	1	1	2	2	0	4	9	4	8	1	2
Bersekediaman	4	19	48	248	176	54	458	361	456	155	181
Request to leave Islam	0	0	0	4	1	0	2	2	1	1	1

Source: Melaka Shariah Judicial Department.

Punishment under the additional *takzir* section is limited to RM 500 and/or six months in prison.

During one of my visits to the Negeri Sembilan Shariah High Court in Seremban, I spoke to the chief registrar, Cik Mamat, about several of the case files I had been reviewing. I first raised a case I found perplexing, concerning a young woman from Alor Gadjah, Melaka, who gave birth out of wedlock at the Kuala Lumpur Hospital. I thought it was a clear-cut case and that she would be punished with a fine and/or prison sentence. He said that the chief prosecutor probably made the decision to retract the charges because the crime occurred in another state. I asked why the prosecutor did not send the case to his counterpart in Kuala Lumpur or Melaka, where she was from. Cik Mamat said the notes do not state his reasons but that the chief prosecutor has the prerogative to retract the charges in any of the cases, and it appears it was done in this case because of the matter of where the crime took place. Another case I asked him about involved a man who was caught by a religious enforcement unit smoking a cigarette in the afternoon during Ramadan in a snooker center. I asked why he was found guilty and sentenced to imprisonment even though it was his first offense and he claimed he was not fasting that day because he had an illness in his gums. The defendant requested a lower fine because he did not have a permanent job and had to support a large family. Cik Mamat explained that it was perhaps because the defendant was loud in court or disrespectful, which reflected poorly on his character. Therefore, the judge did not believe that the sickness in his gums warranted him not fasting and wanted to teach him a lesson with a prison sentence, even for a first-time offense. He was sentenced to fourteen days in prison, beginning that very day, but the appeal court

TABLE 3.4. Criminal cases of the Negeri Sembilan State Shariah Court, 2000–2010

Violation	'00	'01	'02	'03	'04	'05	'06	'07	'08	'09	'10
Gambling	0	0	0	0	0	10	27	34	23	67	24
Drinking	0	0	0	9	6	3	1	11	34	52	171
Attempted *Zina*	2	28	128	427	391	373	261	172	256	1000	445
Zina	0	0	1	0	0	0	0	0	0	2	29
Request to leave Islam	8	14	13	15	14	22	24	13	21	27	6

Source: Negeri Sembilan Shariah Judicial Department.

overturned this sentence, changing it to a fine of RM 500 and no prison term. Although sharia law is codified, these sorts of cases indicate the latitude sharia court judges have in deciding to mete out particular forms of punishment. Agrama (2010) argues that the Al-Azhar muftis' fatwas, in contrast to the personal status court judgments in Egypt, are involved in a process of ethical cultivation as they provide *tarbiah* (education) for those seeking answers to questions in their personal lives. In Malaysia, I think muftis and sharia court judges are both engaged in the process of developing character and instilling ethical values in members of the Muslim community. The leeway sharia court judges have to perform *ijtihad*, retract charges, and decide the form of punishment allows space for them to participate in the cultivation of pious selves.

The Kedah and Kelantan Shariah Courts provided me with more extensive lists of violations over the last thirteen and six years, respectively (see tables 3.5 and 3.6). Both of their sharia criminal law enactments include provisions for indecent acts and the utterance of indecent words. These offenses are punishable by up to RM 1,000 and/or six months in prison. Otherwise, most of the provisions in these enactments cover the same normative prohibitions as all the other state enactments. However, only Kelantan, Pahang, and Perlis have provisions punishing the consumption of alcohol with the maximum penalties allowed under sharia jurisdictions, including up to six strokes of the cane. From examining these extensive lists, we can note that in both states there are relatively high frequencies of violations relating to marriage and divorce, including improper polygamy and contracting a polygamous marriage without court authorization. This would appear to confirm some of the SIS activists' criticisms and the need for reform in sharia family laws discussed in chapter 2.

TABLE 3.5. Criminal cases of the Kedah State Shariah Court, 1997–2009

Violation	'97	'98	'99	'00	'01	'02	'03	'04	'05	'06	'07	'08	'09
Impolite action	81	53	7	21	42	38	16	8	1	51	35	4	6
Pondan	0	5	0	1	4	0	0	1	1	0	0	0	0
Khalwat	496	568	312	348	425	306	309	456	458	503	337	381	333
Indecent behavior	1	0	0	0	0	0	0	0	0	0	0	0	0
Zina	4	4	2	2	0	0	0	0	0	0	0	0	0
Pregnant outside marriage	3	2	0	1	0	0	0	0	0	0	0	0	0
Prostitution	0	0	0	0	0	0	0	0	0	0	0	0	0
Drinking	2	1	0	0	0	0	0	0	0	0	0	0	0
Eating/selling food during Ramadan fast	16	16	10	5	18	11	9	15	0	2	6	4	0
Insulting religious official	0	1	0	0	1	0	0	0	8	8	0	0	0
Disobeying court order	0	8	0	0	0	0	0	0	0	0	0	0	0
Marriage by someone without authority	0	0	0	0	0	10	3	0	0	0	0	0	0
Improper marriage	321	342	294	431	400	364	356	235	525	515	500	564	602
Improper polygamy	8	9	17	21	19	32	92	41	135	138	128	148	148
Divorce without court permission	1	2	0	0	2	2	0	0	0	0	0	0	0
Abetment	4	10	21	15	15	11	10	7	3	13	2	0	10
Failure to list a marriage	1	0	3	10	9	7	48	68	110	84	120	92	143
Other violations	2	2	4	5	6	1	3	4	5	7	0	1	0

Source: Kedah Shariah Judicial Department.

When I visited the two northern states of Kedah and Kelantan in 2010, both were under governments led by the Islamic Party of Malaysia (PAS). Kelantan, of course, had been under PAS control for around two decades, but the party had recently gained power in Kedah following a hard-fought election in 2008. However, despite the large majority of Malay Muslims and the extensive network of Islamic schools there, similar to Kelantan, the social and cultural milieu in Alor Setar was quite different from Kota Bharu, the respective state capitals. As I walked around the city in Alor Setar, I passed some gambling and snooker halls and noticed some Malay youth selling and buying drugs near the malls. I also got the impression that both state bureaucracies were filled with civil servants of different political orientations. Many of the government officials and clerks in Kedah, including those in the sharia courts, seemed to still be affiliated with UMNO, whereas in Kelantan they were much more oriented toward the PAS ideology and worldview. During my interview of Dato' Wira Sheikh Yahaya bin Hj. Jusoh, chief justice of the Kedah Shariah Court, I shared with him with the contrast I perceived between the atmospheres in Kedah and Kelantan.

I told him, "I noticed many cases of *khalwat* and some youth selling drugs here. There is also a gambling hall on the road in the back that I saw when I was walking around. When I went to Kota Bharu I did not see any of these things. Is there a plan to clean everything up here?"

A bit exasperated but without any hesitation, the chief justice responded, "*Inshaallah*, in the future, we want things like that. The problem is that Malaysia is a diverse society; there are all kinds of people here. If the government authorities say that Muslims don't want these kinds of places, but you can sell those things to your people if they want it, you can do it. This was the kind of arrangement we had before. . . . I don't know but I think the government did this for maintaining harmony. In Kedah, *Alhamdulillah*, in this effort they don't want everything, so we do it little by little. We can't leave all things behind. The situation in Kelantan is different. In Kelantan, for twenty years, the PAS government has been under Tok Guru [Nik Abdul Aziz]. Kedah just had the election in 2008. It has definitely been a longer time there. A big change to society is difficult for the people. Changes have to occur little by little. Islam came down little by little right."

I also shared these perceptions with the JAKIM legal experts mentioned in the previous chapter and learned that many of them share an often unspoken positive outlook about Kelantan. I told them, "I've noticed on a state level a different atmosphere, especially when I've gone to the east coast, in terms of the implementation of some sharia laws. I spent some time in Kota

TABLE 3.6. Criminal cases of the Kelantan State Shariah Court, 2005–2010

Violation	'05	'06	'07	'08	'09	'10
Indecency	0	2	0	0	0	1
False accusation	1	0	0	0	0	0
Disobeying court order	0	1	1	0	0	0
Improper behavior toward close relative of the opposite sex (*Mahram*)	1	3	1	0	2	0
Attempted *zina*	3	2	2	1	4	0
Causing enmity to break up married couple	1	0	0	0	0	0
Drinking	2	3	9	3	0	1
Khalwat	471	463	645	545	494	466
Abetment	0	0	0	0	7	0
Attempted violation of sharia laws	0	0	0	0	2	2
Disrespecting Ramadan	48	42	23	18	27	31
Not performing Friday congregational prayer	0	1	0	0	0	0
Male acting like female	1	1	3	3	1	5
Impolite behavior in public	473	569	402	273	274	501
Marriage by someone without authority	9	4	1	0	6	1
Improper marriage	6	14	13	10	52	95
Mistake with marriage	254	244	198	218	284	550
Polygamy without court authorization	107	145	97	99	80	190
Divorce without court authorization	305	326	304	310	464	513
Zina	0	0	1	0	0	0
Resuming intimacy with divorced wife (*rujuk*) without her agreement	0	0	0	0	0	0
Failure to report resumption of intimacy with divorced wife (*rujuk*)	0	0	2	1	0	1
Giving false information/statement	1	0	0	0	0	0
Pregnant outside of marriage	4	1	6	1	3	2
Other violations	3	5	4	1	0	0

Source: Kelantan Shariah Judicial Department.

Bharu and I noticed that there were no nightclubs and none of the gambling places [they laughed at this], there was no visible alcohol in public places. . . . It was a very peaceful environment. But it seems that on a state level they have implemented some more regulations or done some things to restrict some licenses to certain types of businesses that engage in *maksiat* [sinful activities] in Kelantan. Is there any sort of program to try to extend that as you further develop and progress more with Islam in Malaysian society?" I asked.

There were several moments of silence, so I expanded on it and tried to dispel some of the politics: "I'm just thinking on the level of sharia. I know that it has been intertwined with some politics, there is an opposition and everything, but just looking at the level of sharia, has there been some interest in extending that model because it of course relates to the issue of *murtad* as well? . . . In some places I've been, in Penang, Melaka, and Kuala Lumpur . . . I even noticed some Muslims going to gambling places, playing numbers, and drinking alcohol, um, so is there an interest in extending that model that would further implement Islamic principles and ethics in society?"

There was some uncomfortable laughter but I remained silent this time. None of the women appeared ready to answer this question. Zawati finally opted to ask me a question to gauge my views: "Among the states which you've visited, which is the best model of the Islamic state?"[8]

"Well, in terms of Islamic morality and sharia, I would have to say I was quite impressed with Kelantan. I was able to sleep. When I was in Penang, I stayed in Hotel Malaysia or Hotel Continental on Penang Road, and there were nightclubs all down the street, there were parties, and there was music, cars, and people were shouting. . . . Some of the windows were open at the bars and people were drinking inside. . . . None of that was happening when I was in Kelantan . . . so I have to admit that I felt very peaceful and that I was in a very Islamic environment."

Aisha offered an explanation: "Actually it depends on the local authority to enforce the laws that have been provided. The law is there. The main thing is in terms of enforcement. I think that is the major reason why it differs from state to state. Each state has laws on gambling, nightclubs, and alcohol, but the difference is in enforcement. We are still working to improve on that area, of enforcement."

"But when I think about sharia and Islamic morals, that is how I felt. It was a good feeling in that environment in Kelantan," I added hoping to get them to extend on their perception of this model.

Zawati carefully shared her take on my feelings and exposed their own, generally unstated support of the Kelantan model: "It is like we are in our own country." She smiled.

RAISING *TA'ZIR* PUNISHMENTS, *HUDUD*, AND *QISAS*

Although many conservative Muslim *ulama* and civil servants fill positions in the government Islamic bureaucracy, there are intense ongoing contests over the current implementation of sharia criminal laws and proposals to ratchet up penalties or to fully enact a *hudud* and *qisas* penal code. Muslim human rights activists, such as the Sisters in Islam and their supporters, argue that any level of state punishment of personal violations of Islamic ethical values constitutes an unwelcome intrusion of the state into what should be individual moral affairs between a Muslim and Allah. Shanon Shah, coeditor of the SIS bulletin and the first male associate member, in an article titled "Can Personal Expressions of Faith Be Treated as Crimes against the State?" (2007, 15) criticized state-enforced sharia criminal laws as follows: "In effect, turning personal sins into crimes against the state radically alters the relationship between the believer and his or her God from one of personal piety to one of duress. Furthermore, an individual's personal relationship with God is transformed into a matter of public policy. In any sensible democracy, when policies have such far-reaching implications, the public has the right to debate them extensively and offer as many divergent viewpoints as possible in a civil manner." Although the Federal Constitution gives sharia courts the authority to punish individual Muslims for personal sins that violate the precepts of Islam, Shanon opines that it would be better if these state institutions were to leave such "sins" out of public policy and allow individuals to freely work on their own private relationships with God. Norani Othman, one of the cofounders of SIS, expressed strong opposition to any unnecessary corporal and capital punishment, viewing such actions as undermining human dignity and justice, which are fundamental values of sharia. She argued that Muslims should follow the ethical norms due to their own free will and choice rather than out of fear of state penalties.[9] In 2005 the Sisters in Islam called for a repeal of sharia criminal laws, arguing they have no basis in Islamic legal theory and conflict with civil criminal laws (VNC 2009). Likewise, the secular human rights organization Suara Rakyat Malaysia (SUARAM) consistently criticizes the "codification of Islamic 'norms,' 'values,' and 'morals' into state legislation" as imposing restrictions on the religious freedom of Muslims (SUARAM 2009, 119–20).

Muslim and secular human rights NGOs and supporters are also critical of both the controversial "gray areas" in which sharia law affects non-Muslims and the unfair enforcement of sharia criminal laws along gender and class lines. Norani Othman pointed out in my discussion with her that in Malaysia's "multiracial and multireligious society people live and interact as fellow human beings," so Muslims and non-Muslims are often implicated together when it comes to both sharia family and criminal laws. She views these "controversial gray areas" as unintended consequences of "the Islamization policy under Dr. Mahathir" and "the global resurgence of political Islam" that has affected Malaysia. SUARAM also pinpoints the dominant "conservative sector" of Muslims as both stifling interfaith dialogue between Muslims and non-Muslims and targeting human rights advocates. They are concerned about areas in which members of Malaysia's diverse society collide in controversies over conversion, religious status, and the religious freedom of non-Muslims. These human rights NGOs are also critical of gender and sexual discrimination in sharia criminal laws and enforcement that stresses the "indecent" attire of women in public and restricts "cross-dressing" (SUARAM 2009, 120–21).

Similarly, the "drama of contention" that captured public attention surrounding the case of Kartika Sari Dewi Shukarno, a thirty-two-year-old Malaysian woman caught drinking alcohol in a nightclub in Pahang, entailed local and international outcry.[10] Kartika pleaded guilty of drinking alcohol and was fined RM 5,000 and sentenced to six strokes of the rattan. While civil criminal procedure exempts women from whipping penalties, there is no such exemption in sharia law procedures. Norani pointed out to me that given the differences in civil and sharia law in relation to gender, Muslim women are often at the bottom of graded forms of citizenship. The Joint Action Group for Gender Equality, of which SIS was a member, claimed that Kartika's case should be reviewed based on sharia, constitutional and legal grounds, international human rights principles, and sentencing guidelines (*VNC* 2009). Kartika lost her appeal, and as the time approached for her to be whipped she stated that she was prepared to accept her punishment, which authorities viewed as a form of education for the Muslim community. Eventually Sultan Ahmad Shah, the sultan and head of Islamic religion in Pahang, commuted the caning sentence and ordered Kartika to perform community service for three weeks at a children's home.

Furthermore, many activists are critical of what they consider class bias in the enforcement of sharia criminal laws. One of the cases often mentioned as exemplifying such bias is that of Nazarudin Kamaruddin, a forty-six-year-old lower-class Indonesian with permanent residency in Malaysia. Islamic authorities in Pahang caught him consuming alcohol in public during Ramadan, and Hakim Abdul Rahman Mohd Yunos, the same judge that sentenced Kartika, sentenced him to one year in jail and six strokes of the cane. According to a newspaper report Hakim Abdul Rahman was quoted as saying, "The sentence meted out to him is not meant as a punishment but to serve as a lesson" (*Jakarta Globe* 2009). There would be no last-minute commuting of his sentence. On November 12, 2009, his caning was carried out and he was subsequently sent to jail. Referring to this case, Norani Othman told me, "Look, we all know, the upper classes, the British and the sultans, are free to drink and to party, you know, and to do whatever, and that is fine, it's a personal thing, but then to be unnecessarily harsh to this Indonesian worker who drank . . . and to fine him five thousand ringgit and then to whip him six times . . . This is not just in Pahang. . . . The nature of it is so unjust, even the whole context of who this person is, it's their first offense and they don't drink and drive, or beat up somebody." Indeed, in many of my discussions with sharia judicial experts in Malaysia, they emphasized the educational functions and religious instruction sharia criminal punishment provides for the Muslim community. For instance, Hakim Suhaily stated, "The power given to us is very limited in the sharia court. They should give us the similar power in our jurisdiction that they give to the civil court, because we are not punishing people because of our perspective. We give a punishment based on Islamic teachings, just to advise people, just to give people a lesson not to repeat the same bad things." Similarly, the deputy chief prosecutor in the Jabatan Agama Islam Melaka, Hajjah Haznita, told me that any laws the Malaysian government enacts are for *maklumat* (statement, information) and *tarbiah* following the Qur'an and *hadith* and preventing forbidden and immoral acts.[11] In contrast to the shift from public penal punishment to self-disciplinary technologies in European modernity, the Malaysian sharia judiciary still places high value on the disciplinary technology of public instruction through punishment in their version of Islamic modernity. When I asked a high-ranking sharia expert in the Prime Minister's Department about the case of the Indonesian worker being caned, and shared some of the criticism about class bias circulating in public debates, this member of the close-knit group of sharia judicial elites told me that it was to teach a lesson to the Muslim public. This Islamic scholar opined that it was best to start with the lower class, and then turned the tables, asking me how I would approach it. I stated I would start with the upper class because that would send a more powerful message that no one is above God's law. On the other hand, some judges in the Federal Territories Shariah Court expressed frustration with the political and economic elites expecting special treatment in the courts, which suggested to me a latent desire to enforce equal justice across the class hierarchy.[12]

In addition to rejecting the charge that sharia criminal laws and enforcement unfairly discriminate against women and sexual minorities, the sharia judicial figures I interviewed disputed the contention that personal transgressions of Islamic ethical norms should be outside the purview of state-enforced laws. For instance, when I posed to Negeri Sembilan chief justice Dato Hj. Hussin b. Hj. Harun the liberal rights activists' argument that the state should leave these matters for individuals to work out on their own, he responded:

> I think people that look at things that way are actually just stressing the importance of their own individual selves. There are Muslims who drink alcohol, but actually they know drinking alcohol and other mistakes are enjoyable. Yet, from the perspective of the soul, if we are certain and believe in all the things commanded by God and *Rasulullah* [the Messenger of Allah], then we must put aside all the things they prohibit. This is really the direction they have to follow. Then the responsibility of the government is that it must watch over this. [It] must give guidance to the Muslims under [its] command who drink alcohol and put themselves into a condition of drunkenness, even if just a little, or we don't know how much, they still can't be allowed to do this. . . . Actually, those people who complain that human rights are being violated are in effect challenging religion. . . . How can Muslims be allowed to drink alcohol when it is forbidden in Islam? Behaviors like that are violating and ruining religion. . . . The respect of religion must be defended.[13]

In the dominant view of the sharia judiciary Muslims must follow the commands of Allah and His Messenger, Prophet Muhammad, and it is the state's obligation to *menjaga*, or take care of implementing the *hukum* (laws) from sacred sources. They also stress that Islam is the only religion in Malaysia that is specifically designated in the Federal Constitution with the authority to institutionalize regulations enforcing ethical norms in the nation. The chief justice's discourse also indicates the affront to Islam many Malaysian

Muslims perceive from public claims that the punishment of immoral and indecent behavior violates fundamental human rights. Abu Bakar bin Abdullah Kutty, the chief registrar of the Kelantan Shariah High Court and a former prosecutor for the Kelantan Council of Islamic Religion, presented the counter argument that violators of Islamic precepts are actually the ones trespassing the rights of Islam and fellow believers:

> The issue that arises is that some say that these punishments violate people's human rights. It is not a basic human right to violate the rights of others. When we look at Malays, the constitution places Islam as obligatory for Malays. When they follow Islam, they must obey the regulations of Islam. Under Islamic regulations, *zina* is prohibited, drinking alcohol is prohibited, and Muslims are obligated to obey these rules. When they don't obey these regulations, then they are violating the rights of Islam. They are violating my rights. I am a Muslim. Islam prohibits the drinking of alcohol; if a Malay person drinks alcohol they are violating my rights. . . . If a student breaks the rules at a university, they break the rules and violate the rights of other students. . . . From the perspective of rights, we respect the basic rights of people. . . . This is the reason we make laws to regulate the behavior of people in their everyday lives, in religion, in the country, in society, in the family, and as individuals as well. Let's say I am in my home, which is a personal space. In society, I am obligated to attend Friday prayers in the *masjid*. Islam makes Friday prayers an obligation, which is a social affair. In the country, I am obligated to pay *zakat* [tithe] to help other people.[14]

According to Cik Abu Bakar, there must be restrictions on individual rights in order to protect the rights of others. It is out of concern for basic human rights that Islamic laws must extend from individual spaces to broader social spaces out to the realm of the nation-state and global Islam. Similarly, Kedah Shariah Chief Justice Dato' Wira Sheikh Yahaya spoke of the *hikmah* (wisdom) in Islam to guide social relations along a harmonious course.

> We have relations and connections with other people in society, and must be concerned about the burdens we place on others. . . . Islam provides *hikmah* so that people do not harm anyone else badly and so we collectively communicate about what is the best for society. We each speak out, and express our opinions, about what is the best for society. To me, we do not just live in this world as isolated individuals, not just by ourselves. We must

remember *hablum-minannas hablum-minallah hablum-minannas*. . . . We have a relationship with Allah and, on the other hand, we have a relationship with humans. We still have to live in harmony. We cannot run from humanity. . . . We don't desire to run; we desire to be perfected by Allah *Subhaana wa Ta'ala* [the Glorified and Most High].

Here again, unlawful acts of sexual intercourse, consumption of alcoholic beverages, and other violations of Islamic laws and norms are viewed from the perspective of the damage they can have on the rights of family members and others in society, and therefore these rights must be protected through wise sharia laws that prohibit such harmful acts. Individuals are not viewed as isolated and primarily ensconced in their private lives, but rather in terms of their relationships with other people (*hablum-minannas*) and with Allah (*hablum-minallah*). Islam provides the regulations to direct people along the proper course that will keep them from harming the interests of others. Furthermore, he suggests that following the commands of Allah in our relations with people, instead of retreating into our private indulgences and away from humanity, places us on the path to perfection.

The contra-sharia criminal law discourses of Muslim and secular human rights activists pose a public challenge to fundamental beliefs of the dominant conservative Islamic worldview in Malaysia. These discourses are antagonistic and uncompromising. Rather than making calls for lowering the levels of discretionary punishment, they charge that those punishments' very presence violates basic human rights such as freedom of religion and conscience and claim that sharia criminal laws should be repealed. Some challenge gender and sexual distinctions and the proscription of cross-dressing in traditional Islamic values. Moreover, they suggest that many classical forms of punishment are inappropriate in the contemporary world and argue that more authority should be returned to civil courts and laws. These sorts of public discourses hit at the heart of traditional sharia models that entail notions of eternal directives from sacred sources, which believers must obey and religious authorities must establish. Such challenges to Islam and the legitimacy of Malay and Muslim authorities circulating in media provoke responses from the broader Malaysian Muslim community as well as Malay political elites and religious officials. Kamali (2000, 310) notes that it is generally the case in contemporary Malaysia that "political uncertainty and turbulence tends to enhance the role of the conservative forces in society. Since the Malay community dominates the Malaysian government, there tends to arise a greater need to preserve Malay unity in times when this might be seen to be under threat. Under such circumstances, Malaysian leadership is likely to increase its Islamic orientation." This is even more the case in the second decade of the twenty-first century than it was when he was writing. However, it is unclear at this point whether the Malay political elites and conservative Islamic forces will unite behind a drive to raise the level of sharia jurisdiction and discretionary punishment and to implement a *hudud* and *qisas* code in Kelantan.

Yet, my research indicates that many government *ulama* are pushing for an increase in the sharia court jurisdiction and *takzir* penalties and are in favor of an eventual implementation of *hudud* and *qisas* in Malaysia. The chief justice of the Negeri Sembilan Shariah Court responded emphatically to my question about whether *hudud* should be applied in Malaysia: "It must be implemented." Similarly, the chief justice of the Federal Territories Shariah Court, citing the constitutional expert Aziz Bari, told me that there were no constitutional impediments to the implementation of *hudud* in Malaysia.[15] He expressed the view that *hudud* and *qisas* can be implemented in Malaysia if there is the political will to do it. Likewise, a sharia court judge told me, "Actually, in our society, it is not so easy to implement *hudud*, unless the prime ministers or the top management of the government [are] really, *really* religious." Datuk Haji Mohamad and some other judges also spoke favorably of the establishment of *hudud* codes in Nigeria, Sudan, and in the province of Aceh in neighboring Indonesia and recently in Brunei Darussalam.[16] Judges emphasized the positive effects of a *hudud* penal code on the deterrence of criminal infractions, as exemplified by the criminal offense data they received from Sudanese officials during their visit to the Federal Territories Shariah Court. Moreover, government *ulama* view the spirit of *hudud* as being already present in the limited discretionary punishments, which prepares the road for stricter penalties. For instance, Hakim Shukri, a lower court judge in Melaka, stated, "Now everything is *takzir*. Whatever we can get we implement, although we truly have the clear procedure and law, like *hudud*, which is definitely strict. But from the spirit of the laws we have will grow *hudud*. There will be *hudud*. Because we have low fines, they can be raised . . . the fines are *takzir*. We have to understand that the spirit connected to these laws point us to *hudud*." A gradual increase in discretionary punishments can eventually arrive at the same penalties as prescribed by *hudud* in classical Islamic jurisprudence. This appears to be exactly the course many government *ulama* have been advocating in recent proposals to Malay political elites and to the Parliament.

Rather than moving toward softening the intrusion of the state into violations of Islamic precepts, government *ulama* have gone in the opposite direction in the face of ongoing public disputation from liberal Muslim reformers and human rights activists. Professor Dato' Dr. Zaleha, deputy director of IKIM, informed me that the government is trying to improve the three-five-six *takzir* limits, making them "more stringent, more strict," so that sharia will be respected.[17] In 2012, sharia court judges and civil servants in the Prime Minister's Department told me they had prepared a proposal to "upgrade" the status of the sharia court jurisdiction and court officials, bringing them on par with that of civil courts. Their plan would raise the level of punishment allowable in sharia jurisdictions, making it "just like *hudud*." The issues of overlapping jurisdictions would also be worked out in this amendment to the Federal Constitution. Cik Noor, a researcher in IKIM, suggested that the jurisdiction of the sharia courts would be raised to the same level as civil courts so that sharia judges can sit with corresponding civil judges to deliberate together and issue joint rulings pertaining to cases with overlapping jurisdictions, such as family law cases that involve Muslim and non-Muslim parties. Later, in 2014, the minister in charge of Islamic affairs, Datuk Seri Jamil Khir Baharom, announced that the plan to upgrade the three-tier sharia judiciary system to a five-tier system is nearing its conclusion, since it's been agreed on by all the states. The proposed new system would shift the current Sharia Subordinate Court, Sharia High Court, and Sharia Court of Appeal three-tier structure to five tiers that would run from the Sharia Lower Court, Sharia Middle Court, Sharia High Court, and a Sharia Court of Appeal for each state, to the Sharia Appeal Council, which would be the highest sharia court. However, according to some constitutional experts, to make this five-tier system on par with the civil court system, operating beyond each state boundary, will require a carefully drafted constitutional amendment that would not "offend the basic structure" of the Federal Constitution (Boo Su-Lyn 2014).

In addition, many government *ulama* have expressed support for the 2015 PAS private member's bill in the Parliament to amend the Syariah Courts (Criminal Jurisdiction) Act of 1965 to pave the way for implementation of *hudud* in Kelantan. PAS passed a *hudud* bill in Kelantan in 1993 and a *hudud* and *qisas* bill in Terengganu in 1999, but neither was implemented due to restrictions in federal law and constitutional constraints. In 1994, the Shariah and Hudud Laws Committee of the Malaysian Bar Council announced that Kelantan's *hudud* bill was consistent with Islamic law and that its inconsistencies with the Federal Constitution could be overcome by amending the latter document (Kamali 1998, 208). PAS has actively campaigned for several decades around the issue of *hudud*, even when their opposition coalition partners were strongly opposed to it. The Kelantan state assembly unanimously approved the Shariah Criminal Code (II) 1993 (Amendment 2015) on March 18, 2015. Now, in their new effort to establish a *hudud* code in Kelantan, PAS found that their allies in the opposition coalition Pakatan Rakyat—DAP and PKR (Parti Keadilan Rakyat; People's Justice Party)—were committed to not supporting the bill in Parliament. Tensions over the PAS move to clear a path for the realization of a *hudud* code in Kelantan led to PAS severing ties with DAP in 2015. In contrast, government *ulama* in JAKIM and IKIM made public statements in support of the PAS effort to amend the federal act limiting sharia jurisdiction, while stressing that the decision rests with the Parliament. Datuk Othman Mustapha, director-general of JAKIM, expressed support for the PAS bill and stated that making this amendment to the federal act has long been part of JAKIM's efforts "to increase the punishments according to the Al-Quran" (Jamilah 2015). IKIM director Datuk Seri Jamil Khir Baharom also made positive comments about the PAS plan but added the caveat that "the implementation of Islamic law should only be applicable to Muslims in order to maintain stability and national harmony" (*Astro Awani* 2015).[18]

While these supportive statements and broader agreement from many conservative government officials and *ulama* are significant as a rebuttal to public challenges from liberal Muslim reformers and human rights activists, political backing from the Malay political elites will be required to make any of these amendments in federal and constitutional law. At this point, it does not appear that prime minister Najib Abdul Razak and his government ministers support paving a way for *hudud* and *qisas* to be implemented in Malaysia.

APOSTASY LAW, CASES, AND PROJECTED STANDARDIZATION

There is a moral panic in the majority Malay Muslim community that large numbers of *murtad* (apostates) are prepared to flee from Islam. I have often heard and felt the panic conveyed in Friday prayer sermons (*khutbah*) and mosque religious talks (*kuliah masjid*) and in discussions with some of my interlocutors in various cities in Malaysia. However, the figures I received from the sharia judicial departments did not reflect the high numbers of *murtad* mentioned in these contexts. Half of the state sharia departments from which I requested data did not include any figures of Muslims trying to leave Islam. The three states that did—Melaka, Negeri Selangor, and Negeri Sembilan—reported only 227 Muslims trying to leave Islam over roughly the first decade of the twenty-first century. There were 12 from Melaka between 2000 and 2010, 83 from Negeri Selangor between 2003 and 2010, and 177 from Negeri Sembilan between 2000 and 2010. Sharia court officials in Kelantan and Kedah told me in interviews that they had only a few cases over roughly that same period. However, judges in the Federal Territories Shariah Court reported that there were numerous requests from Muslims asking to convert out of Islam. These cases are heard in the Shariah High Court. I sensed that *murtad* was a problem about which court officials, especially in Kuala Lumpur, felt uncomfortable sharing any official figures. Granted, any number of *murtad* is disheartening to the Muslim faithful; nevertheless, the numbers disclosed hardly amount to a deluge of Muslims trying to leave the faith or to change their religious status. Yet, many people may be deterred by the difficulty and dangers of approaching a sharia court to request a declaration of their status as a non-Muslim. In fact, one of the judges who used to work as a researcher at a sharia court told me that he found there were over fourteen thousand Malay Muslims across Malaysia trying to convert out of Islam in 2004. He was convinced there were many more when we discussed this in 2011.

I also broached the topic of apostasy in my discussion with legal experts during my excursion to JAKIM. Regaining the floor in part of our group discussion, Zawati said:

> I am not going to touch on marriage. . . . Maybe we can look at the provision of the convert out from Islam. In other states you have a provision that under the High Court in the states, they have a power to declare the status of religion of somebody. They have drafted it differently in Negeri Sembilan. The procedure is much more clear. They state in the provision the complete procedure of what the person has to follow to apply to convert from Islam. But other states don't have that provision in their law. . . . In the other cases, perhaps, the judge can practice their *ijtihad* because they don't have the clear procedure . . . to handle that kind of matter when someone wants to convert out of Islam.

Halimah (2009, 30–32) reports that there are three types of laws concerning converts out of Islam across the states of Malaysia. In Perak, Melaka, Terengganu, Pahang, and Sabah apostasy is a *kesalahan*, or crime with a definite punishment. Perak and Terengganu have laws punishing *murtad* with fines and/or prison sentences. Pahang has the strictest punishment, set at the three-five-six limits of discretionary punishments for sharia offenses: three years of imprisonment, a fine of RM 5,000, and/or six strokes of the cane. Melaka, Kelantan, and Sabah have the second type of law, which requires people attempting to commit apostasy or to be *murtad* be held at the Center for Correcting Akidah (religious beliefs), for not more than thirty-six months in Kelantan and Sabah and six months in Melaka. Negeri Sembilan has the third type of law, and the only one that provides a "remedy" for those who want to convert out of Islam. It requires the person to request a declaration from the sharia court that they are outside of Islam. While the court is considering the request, it may advise the person to attend counseling and to *bertaubat* (repent for the sin of apostasy). Halimah states that eighty-nine people requested such declarations in Negeri Sembilan from 1994 to 2003 and sixteen obtained them. The records I received from the Negeri Sembilan Shariah Judicial Department indicate that from 2003 to 2010 there were a total of 142 cases of people requesting declarations that they were outside of Islam and nineteen people obtained them. There were still eighty-three cases pending, and the others had been rejected, canceled, withdrawn, or mentioned (but encountered problems with proceeding). Selangor, Kedah, Sarawak, Perlis, Penang, and the Federal Territories do not have any laws pertaining to *murtad* in their administration of Islamic law acts. However, even without clear laws in their specific legal codes, sharia court judges in these states and in the Federal Territories do consider making a ruling on the religious status of a Muslim or whether a person can convert out of Islam as being within their jurisdictions. They can also decide to adopt the clear law within the Negeri Sembilan Administration of Islamic Affairs Enactment of 2004, which is what happened in some cases discussed below.

"From my research on the variations on the laws of converting outside of Islam, I read that there are three different types of *murtad* laws in Malaysia. . . . Are you working to bring those into a general form, or has your department decided to just leave that to the states to manage?" I asked.

"Actually, this matter is under the purview of the Attorney General's Chambers, and they are still [deciding] whether we should have that kind of law regarding converts out of Islam or not," Zawati replied. "We should not have that kind of law, because as we know in Islam . . . there should be no law to regulate that because Allah prohibits us from becoming *murtad*. So it is still under review in the AG's Chambers."

According to classical Shāfi'ī, Ḥanbalī, and Mālikī schools of jurisprudence, apostasy (*ridda, irtidād*) is one of the *ḥudūd* crimes with a fixed punishment mentioned in the Qur'an and/or *hadith*, and the punishment prescribed is death (Peters 2005, 64–65). Much of the deliberation in the Malaysian Attorney General's Chambers will likely revolve around deciding how to legally establish the status of a person as Muslim or not, and whether and how to recognize any difference in status between Malay Muslims (and other "born" Muslims) and Muslim converts. In fact, the reasoning of sharia judges in several exemplary cases and my interviews with government *ulama* indicate the way the Malaysian sharia judiciary is leaning in deciding these matters related to apostasy.

Several cases in which sharia judges decided that people registered as Muslims were not Muslims show that they review and evaluate evidence relating to their family background and whether they ever actually embraced and practiced Islam in their everyday lives. In the case of Janisah binti Abd Rahim alias Bigul heard at the Shariah High Court in Keningan, Sabah, in 2004, Janisah asked the court to declare that she was not a Muslim and that she never embraced the religion of Islam. She filed this request because of the confusion that ensued when she went to the Department of National Registration in Keningau as a non-Muslim with her and her father's name appearing like those normally used by Muslims. The court heard statements presented by witnesses that told the story of Janisah's father helping a Muslim traditional healer treat the illnesses of people in the village. This healer invited her father to become a Muslim, but according to the witnesses he never actually embraced and practiced Islam and never filed any conversion of himself or his daughter to Islam with the Registrar of Muslim Converts. Therefore, the Shariah High Court decided and declared that Janisah was not a Muslim and had never embraced Islam (*Jurnal Hukum* 2006b). Similarly, in the case of Mohammad Shah alias Gilbert Freeman heard at the Shariah High Court in Seremban, Negeri Sembilan, in 2009, Mohammad Shah requested that the court declare that he was not a Muslim and never was a Muslim, so that he could clear up the contradiction between the religion of his family life, which is the religion he practices, and the religion on his national identity card. The petitioner's father was a Muslim and his mother a Christian. According to a witness statement, his parents lived together and had several children but never had a marriage registered with the civil or sharia court. Mohammad Shah never knew his father: when he was around two years old his father left them and they did not know where he went. He was baptized as a Christian when he was three years old, and there was no evidence his mother ever converted to Islam. Based on the statements of non-Muslim witnesses, the Shariah High Court decided he was not a follower of the religion of Islam.

Two recent cases in the Federal Territories Shariah High Court also reflect similar logic as the Janisah and Mohammad Shah cases. In the case of *Surath A/L Maniram v. the Islamic Religious Council of the Federal Territories* in Kuala Lumpur in 2010, Surath asked the court to change the religion listed on his national identification card from Islam to Hindu as quickly as possible. Following the procedure outlined in the legal code of Negeri Sembilan, the court ordered the plaintiff to attend three months of counseling. But after only four sessions the counselor concluded that Surath never practiced Islam because his father was a *murtad* when he was only six years old. The counselor also stated in his report that the plaintiff had been given information and knowledge about Islam in these sessions, but he maintains his determination to remain outside of Islam. The plaintiff testified that his father was a Muslim for a time when he lived with a Muslim family that took care of him, but after members of this family passed away he married the plaintiff's mother, who was a Hindu. His father tried to change his own name and religion and after several years succeeded, but only after fathering two children. Surath was five years old when his father officially changed his religion to Hindu. The statements of two non-Muslim witnesses supported the plaintiff's testimony. Based on this evidence about his background, the judges decided he never practiced Islam in his life, declared he was not a Muslim, and granted him permission to change his religious status on his identification card, which is under the jurisdiction of the Department of National Registration. Likewise, in the case of *Faridah Ching binti Amin v. Islamic Religious Council of the Federal Territories* heard in the Shariah Appeal Court in Kuala Lumpur in 2012, the plaintiff filed a request to have the religious council recognize her as outside of Islam and to change her name to Ching Lee Yen. She originally filed this request with the Shariah High Court in 2007, but after sending her to counseling and considering the evidence presented the court decided to reject her application in 2011, and subsequently she appealed its decision in the Shariah Appeal Court. Similar to Surath's case, Faridah's father was a Muslim and her mother was a Buddhist when she was born. However, her father was not in the process of trying to change his name and religion. The fact that he was still a practicing Muslim at the time of her birth led the High Court to decide that she would obtain her religious status from her father. Thus, even if she has been practicing Buddhism all her life, her religion would descend (*nasab*) from her father, since he was still apparently a practicing Muslim (and not a *murtad* like Surath's father was when he was born). This posed a complex problem for the Shariah Appeal Court to figure out. The three judges hearing Faridah's appeal considered when the father converted to Islam and the status of her parent's marriage in relation to the time of her birth. They concluded that her father converted to Islam five years before she was born but her mother continued to be a Buddhist. According to sharia law, three months after he converted to Islam, the *'iddah* period of the plaintiff's mother, any children born from this union would get their *nasab* or descend from the mother because the marriage was no longer valid. Therefore, the appellate court judges ruled that the High Court decision that the plaintiff was a Muslim, based on the interpretation that her father was a Muslim when she was born, could not be defended. They also heard statements from four witnesses who were relatives or friends of the plaintiff and could vouch for the fact that she has always practiced Buddhism, not Islam. The Shariah Appeal Court decided that the plaintiff was not a Muslim from the time of her birth. In all these cases, the sharia court judges ruled that these petitioners were not Muslims based on certain aspects of their family backgrounds—such as having at least one non-Muslim or *murtad* parent and an invalid marriage of their parents—along with evidence that they had never embraced or practiced Islam in their lives. Through considering this sort of information about the applicants' lives, these Muslim jurists were able to discern that they were not "born Muslims" with valid descent from a Muslim parent and at no point in their lives did they become Muslim.

On the other hand, there are many other cases when reasoning about this sort of information about the lives and experiences of petitioners asking to leave Islam results in the decision that they are Muslims and therefore are not allowed to be *murtad*. The most well-known example of this is the case of Lina Joy discussed in chapter 2. It is important to note here that she was born into a Muslim family and therefore had a valid line of descent of Islam from her Malay Muslim parents. The fact that at some point in her life she began to embrace and practice a different religion means that she was trying to move from Islam to another religion or to become a *murtad*, which is prohibited according to traditional Islamic jurisprudence. This logic would also apply to non-Malay Muslims who had a valid line of descent from one or two Muslim parents when they were born. On top of this reasoning about *nasab* or lineage, many Malaysian jurists consider the fact that Malays are defined as Muslims in the Federal Constitution as placing an additional restriction on the movement of Malays out of Islam. On the other hand, we must consider cases in which applicants are not born Muslims but at some point in their lives converted to Islam. For instance, the case of Muhamad Ramzan Maniarason heard in the Pahang Shariah High Court in Kuantan, Pahang, in 2005 involved a man who was born into a Hindu family in Penang in 1973 and decided to convert to Islam in Terengganu at the age of twenty. His conversion to Islam took place in the *kadi*'s office and was later registered at the Terengganu Department of Islamic Religious Affairs. Subsequently, still as an unmarried man, he moved to Pahang and worked as a taxi driver living with other Indian men. After twelve years of being a Muslim convert, he approached the Pahang Shariah Court and requested to leave the religion of Islam. Without representation by a sharia lawyer and without any supporting witnesses, he testified that he wanted to leave Islam and return to the religion of his father, Hinduism, because he had lost interest in Islam and did not have a good understanding of it. In consideration of this case, the judge noted that Article 11 of the Federal Constitution provides the right of religious freedom to Malaysian citizens from non-Muslim backgrounds to choose a religion of their liking, but it does not give them the right to change religions willy-nilly. After the applicant was a Muslim for twelve years, the court could not accept his petition to return to Hinduism. The Penang Shariah High Court rejected his request to leave Islam and ordered the Kuantan Office of Islamic Religion to help Muhammad Ramzan. It also ordered the local Islamic religious office to seek the service of the Pahang Department of Islamic Religion and the Malaysian Muslim Welfare Organization to guide him (*Jurnal Hukum* 2006a). Similarly, in the 2012 case of *Muhammad Khairil David bin Abdullah v. Majlis Agama Islam Wilayah Persekutuan*, the Shariah High Court of the Federal Territories considered the request of a Muslim convert to leave Islam and return to his previous religion, Christianity. Muhammad Khairil converted to Islam in 2005 in order to marry a Muslim woman from a Dusun ethnic background. They were married in 2006 and divorced in 2010, at the request of his wife. During the time he was married, he attended several Islamic religious classes for Muslim converts. The petitioner testified before the court that he has not gone to a *masjid* or *surau* (prayer hall) to pray since 2010 because he had already requested to leave Islam.[19] He also mentioned that he attended several counseling sessions and that he recently married a woman who works with him but they live apart. One of his witnesses told the court that Muhammad married a Christian woman in a village in Kota Kinabalu, Sabah, following local customs, and did not register the union. His other witness informed the court that he had seen Muhammad in a church more than once. The applicant attended four court-ordered counseling sessions, and the counselor reported to the court that the petitioner stated he only converted to Islam to marry a Muslim woman. In these sessions he was taught many core Islamic concepts but held on to his determination to request leaving the religion. The Federal Territories Shariah High Court decided that the petitioner was a Muslim, thereby rejecting his request, and ordered that he begin a six-month process of *taubat* (repentance) in the Selangor Center for Correcting Akidah. These two cases demonstrate that when sharia judges have evidence that Muslim converts made valid and registered conversions they will view them as Muslims, and as Muslims such converts will not be permitted to leave Islam. In sum, people whom the court recognizes as Muslims, either through descent or conversion, who want to shift from Islam to another religion fall under the rubric of apostasy.

Several sharia court judges and other government *ulama* have discussed and described their efforts to unify the various laws and procedures in regard to dealing with cases ostensibly connected to the issue of *murtad*. They often point to the complexity of dealing with the variety of people applying to be recognized as non-Muslims and to change their religion on their identification cards. Government *ulama* from IKIM and JAKIM informed me that the Attorney General's Chambers is spearheading the effort to standardize the laws on apostasy-related cases across the states. Despite complaints from liberal rights activists about restrictions on religious freedom and time-consuming procedures for applying to convert out of Islam and/or to change one's religious status, the general contours of the proposal formulated through the research of IKIM and conferences of sharia experts shows they are trying to take a middle path, upholding the general spirit of traditional Islamic jurisprudence forbidding apostasy while allowing a path to change religious status for Malaysian citizens from diverse backgrounds who have come to be mistakenly identified as Muslims. Their proposal makes several distinctions between applicants that reflect the reasoning in the sort of cases discussed above. First, there would be a law pertaining to *murtad*. If the petitioner is Malay, as in Lina Joy's case—and given that the Malay category is defined as Muslim under the Federal Constitution—the person would not be allowed to convert out of Islam. The same would apply to people from other ethnic groups who were born into Muslim families. These Muslims would be arrested before they make an application in the court and charged with an offense under sharia criminal law—and if found guilty they would be ordered to attend counseling in a Center for Correcting Akidah for at least one year. The religious officials are planning to separate the more hardcore apostates in these centers from the newer converts, so as to check the spread of anti-Islamic sentiments and negative influence on *mualaf* who lack a strong understanding of Islam. Second, there would be a law pertaining to determining the religious status of persons who are not Malays or from Muslim backgrounds. The courts would entertain their petitions and try to determine their status through considering their practices and experiences. IKIM deputy director Dr. Zaleha stated that they are trying to convince the states to adopt this proposal and will have sharia experts well versed on these issues explain them to the sultans (Malay rulers). In 2010 she told me that trying to unify laws relating to *murtad* and determining religious status is a "very difficult and painful process" that may take around five to ten years to complete.[20]

LAWS CONTROLLING PROPAGATION AMONG MUSLIMS

In addition to wrangling over the issues of sharia criminal law punishment and apostasy, liberal rights activists and conservative Muslim forces often collide over the restriction on non-Muslims propagating religion among Muslims. Federal and state laws restrict the propagation of Christianity, Hinduism, Buddhism, Sikhism, Judaism, Ahmadiyyah, Shi'i Islam, and other religions and creeds considered "non-Islamic religions" or "deviant" sects. Federal laws, such as the Sedition Act 1948 (Act 15; rev. 1969), the Printing Press and Publications Act of 1984 (Act 301), the Societies Act (Act 335), the Internal Security Act of 1960 (Act 82), the Police Act of 1967 (Act 334; rev. 1988), and the Penal Code, can be used to restrict the propagation of religions to Muslims (Zuliza et al. 2013). The states of Kelantan, Melaka, Selangor, Johor, Kedah, Negeri Sembilan, Pahang, Perak, Perlis, and Terengganu have passed enactments to control and restrict the propagation of non-Islamic religion. Terengganu was the first to do so in 1980, followed by Kelantan in 1981; Johor was the last to do so, in 1991. These state enactments consist of provisions prohibiting the proselytization of other religions to Muslims and the use of several words and phrases seen as uniquely Islamic. Malay government officials and religious leaders view these enactments as consistent with constitutional articles on state-level sharia jurisdiction, religious freedom, and the prohibition of the grave offense of apostasy in sharia law (Zuliza et al. 2013). However, the states of Penang, Sabah, and Sarawak do not have any enactments controlling the propagation of non-Islamic religions. Christian leaders and liberal rights activists argue that these state enactments are too broad and run counter to rights of religious freedom for

Malaysia's large non-Muslim communities enshrined in the country's supreme law, the Federal Constitution. In fact, the Christian Federation of Malaysia asked prime minister Najib Razak for a public commitment to repeal these enactments in BN-controlled states (*Malay Mail Online* 2014b).

The Selangor Non-Islamic Religions (Control of Propagation among Muslims) Enactment of 1988 includes six offenses: persuading, influencing, or inciting a Muslim to change faith; subjecting a minor who is a Muslim to influences of a non-Islamic religion; approaching a Muslim to subject him to any speech on or display of any matter concerning a non-Islamic religion; sending or delivering publications concerning any non-Islamic religion to a Muslim; distributing in a public place publications concerning non-Islamic religion to Muslims; and using certain words and expressions of Islamic origin. The punishment for the offenses of inciting a Muslim to change faith and subjecting a Muslim minor to non-Muslim religious influence is the strictest, a prison term of up to one year and/or a fine up to RM 10,000; whereas punishment for the other offenses are lower, ranging from no prison term to six months, and from RM 1,000 to RM 5,000 in fines. Cases relating to the offense of exposing a Muslim minor to non-Islamic influence often arise when custody is given to a non-Muslim parent, but they are difficult to prosecute because children are easily influenced by close relatives (Zuliza et al. 2013). Cases relating to the offense of distributing non-Islamic publications to Muslims can involve the confiscation of Malay-language Bibles. Juliana Nicholas, a Christian missionary from the Philippines, had most of the Bibles he brought into the Kuala Lumpur International Airport confiscated, but he was later able to reclaim them on the grounds that they were for use in his church (ibid. 15). The section pertaining to the offense of using certain words and expressions of Islamic origin relates to cases such as the *Herald*'s use of the word *Allah* in its Catholic weekly paper. There are two schedules at the end of this enactment that list twenty-five words and ten phrases prohibited from use in reference to non-Islamic religion.[21]

In 2011 great drama surrounded a raid of a Christian church dinner by Selangor religious authorities who had heard that Muslims were in attendance. On August 3, 2011, Selangor Department of Islamic Religion officials and police disrupted a dinner organized by the Damansara Utama Methodist Church (DUMC), collected information, and found twelve Muslims present. The dinner was reportedly meant to express gratitude for the efforts of a community-based benevolent association that aids women, children, victims of HIV/AIDS, and natural disasters. Subsequently, reports and responses to this event appeared in various media and on the streets. The youth wing of PAS and twenty-two nongovernmental organizations made public statements expressing their commitment to defend the faith of Muslims and revived calls for a law banning apostasy (*Jakarta Globe* 2011). Mohd. Ezam Mohd. Nor, a BN senator, declared an "all-out war" against those that attacked the Islamic faith, and Gerakan Cegah Murtad, a new coalition of twenty-five apparently UMNO-affiliated and Malay rights organizations, expressed support for the JAIS action and announced that they would be doing their own monitoring of churches to prevent proselytizing of Muslims. Pertubuhan Perkasa Malaysia organized a rally at the Shah Alam Stadium calling on people to fight Christianization (*Malaysian Digest* 2011).

On the other hand, Daniel Ho, senior pastor of DUMC, issued a statement expressing disappointment at the religious officers' actions that subjected their dinner guests to "undue harassment" (*Christian Post* 2011). Bishop Ng Moon Hing, chairman of the Christian Federation of Malaysia, complained about an increase in incidences of Christians being targeted with "unjustified accusations and prejudice" and questioned the legality of the raid. Moreover, Dr. Ng Kam Weng, research director at the Kairos Research Centre, argued that "the powers granted by the state enactments 'cannot be taken as license' for Muslim religious authorities to intrude or trespass onto the premises of a church." The Islamic Renaissance Front, a liberal Muslim group, called on Muslims "not to blame others but to examine the root causes of apostasy and to consider their own shortcomings" (ibid.). With the Selangor state government under control of the opposition coalition Pakatan Rakyat, this incident placed the Selangor chief minister Khalid Ibrahim, hailing from PKR, and his coalition partners in a quandary. They had gained control of the state in 2008 campaigning as a tolerant, multiethnic, multireligious alternative to the racialized politics of UMNO. This church raid, executed under their state administration, smacked of religious intolerance to many non-Muslims. PAS leaders' initial questioning of the grounds and legality of the raid quickly gave way to deafening calls to defend Islam from Christianization and to pass an apostasy bill.

However, the head of religion in Selangor is the sultan, not the chief minister. The sultan of Selangor, Sharafuddin Idris Shah, issued a ruling that neither the Christians nor state religious officials would be prosecuted. He stated that the Selangor Department of Islamic Religion authorities were acting within the powers granted them by the Selangor criminal law enactments, including the Selangor Non-Islamic Religions (Control of Propagation among Muslims) Enactment of 1988. In his ruling the sultan noted that, according to the JAIS investigation, there were attempts made to "subvert the faith and belief of Muslims," but there was insufficient evidence to take legal action against the alleged Christian perpetrators. He called for all actions aimed at propagating other religions to Muslims to "cease immediately," and commanded JAIS to "provide counseling to the 12 Muslims present at the dinner in order to restore their faith and belief in Islam" (ibid.).

CONCLUSION

In Malaysia, as in many other Muslim societies, the "modern" concepts of nation-state, nationalism, citizens, and state-enforced "criminal" law articulate with traditional Islamic notions of an omniscient and powerful God, public morality, and Muslim community (*umma*). The Federal Constitution gives state-level sharia officials the authority to enforce Islamic ethical norms and public morality among Muslim citizens of the Malaysian nation-state. Sharia "criminal" laws are codified into acts, enactments, or ordinances passed by legislative bodies like sharia family codes, but they are not as standardized across the states. Thus, Muslim citizens are subject to civil and sharia law criminal codes; their individual sins and violations against Allah are also crimes punishable by state authorities. Non-Muslim citizens are also subject to federal and state restrictions on propagating their religions to Muslims. In addition, when non-Muslims are mistakenly registered or conventionally considered Muslims, they must apply to sharia authorities that have the jurisdiction to determine their religious status. From the perspective of state authorities, the Muslim *umma* is properly contained, together with other religious communities of citizens, within the boundaries of the nation-state and under the regulation of the bureaucratic state apparatus. Clearly, many social forces contest the hegemonic manner of combining these "modern" and Islamic notions.

However, Malaysian political and religious elites have had a more difficult time combining the concepts of international human rights, liberal rights of citizens, and secular-pluralism within a traditional Islamic framework. As a rule, they accept the elements of international human rights that do not contradict Islamic principles and law. Similarly, they accept the liberal rights of citizens but limit them when it comes to upholding divine directives and preserving the Islamic faith. They also have trouble with secular-pluralist conceptions of the nation-state that would seek to rearrange official racial and religious hierarchies and remove the special status of Malays and Muslims. Thus, while they adopt the general notion of a "modern" nation-state, Malaysian political elites hold at bay the secular-pluralist paradigm often promoted by the United States and many European countries (cf. Hallaq 2013). The fact that Malay government officials and religious leaders do not wholeheartedly embrace these contemporary Western concepts is evident from the discursive skirmishes they engage in with liberal Muslim and non-Muslim opponents of state enforcement of sharia criminal laws.

In the context of increasingly intense public confrontations with liberal activists, government *ulama* have moved in the direction of strengthening sharia implementation and pushing against the secular format inherited from the British colonial period. They have been working on plans to institutionalize another increase in the level of discretionary punishments and the status of the sharia court system, and some PAS *ulama* are striving to finally implement a version of their 1993 Hukum Hudud. They are finding some public rhetorical support from UMNO-affiliated *ulama*, but it is not likely they will find sufficient political approval in the Parliament from UMNO politicians under the sway of prime minister Najib Razak's Cabinet. Government *ulama* are also working to unify the laws across the states and Federal Territories through gaining support for legal provisions that would not allow apostasy for Muslims while providing a clear method to determine the religious status of individuals, mistakenly considered Muslims *or murtad*, as non-Muslims. Both government and PAS *ulama* continue to struggle with combining notions of the nation and its plural citizens in their traditional Islamic worldviews.

4 ECONOMICS

The Malaysian State, Darul Arqam, and
the Islamic Party of Malaysia

"DEVELOPMENT NEEDS TO PROCEED BECAUSE THIS WORLD WAS
made by Allah for humans, not for angels or other creatures," Nik Abdul
Aziz (2010, 28), chief minister of Kelantan and spiritual leader of PAS, told
an audience at the Kelantan Trade Center in Kota Bharu. "However, development that is spiritually empty is like a large tree with hideous and rotten
roots. Even the abundant leaves will not cover it for long; they will very
easily fall flat." The Malaysian state and other social forces have infused
sharia law and ethics into a variety of economic activities in Malaysia. Traditional jurists of Sunni schools of jurisprudence developed laws for contracts, property, and ownership based on the Qur'an and *hadith* and several
other sources and reasoning methods (Auda 2008; Hallaq 2009). Given the
notion of Islam as a "way of life and polity" (*Din wa Dawla*) rooted in early
Islamic history, these laws involved the diffuse implantation of religious
principles and ethics into various domains of everyday life, including politics and economics. Wael B. Hallaq (2013, 148–49), a scholar of Islamic legal
studies, estimates that around a quarter of the vast written records of sharia
were devoted to contract, trade, and financial transactions. Since these laws
pertaining to economic affairs concentrate on the moral qualities of exchange,
trade agreements, and property ownership rather than specifying a particular kind of system, Islamic ethics have been applied in a wide range of economic systems. When the established legal opinions were in conflict with
elite interests and/or the practical needs of life, jurists could adopt less strict
positions within their school or from other schools, and political rulers
appointed judicial officials to make rulings on economic matters (Coulson
1969, 66; Ibrahim 2015). During the British colonial period, secular commercial codes replaced the combination of sharia ethics and sultanate rulings in public commercial codes. Nevertheless, precolonial Malay Muslim
ethical values continued to circulate in family and community circuits (Raymond Firth 1946; Rosemary Firth 1943; Scott 1979). In the postcolonial
period, under the influence of resurgent Islamic movements and campaigns,

Islamic ethics are playing an increasingly public role in distribution, consumption, and production activities. As in many other Muslim societies, social forces in Malaysia with different ideological orientations are combining Islamic ethical notions with a variety of other ideas to formulate and promote diverse approaches to economics (see Tripp 2006). Moreover, the Islamic economic discursive tradition entails a range of ethical notions from prohibitions on *riba* (usurious interest), excessive uncertainty, and gambling to an emphasis on social welfare based on mutual help, character building, *riḍa* (wholehearted consent), charitable giving, and care and dignity for the poor (Black, Esmaeili, and Hosen 2013, 181; Hallaq 2013, 146–52).

Muslim social forces stress different aspects of this broad discursive tradition. In contrast to the skirmishes between liberal Muslim and secular human rights activists, on the one hand, with conservative Muslim forces, on the other, over sharia family and criminal laws, there is no entrenched opposition to sharia economics being implemented in contemporary Malaysia. In fact, many non-Muslims enthusiastically participate in several forms of sharia economics, although some activists have expressed concerns about halalization and sharia compliance being used to deepen ethnic and religious divisions.[1] On the other hand, there are significant debates amongst pro-sharia Muslim social forces on how best to implement sharia economics and about whether certain forms of economic activities and investment vehicles are properly sharia-compliant. Four different sharia economic models are of concern here: those of the Malaysian state, leaders of some government-linked corporations, Darul Arqam and its successor Global Ikhwan, and the PAS-led state government of Kelantan. This broader perspective stands in contrast to overemphasis on the state in studies of Islamic economics in Malaysia.[2] Explicating cultural models helps to delineate the diverse approaches to sharia economics. However, when taken together these four influential sharia models facilitate greater infusion and emplacement of sharia values and ethics in otherwise mundane dimensions of life and thereby serve to de-secularize the economic domain.

MALAYSIAN STATE AND CORPORATE CALIPHS: INFUSING ISLAMIC ETHICS INTO GLOBAL CAPITALISM

Under the influence of the Islamic resurgence of the 1970s and sociopolitical pressure from *dakwah* movements and the Islamic Party of Malaysia, the UMNO-led Malaysian state began to infuse Islamic ethics into its ongoing project of economic development and modernization within the global capitalist system. Amid the proliferation of free-trade zones and industrial and commercial sites entailing the flow of transnational capital investments and the government's affirmative action policies for Malays moving from rural to urban spaces, elite Malay politicians promoted developing an alternative form of capitalism that incorporates some pious Islamic ethics and principles—notions they argued were consistent with modern capitalist values of efficient productivity and capital accumulation (Ong 1987; Mearns 1995; Daniels 2005). One of the key notions of pious Islamic ethics, borne out of anxieties over accruing *amalan soleh* or "good works" toward salvation, is the imperative to avoid *riba*. Combining these concerns with a drive to accumulate capital, the Malaysian state passed the Islamic Banking Act of 1983 and the Government Investment (or Funding) Act of 1983, and established the nation's first Islamic bank, Bank Islam Malaysia Berhad. These acts facilitated the concentration of capital in Islamic banks, which joined their conventional counterparts as powerful capitalist financial institutions, and the funding of the government through investment instruments that must be approved as being in accordance with sharia principles by the Shariah Advisory Council. Malaysia's Central Bank, Bank Negara, regulates and supervises the Shariah Committees of Islamic financial institutions and, together the sharia experts in these institutions, performs *ijtihad* (religious interpretations) that designate financial instruments and practices as sharia-compliant. Malaysian jurists in regulatory agencies have engaged in reasoning about how to best take account of Islamic prohibitions on *riba*, risk and uncertainty (*gharar*), and gambling or speculation (*maysir*) while still making business activities profitable.

Similarly, Islamic insurance (*takaful*) companies, established following the Islamic Insurance (Takaful) Act of 1984, were also officially placed under the supervision of the Shariah Advisory Council of Bank Negara. These insurance operators provide risk- and profit-sharing *mudarabah* (profit-margin sales) contracts to policyholders who mutually agree to insure one another against losses and damages and share in any surplus based on agreed-on profit-sharing ratios (Rudnyckyj 2013, 840). In the 1990s, Islamic "windows" offering sharia-compliant loans and savings accounts were opened in conventional banks, and Islamic debt securities and equity markets were established. In 2004, the Central Bank required conventional banks with Islamic financial operations to establish full-fledged Islamic subsidiaries, and in 2009 the country's stock exchange Bursa Malaysia launched Bursa Suq Al-Sila', a commodity trading platform that facilitates liquidity management in Islamic banks through commodity *murabahah* contracts and secondary trading of government-linked corporations' *ṣukūk* (Islamic bond) offerings (842; Elder 2017).[3] The Central Bank of Malaysia Act of 2009 established the Central Bank's National Shariah Council (NSAC) as the most authoritative sharia financial body in the country. Its rulings prevail over the rulings of "any Shariah body or committee constituted in Malaysia by an Islamic financial institution," and any court or arbitrator must take into consideration any rulings of the NSAC, which are binding on Islamic financial institutions and courts. Nevertheless, according to officials in the Malaysian Shariah Judiciary Department in Putrajaya, the NSAC must still "refer to and go through" the National Fatwa Council that issues rulings on all categories of sharia law, including *muamalat* (cf. Rudnyckyj 2013, 842). The National Fatwa Council has issued forty-four rulings under the category of *muamalat* from January 21, 1971, to February 11, 2015.[4] Section 60 of the act states that the Central Bank shall in cooperation with the government and government agencies develop and promote Malaysia "as an international Islamic financial centre."

Similarly, the Malaysian state promotes "proper" Islamic consumption and the regulation, production, and distribution of *halal* (permitted) goods as part of its national and international project for development and modernity (Fischer 2008; Lever 2016). Fischer (2008, 37) argues that the Malaysian state combined authoritarianism and responsiveness to outmaneuver *dakwah* groups such as Darul Arqam and PAS; it used its authoritarian powers to ban Darul Arqam, popular for its production and distribution of *halal* products, and responded to Muslim concerns by forming government institutions to regulate *halal* goods. He suggests that the Malaysian government's vision of proper Islamic consumption linking shopping to state-led nationalism held sway with a large segment of the Malay middle class who conceived of themselves as Melayu Baru (New Malays). The Malaysian government also sought to make Malaysia an international hub for the certification, production, and distribution of *halal* products. And Malaysia, in fact, has become one of the largest global exporters of *halal* products and has emerged as a major player in setting international *halal* standards, fusing Islamic traditions with the demands of international markets (Lever 2016).

The Malaysian state has recently strengthened its regulation of *halal* certification and the display of *halal* logos. During my visit to JAKIM, Zainul and Hamidah expressed their anticipation of the passage of a new federal act that would rectify the lack of standardization in *halal* certification. Speaking to Zainul, an Islamic scholar in the *halal* certification division at JAKIM, I told him, "I'd like to learn more about *halal* businesses in Malaysia."[5]

"In Malaysia, you need a *halal* certificate because if you don't have it sales will go down more than ten percent. . . . There is an American company . . . that makes bread, and when somebody questioned about his *halal* certificate, his sales went down. Now, he has it, and his sales have increased."

"I've noticed that a lot of restaurants will have Islamic-related pictures and symbols up, sometimes plaques, but there is no sign stating that the food is *halal*."

They both laughed at this. Zainul said, "Actually, now, we have standard *halal* in Malaysia: JAKIM *halal*. But the problem we have until now is that there is no *akta*, no law about *halal*, *halal* law."

"Is it very expensive to get the certification, because I noticed that several of the small Indian Muslim restaurants . . . in Penang, on Penang Road, Burma Road, don't have the *halal* certification logos up. But I can see that there are Muslims making the food and managing the restaurants."

"They put signs with Al Qur'an [the Qur'an] there . . . so they are responsible for the *halal*." Zainul laughed at the apparent inefficiency of the current state of *halal* certification.

Hamidah further clarified that they are working on implementing new policies on halal: "Right now, our act allows for self-decoration of *halal*. That means they can put there Al Qur'an or decoration or whatever, showing they are Muslims and that all those things are *halal*. But right after this we are going to amend our act about *halal* so that all these stores and restaurants cannot do the self-decoration of *halal*."

"[In] March of next year, *Inshaallah*, next year, we pray together to Allah," Zainul said, projecting the planned timing for the new act on *halal* regulation and calling for prayer, with his bright smile radiating piety. The Trade Descriptions Act of 2011 and its subsidiary legislation that provided a definition for halal and required certification by the competent authorities (JAKIM/MAIN [Islamic Religious Council of the States]) and marking with the logo issued by these authorities were passed the following year. Any individual convicted of violating this act may be fined up to RM 100,000 and/or three-years in prison, and the penalty for a corporation is a fine up to RM 250,000.

Several Malaysian Muslims and international scholars teaching at Islamic institutions were critical of government projects regulating Islamic finance and *halal* certification. For instance, Cik Firdaus Koh, a Chinese Muslim, told me that *mukmin* (pious Muslims) in Malaysia generally avoid the products from certain banks because they know those institutions are not Islamic and they are aware there are many companies listed on the Islamic index that engage in *haram* (prohibited) activities. Moreover, he said that the "so-called Islamic finance is not Islamic." Islamic financial advisers are even less fair than conventional bankers are because they say that there is no *riba*, but if a person cannot pay it off and defaults they want the full amount to be paid, which includes their calculation of profits. "It is just *riba* given another label," he exclaimed. "There is also a problem with marketing *really* halal products in Malaysia," he said, "because it is hard to break into the marketing networks." Cik Firdaus gave the example of a *halal* toothpaste distributor that was not able to place its product in the Giant chain of stores because of the sum of money it was required to pay Giant; whereas Colgate, using *haram* (forbidden) ingredients in its toothpaste, was on the shelves in most of the big stores and chains.[6]

Likewise, Cik Tariq, an Indian Muslim, told me that he went to the "supposedly sharia-compliant branch" of a bank to finance his purchase of a car. He asked if they were charging him *riba* in the form of a large administrative payment or if they would be buying the car from the dealer and reselling it to him, but they told him that they were actually taking out a loan with interest and that he would be paying the *riba* indirectly from what they worked out. "There is only Islamic finance in name for the most part in Malaysia," he declared.[7] Dr. Burhan, an international scholar who has trained many of the sharia experts sitting on the bank's Shariah Committees, told me that in some Gulf States they are really trying to implement Islamic finance, but "they can't do it here in Malaysia now because they don't want sharia regulations to stand in the way of profit."[8]

"But they have to hire sharia experts, right?" I asked him.

"Yes, but they are not highly educated in Islamic finance. They just want someone to rubberstamp what they want to do to make profit. It is just conventional economics with an Islamic label." As an informed observer of Islamic finance in Malaysia, Dr. Burhan was convinced the Central Bank would not approve any sharia experts to sit on the Shariah Committees who would tell them to work the finance out in the "right way"—the properly sharia-compliant way—and disrupt the drive for profits.[9]

Laura Elder (2017) argues that in the wake of the Asian financial crisis in the early 2000s, the Malaysian state and regulatory agencies exerted their authority to push for a merging of Islamic financial practice with a heavily efficient, market-oriented version of neoliberalism. She demonstrates how market-driven reasoning enters into the *ijtihad* of the Bank Negara's Shariah Advisory Committee. For instance, one of her interlocutors, a woman that sits on the Shariah Advisory Committee of both the Securities Commission and Bank Negara claimed her innovative interpretation that *wa'ad* (promises) could be used to structure derivatives is justified because a certain degree of *gharar* (uncertainty, speculation) is unavoidable and acceptable. This Islamic scholar argued that financial instruments entailing these sorts of speculative promises would bring benefits to the industry. Similarly, a researcher at a government think tank, in line to be chairman of a bank's Shariah Committee, informed Laura Elder that *bai' al 'inah* (sales/buy-back) contracts are accepted in Malaysia because they follow the Shāfi'ī ruling that focuses on the structure rather than the intention behind the two sales. He states that the Gulf Cooperation Council, stressing intention, consider the sales/buy-back contracts to be a "backdoor to *riba*." In addition, the standards of sharia compliance for equities in the Islamic Financial Services Act of 2013 has allowed the Shariah Advisory Committee to certify Malaysian Airlines, a government-linked company, as sharia-compliant despite its practice of serving liquor on its flights.

Badlisyah Abdul Ghani, executive director and chief executive officer of the CIMB Islamic Bank Berhad, tried to dispel some critical ideas about Malaysia's Islamic financial industry by pointing out that it is the most regulated and institutionalized framework for Islamic finance in the world; furthermore, he claimed that variations across Muslim jurisdictions are minor and based on local laws, market conventions, and customs (Ee Ann 2010). He claims, contrary to popular misconceptions, that Islamic finance is not better in the Middle East, where it is governed in a less institutionalized and regulated fashion. Their poor understanding of Islamic finance, he adds, leads to Muslims missing financial opportunities, in contrast to non-Muslim customers who are more interested in the "value propositions" offered by Islamic finance. He contends that instead of being fixated on the differences across jurisdictions in the global Islamic financial market, Muslims should revel in the benefits they gain as customers from the increasingly stiff competition between Islamic financial corporations to deliver new, unique financial instruments. Badlisyah's discourse suggests a model of sharia economics that emphasized institutionalized control of the Islamic financial industry and values of accumulating wealth rather than the persisting moral concerns of many Malaysian Muslims about whether the products are properly sharia-compliant.

After hearing from many of my Malaysian Muslim interlocutors that Islamic banks were charging interest on loans when it is clearly prohibited according to traditional Islamic jurisprudence and the National Fatwa Council, I decided in August 2012 to investigate on my own by visiting some banks. I took the monorail to the Bukit Bintang stop and walked to the Islamic subsidiary of Maybank. A middle-aged Chinese bank representative told me to go upstairs to speak to Suha. I went upstairs, approached a Malay woman wearing a *tudung*, and asked if she was Suha. She said she was and asked me to take a seat. I told her I was looking for information on Islamic housing loans. "For how much?" she asked. "Well, perhaps one for RM 150,000 if I get an apartment or RM 250,000 for a house," I answered. She told me that the terms would depend on my immigration status. If I were a permanent resident I may apply for different amounts of money, but a foreign investor would have to buy a house valued at RM 500,000 or higher. As a permanent resident I would be able to buy a house valued at less. She wrote the terms of the loan down on a sheet of paper and explained to me that there would be an interest rate on the loan; after looking up the latest rate, she informed me it would be between 6.2 and 6.6 percent. The rate came from Bank Negara. I asked how it was different from a conventional loan, and she explained that they both have interest rates but the conventional loan is capitalized, so there would be less interest accruing on the Islamic loan. But there was still the same basic interest rate. Recalling that a close Malaysian friend told me that if I planned to buy a house in Malaysia it would be best to put it in his name and to have a lawyer draw up a power of attorney document stating that I am the actual owner, I asked Suha if this would be possible. She stated emphatically that it would be illegal because it would bypass the regulation concerning foreigners buying property in Malaysia. "Besides, there would be problems with inheritance if something were to happen to you," she added.

After meeting with Suha, I walked around in Bukit Bintang, passing several sleek malls and eateries, until I found the OCBC (Oversea-Chinese Banking Corporation) Al-Amin Bank branch. I entered and asked a young Malay man for information on Islamic housing loans. He told me that they could give me some information but to process the loan I would have to go to a larger Al-Amin branch. A woman came out from an office in the back to help him, and they both explained to me that the interest rate they use is the one from Bank Negara, just as Suha had informed me. They showed me on their computer monitor that the terms of the loan would be the same regardless of whether I were a permanent resident or a Malaysian citizen. The loan would cover around 80 percent, and the rest would have to be paid in cash if the purchase were made in Melaka or 90 percent if it were in Kuala Lumpur. My visits to these two Islamic bank branches demonstrate that there are some significant differences between conventional and "sharia-compliant" loans, but indeed they both impose interest at rates set by Bank Negara.

Although Malaysian jurists on Bank Negara's Shariah Advisory Council and many on other banks' Shariah Committees appear to share the Malaysian state's cultural model of merging pious Islamic ethics with neoliberal capitalist values, the corporate executives and managers of many government-linked companies applied a different cultural model to organize workplaces and to understand their activities within the global capitalist system. Sloane-White (2017) notes that many of the "corporate elites of sharia" in Islamic banks, *takaful* companies, and some government-linked and -owned corporations are members of an overlapping network of Qur'anic study groups and Islamic nongovernmental organizations. Many of them were members of three organizations of the Islamic resurgence—Pertubuhan Jamaah Islah Malaysia, Malaysian IKRAM Organization, and Muslim Professionals Forum—and conceived of the corporation as a "small Islamic state" and of themselves as its *khalifah* (caliph). Viewing the corporate workplace as their field of social responsibility, these corporate leaders implement and enforce a set of rules and obligations, which Sloane-White calls "personnel sharia," based in their orthodox understandings of Islam. Many of these companies broadcast prayers over loudspeakers, established separate prayer rooms for men and women, organized lunchtime sermons, enforced payment of *zakat*, and deposited employee salaries in Islamic banks (Sloane-White 2011). They also directed employees to participate in their pious Islamic ethical projects such as building orphanages and religious schools and doing community service, which they considered to be part of their collective responsibility (*fard kifayah*). These sharia corporate elites of the Islamic resurgence distinguish their identities and practices as Muslim businessmen from those of Bumiputera businessmen, emphasizing simple lifestyles and moderate consumption (like PAS leaders), equitable relations with subordinate workers, and counting good deeds along with profits. Indeed, these Muslim corporate leaders value the way they perform *dakwah* in their relations with less religious, or even "sinful," Malay Muslim businessmen, and stress a *barakah* (divine blessings)–driven corporate life in which they work to accumulate wealth and enhance the public good (*maslaha*) while producing more Islam.

Nevertheless, they defer to the guidance of sharia advisers operating with more market-driven models in terms of how to manage their businesses in the broader economic environment. They seek input from sharia advisers not only about how to avoid *riba*, uncertainty, and speculation, but also about how to relate to corrupt businesses and deal with bribes and patronage money. For instance, a sharia adviser ruled that it was ethical for a subcontractor to work for a contractor that secured the job by paying a large bribe to a politician. They also advised pious Muslim businessmen to accept "dirty money," such as bribes and profits from political patronage, and donate it to charities (Sloane-White 2017). Thus, these sharia corporate elites were able to emplace their relatively rigid models of piety in the workplace, but as they operated in the broader world they were advised to adjust to the exigencies of doing business.

Hefner (2010, 1038–39) reminds us that although most popular new religious streams in East Asia have expressed market, materialistic, and consumer-oriented discourses, "there continue to be significant areas of tension between Islamic social ethics and late modern capitalism." This is certainly the case with Darul Arqam, PAS, and some other Islamic revival movements and political parties (see Deeb 2006; Daniels 2009).

DARUL ARQAM: CREATING AN ISLAMIC ECONOMIC SYSTEM

Darul Arqam grew out of a religious study circle Ashaari Muhammad organized in Datok Keramat, a Malay suburb of Kuala Lumpur, in 1968. Ashaari was formerly a government religious teacher and member of PAS (Kamarulnizam 2003, 99). The group adopted the name Darul Arqam in 1971 and established its main base and model Islamic village in Sungai Pencala in the mid-1970s on a five-hectare plot of land that encompassed a mosque, lecture hall, dormitory offices, school, houses, and shops. It was a Sufi movement following the spiritual practice of Aurad Muhammadiah, an order founded early in the twentieth century by Sheikh Muhammad Abdullah As-Suhaimi, who was born in Central Java, Indonesia, and studied *taṣawwuf* in Mecca for twelve years. Muhammad Syukri Salleh (1994, 27), a member of Darul Arqam and scholar on the faculty of the Science University of Malaysia, characterized this group as a "progressive Sufi movement" with the fundamental aim to "revive Islamic religious belief and values into a comprehensive pattern of living." He argues that in contrast to the Malaysian state, which inserts some Islamic ethical values into a neoclassical economic paradigm, Darul Arqam has established an ethical approach to development based on an Islamic worldview outside the dominant development framework. That is, he asserts that they have successfully established an all-embracing Islamic system within the dominant Malaysian secular system but apart from its values and worldview. Moreover, their sharia model for developing an Islamic life based on the Qur'an and *hadith* did not require an Islamic state as a geographical entity to administer educational, information and welfare services, *dakwah* and international relations, or economic and financial affairs (Kamarulnizam 2003, 104). In other words, they conceive of "Islamic states" as "evolving from within themselves to their own family, society, state, and eventually to a global level" (Muhammad Syukri 1999, 236). According to Ustaz Ashaari, Islamic movements needed to do less theorizing and shouting slogans about establishing an Islamic state and more work creating an Islamic society that truly practiced Islam, which is a precondition for establishing an Islamic state (Jomo and Ahmad 1992, 82).

Darul Arqam's sharia economic model entails the notion that improvement of the individual by means of inner spiritual revival is entangled with, and essential for, economic improvement of the wider society. Their leaders stress that the basis for individual spiritual revival lies in the individual's relationship with God (*hablum-minallah*), which nurtures Islamic values and ethics within members through worship (*ibadah*). The group adopts Sufi methods to attain *iman* (Islamic faith) and *taqwa* (Islamic piety) through eliminating unworthy attitudes (*mazmumah*) in oneself and replacing them with good attributes (*mahmudah*). Successful social and economic development, integral to relationships between humans (*hablum-minannas*), depends on proper attention to the domain of relations with God. Thus, the legitimacy of the outward forms of human sociopolitical and economic activities, according to Darul Arqam, is determined by the fulfillment of these basic guidelines: the intention is for the sake of God alone; compliance with sharia in their aims and implementation; positive consequences from the Islamic viewpoint; and not neglecting the basic tenets of Islam as expressed in the *hablum-minallah*. In their scheme of economic development, material and spiritual development are interdependent; yet its members place higher value on embracing *amalan soleh* aimed at the next world rather than seeking material success alone. They are taught that every one of their actions aimed at development—which results from integrating *hablum-minallah* and *hablum-minannas* and conforming to the basic guidelines above—can become an act of worship (*ibadah*) of God (Muhammad Syukri 1994, 31–32).

The economic principles of "Arqamnomics," a term found in the writings of its members, include aiming to realize Islamic ethical goals rather than striving for excessive profits or the accumulation of wealth; basing the Islamic economy on *taqwa*, human energy, natural resources, *istiqamah* (steadfastness), and prayer; and keeping the Islamic economy free from *riba*, monopoly, haram sources, unpaid loans, fraud, and deception (Kamarulnizam 2003, 104–5). Darul Arqam divided its economic activities into three categories: the *fard kifayah* economy, fulfilling the collective obligation to offer sanctioned activities such as *halal* foods; the commercial economy, aimed at making profits that are not excessive and out of the recognition that gains belong to Allah; and the strategic economy, used as a strategy of achieving the movement's struggle such as uplifting the morale of Muslims and instilling confidence in the ability of Islam to bring prosperity (Muhammad Syukri 1994, 44–45; Kamarulnizam 2003, 105).

Darul Arqam implanted its sharia economic model into production, consumption, and distribution activities. They established an extensive network of businesses in Malaysia and abroad beginning with the founding of the Darul Arqam Ummah Service in 1977, which started sundry shops, a wholesale store, and noodle factory and produced soya sauce and chili sauce. As their economic activities expanded they formed the Department of Economic Affairs, which concentrated on the *fard kifayah* economy by producing and distributing *halal* goods. Darul Arqam, similar to ABIM (Angkatan Belia Islam Malaysia; Malaysian Islamic Youth Movement), clearly promoted the consumption of halal products produced by Muslims under reliable conditions (rather than by non-Muslims) (Kamarulnizam 2003, 106). They also owned industrial factories, mini-markets, grocery shops, bookstores, tailor shops, workshops, restaurants, and taxis and express coaches. In 1993 they launched the Al-Arqam group that expanded their activities in the commercial and strategic economies of the Arqamnomics framework, with twenty subsidiaries dealing with groceries, mini-markets, food and beverages, clothes and tailoring, animal husbandry, medical services, and many other areas of business. Its technology company, Spectra Technology, provided services to ExxonMobil, Shell Oil, Petrolium Nasional Berhad, and Tenaga Nasional Berhad. While Darul Arqam's state and department units continued to manage other economic projects, the Al-Arqam group operated under the central management of a board of directors led by Sheikul-Arqam Imam Ashaari Muhammad. Companies at the central level were also able to merge with the state and department levels in certain projects through a risk- and profit-sharing (*mudarabah*) arrangement (Muhammad Syukri 1994, 44–45; Kamarulnizam 2003, 106). They also organized large-scale agricultural enterprises in several states and extended their "business empire" overseas, operating businesses in the Middle East, Central Asia, and other Southeast Asian countries. In addition to promoting consumption of *halal* goods, Darul Arqam required women to wear long hijab (headscarves) and robes and encouraged men to wear turbans (attire Sheikul-Arqam considered to be Islamic, based on the Qur'an and *hadith*). They also advocated moderate consumption practices, avoiding extravagance—for instance, in the context of inflationary marriage costs, their marriages usually only cost around RM 1,000 (Muhammad Syukri 1994, 43). Darul Arqam's Department of Finance collects contributions from members and sympathizers and revenue from economic projects, and redistributes a considerable portion of these funds to full-time members for their basic needs through a system called *ma-ash*. According to their notion of justice and equality, this *ma-ash* system distributes funds based on ones' need rather than occupational status; hence, a factory worker with four children would be given more funds than a doctor with one child (46; Kamarulnizam 2003, 109).

After the Malaysian state banned Darul Arqam and imprisoned its leader, Ashaari Muhammad, in 1994, the group's businesses continued and its sharia economic model remained popular and influential among Malaysian Muslims. Kamarulnizam (2003, 110) notes that despite the alleged deviation of the group's Sufi teachings, Darul Arqam's successful Islamic economic projects were widely admired by the Malaysian public. Many of my Malay interlocutors in the 2000s expressed highly favorable views about how Darul Arqam organized economic activities, and some were also impressed with Imam Ashaari Muhammad's charisma. They felt he was even more talented and engaging than was former deputy prime minister Anwar Ibrahim. The way Darul Arqam spurred the Malaysian state to get out in front on matters of *halal* production and certification is often cited as evidence (Fischer 2008; Lever 2016). However, I think many of Darul Arqam's pious economic notions, such as developing individual piety for enhancing human resources, seeking spiritual as well as material benefits, and establishing "Islamic states" at various levels of society, have also influenced the ideas and practices of the "sharia corporate elites" in the small but growing "Islamic economy" (cf. Sloane-White 2011, 2017).

In July 2009 I had several discussions with two of the movement's followers at a small shop in Alor Setar, Kedah. Abdul Latif, the shop operator, told me they are Arqam, but since it is forbidden to use the name they have changed theirs several times and are now using the name Global Ikhwan as a registered company rather than an official organization. Yet the movement continues and has progressed, Abdul assured me. He was critical of the way local Muslims were not practicing Islam, exhorting me to look at the way they were dressing and acting and how their parents were directing them to be doctors and lawyers rather than *ulama* because they valued high salaries more than religious knowledge. Abdul told me that the Islamic economy is not supposed to aim for making profit, but rather for doing good. Capitalists are always looking to make a profit, turning one dollar into one dollar and fifty cents, but a dollar is not just a dollar because Allah gives us these gifts. Abdul continued, telling me that "Abuya" (Father) Ashaari has developed an entire system for education, a complete system for establishing Islam in every area of life, and he pointed to the posters hanging around his shop on culture, politics, social affairs, education, health, and so forth, informing me that Ashaari has written lots of books on all these topics.[10] Abdul Latif gave me a few of these books and allowed me to have some others photocopied at a nearby shop. He clearly saw me not just as a social science researcher but also as a potential recruit, and gradually he began to pressure me to make a commitment. After I told him that I had attended several religious study circles at Masjid Zahir, he stated that many of the *ulama* there are knowledgeable and give excellent talks, but that after the talks are over they do not implement the knowledge in their lives. Abdul apologized for having to say this, and he went on to explain that the knowledge enters their *akal* (intellect) but not their *qalbu* (hearts). However, the educational process Ashaari formulated has the right *tujuan* (objective), and Islam enters into their hearts and is practiced in all aspects of life.

During one of my visits to Abdul Latif's shop I had an opportunity to speak with Ustaz Othman, a higher-ranking member of their movement, who was visiting from Bandung, Indonesia, for some meetings on agricultural business. Ustaz Othman said they have a school up north in the direction of Perlis, and that they produce the bottled prayer water, Air Ikhwan, in Kuala Lumpur and Kelantan and the bread and cakes in factories in Kedah. Abdul invited me to visit their economic enterprises in Jitra, Kedah, informing me that they have lots of students and workers there, living and working in simple conditions. Ustaz Othman exclaimed that Global Ikhwan is truly universal like Islam, and that there are no national or ethnic boundaries in their organization. They are all over Malaysia; in Sumatra, Java, Makassar, Sulawesi, Kalimantan, and Lombok in Indonesia; in Singapore, Brunei, the Middle East, Australia; and hope to establish themselves in the United States in the future. He informed me that a recently aired television program on Astro stated that Global Ikhwan was the only group following the method of education as established by *Rasulullah*.[11] One of the main differences between their Islamic education and secular education, he noted, is that the students who study making bread, cakes, sauces, and other products maintain a relationship with their teachers throughout their lives. Global Ikhwan is like a family all over the world. The fact that they are *saudara* (brothers and sisters) is also reflected in the way they marry across ethnic categories. He has four wives: one from Malaysia, and three from different regions in Indonesia, and one of his wives was about to give birth to his twentieth child. Ustaz Othman assured me that their members have happy and harmonious families, and that their polygamous families can live in the same houses as one happy family without any problems. Some people criticize them and assume that the women must be forced to accept polygamy, but this is not the case, he asserted. Othman added that women in their movement believe in Islam and see the beauty in it, so why would they not accept something beautiful?[12]

Ustaz Othman and Abdul Latif both spoke to me about the special role they believe Global Ikhwan will play in the last days of human existence (*zaman akhir*). They believed that it was prophesied that the *Imam Mahdi* (savior), a man wearing a blue turban, and his followers would emerge in the East, and both of them tried to convince me that Malaysia is the perfect place for this to happen. These members of the movement believed "Abuya" Imam Ashaari has been given supernatural abilities and that he is the most amazing leader of our time. They stated that Allah would determine and select the leaders, the *Mahdi* and *Mujaddid* (Renewer), for the last days, and the pious Muslims will recognize these leaders by their characteristics. For these followers, "Abuya" fulfills the characteristics of a divinely selected leader of *zaman akhir*.[13] In contrast to prophets, Ashaari has been blessed with *ilham* (divine inspiration) rather than *wahyu* (divine revelation). Moreover, since *Rasulullah* will return to the world in this period without his companions, it is the special role of the *ikhwan* to fight for the second coming of Islam in the last days through love, serving as living models of the complete practice of Islam, rather than by way of violence. Therefore, they have to be on a very high spiritual plain. There will only be fifty thousand *ikhwan* around the world that will develop and help in the second coming of Islam.

Although their sharia economic model still enjoys much public support, I perceived that followers of Global Ikhwan were having problems attracting new members; furthermore, I sensed that they felt persecuted. Abdul Latif mentioned several times in our discussions that they have been *haramkan* (banned), and many consider them to be *sesat* or to have deviated from Islam. He told me that they have many enemies. Observing their interactions with local Malays, I noticed that they have very few local supporters in the city. In one exchange with a Malay man that Abdul called an "old friend," the man disputed the movement's interpretation that smoking and selling cigarettes were *haram* rather than *makruh* (reprehensible), and questioned the quality of Air Ikhwan prayer water they sold in their shop. The following statement was written on the water bottles: *Untuk mensucikan dan menye- jukkan hati, minumlah air ikwan* (For purifying and cooling the heart, drink *ikhwan* water). His "old friend" asked him if this Air Ikhwan were so good, then why don't they sell it to the vendors in the food court? Abdul literally backed up, leaned against the wall, and stopped ranting about the spiritual benefits of drinking their prayer water. I perceived this man was making a veiled accusation that there was something unsavory about the nature of Air Ikhwan.

After the passing of "Abuya" in May 2010, I have not had an opportunity to visit the brothers of Global Ikhwan in Kedah. However, there are media reports that Global Ikhwan Holdings Sdn. Bhd. is expanding on the *halal* businesses formerly part of the Al-Arqam group. Ashaari Muhammad's wife, Hatijah Aam (also known as Ummu Jah), continued the group's "business empire" and is famous for starting the Obedient Wives Club. She and nine other group members were detained at the Kuala Lumpur International Airport upon their return from Saudi Arabia and accused of trying to revive the banned religious group. She pleaded guilty to violating the fatwa outlawing Darul Arqam. Later that year she renounced all past beliefs in a public ceremony and apologized to the Selangor Department of Islamic Religion, the National Fatwa Council, JAKIM, and all the Muslims in Malaysia. Hatijah Aam made a statement to the media explaining that Global Ikhwan Holdings Sdn. Bhd. was in the process of securing *halal* certification from JAKIM; furthermore, she stated that Global Ikhwan planned to encourage "all Muslims to unite and defend Islam through economic activities according to the al-Quran and Hadith," and that they needed a series of interconnected projects that cover "all aspects of the life of a Muslim" (Hasbullah 2014). It appears they are publicly distancing themselves from the group's unorthodox teachings about supernatural powers while continuing to promulgate their popular sharia economic model and ideas about Islam as a total way of life, which are widely shared in Malaysian Muslim society.

PAS: SHARIA ECONOMICS UNDER AN ISLAMIC STATE

The chapter opened with the words of Tuan Guru Nik Abdul Aziz, chief minister of the state of Kelantan and spiritual leader of PAS, at an event commemorating the twenty years PAS has controlled the state government.[14] A national opposition party, PAS previously administered the state from 1959 to 1978, after which UMNO took control. This Islamic opposition party regained and maintained power over the state government through electoral victories from 1990 to 2013. It shifted from stressing anticolonialism to pushing Malay communitarianism and eventually "revolutionary Pan-Islamism" with the rise of the *ulama* faction in the 1980s (Farish A. Noor 2004). As his above statement implies, Nik Aziz and the other PAS *ulama* that lead the party and state have tried to implement a pious form of development. PAS has engaged UMNO, the Malay Muslim political party leading the National Front (Barisan Nasional; BN), in tense political contests in the northern states of Kedah, Perak, Terengganu, and Kelantan over the last few decades.[15] These states of West Malaysia have large, mostly lower-class, Malay majorities and extensive networks of Islamic schools. Malaysians widely view Kelantan, even more so than these other states of the "Malay heartland," as staunchly Islamic. While UMNO has campaigned on their version of Islamic proselytizing coupled with promises of capital infusion and infrastructural development, PAS has targeted the UMNO-led federal government's form of development as "spiritually empty" or ethically deficient in their lack of emphasis on fulfilling the requirements of divine directives.

PAS combines Islamic ethics with several related religious notions and a political activist Islamic ideology, producing a "pious worldly consciousness" that brings Islamic ideas and feelings into economic processes as materially transformative forces, a "celestialization" that seeks to provide fulfillment in this world *and* the world hereafter. These religious notions are shaped by material conditions and in turn influence them; theological ideas are intertwined with political economic structures. Here, in the case of Kelantan, PAS *ulama* and state political leaders draw on pious Islamic ethics connecting them to subgoals motivating civil servants toward responsibility, accountability, and efficiency within a sharia-oriented perspective. They also motivate charity, a redistribution of wealth, reform of the financial system, and trade in *halal* products. PAS leaders in Kelantan tend to contest rather than embrace neoliberal norms, which they view as corporate-oriented, elitist, profit-seeking, detrimental to common people, and contrary to divine directives. PAS activists, associating these characteristics with the UMNO-led federal government, try to produce an alternative mode of economic development that puts greater emphasis on Islamic principles.

Following the electoral victory in 1990, PAS elected a popular religious scholar, Nik Abdul Aziz, to be the new chief minister of Kelantan. Deploying the slogan "Developing with Islam" chief minister Nik Aziz set out to transform the state into a model Islamic polity. At the gathering celebrating twenty years of "Developing with Islam," he stated that this slogan means "we develop in accordance to a foundation determined by Allah, the Glorified and Exalted." However, development should not be "spiritually empty," but rather mindful that this world is connected to the hereafter (Nik Abdul 2010). Using the metaphor of an airplane, he explained that a person who focuses only on the material world is like an airplane with one wing, whereas a person who thinks of both the material and the spiritual is like a plane properly equipped with two wings. The chief minister's formulation expresses a pious worldly consciousness that promotes a "sharia-compliant" form of economic development.

PAS set out to distinguish itself from UMNO, which had already initiated its own *dakwah* (proselytizing) campaigns, by demonstrating its commitment to implementing sharia and establishing an Islamic state. As part of fulfilling what they saw as their responsibility as leaders entrusted by Allah with control of the government, Tuan Guru Nik Aziz states that they taught state civil servants the principles of *ubudiah*, *mas'uliah*, and *itqan* (UMI) as the basis of their administration.[16] I found these ideas promulgated in widely distributed government newsletters and bulletins. A government publication states that the concept *ubudiah* (service to Allah) is connected to *aqidah* (religious belief), and reminds the administrators of their position as servants of Allah. Their main goal of administering the state should be to make it a form of *ibadah* (worship). The concept of *mas'uliah* (accountability) is connected to *amal* (good works) and sharia, directing them to be cognizant of the responsibility bestowed on them by Allah and the goals of acting as just and responsible authorities (as *khulafā'*; caliphs). Finally, the concept of *itqan* (skill) is connected to piety and ethics, reminding civil servants to perform quality work with skill, concentration, and sincerity (Kerajaan Negeri Kelantan 2007, 23). With these religious concepts, PAS leaders draw on and extend core Islamic beliefs in monotheism, the hereafter, and the ultimate cosmic significance of performing good works in this world. Nik Abdul Aziz (2010, 29–30), after declaring UMI the foundation of their state administration, announced that "civil servants are taught that their work is broadcast on Almighty Allah's closed circuit television through His secret police, the Angels." State government civil servants and employees in state agencies with whom I spoke all expressed a strong commitment to UMI.

Soon after regaining control of Kelantan, PAS leaders also implemented policies aimed at cleaning up "sinful" activities (*maksiat*) in the entertainment service sector, which they argued were allowed to continue under the UMNO-BN state. Although there were many Islamic schools and institutions, there were also many centers of "sinful" behavior.[17] Many of my local interlocutors informed me that before PAS came to power, there was an area in the middle of town with numerous nightclubs, billiard halls, movie theaters, gambling dens, and prostitution lairs. They report that PAS immediately, and triumphantly in their opinion, eliminated these venues from the urban landscape. State authorities refused to issue licenses for businesses engaging in these sorts of entertainment activities. The sale of alcohol in public places, including hotels and restaurants, was restricted, though some limited circulation of alcoholic beverages is allowed in the Chinese non-Muslim community. Of course, there is a gap between the state-promoted pious ideals and local people's everyday practices. Although I discovered occasional reports of "sinful" behaviors, most of the people I observed and interviewed in Kota Bharu expressed and embodied a strong sense of religiosity. My ethnographic evidence suggests that such ethical schemas are widespread in the urban context of Kota Bharu.

In addition, state government officials promoted the reduction of "wasteful" consumption and tried to embody this in their practices. Government officials accepted lower salaries and avoided extravagant events. In contrast to the forms of "proper" Malay middle-class consumption promoted by the UMNO-led federal government, PAS leaders advocated more modest and restrained consumption. These moderate values appear to resonate with both middle-class residents in Kuala Lumpur and corporate sharia elites of the Islamic resurgence (see Fischer 2008, 90; Sloane-White 2017). From this pious Muslim perspective, "wasteful" consumption and use of God-given resources is associated with *Shaitan* (Satan) and is therefore unethical behavior. In addition, in 1991 Kelantan state leaders banned performances of *mak yong* and *wayang* (traditional dance drama and shadow puppet arts)—which they interpreted as entailing elements of "superstition" and "un-Islamic beliefs"—as well as inappropriate attire and mixing of genders. With the official 1998 Enactment Controlling Entertainment and Places of Entertainment, they codified restrictions on traditional arts and entertainment venues deemed to be flouting Islamic values and norms. I did not witness

Friday morning religious instruction, Kota Bharu, Kelantan

any performances of these traditional arts in the Kota Bharu; however, Hardwick (2013) reports their continued existence and transformation in rural Kelantan, where they embody diverse senses of personal and normative piety.

My local interlocutors often referred to the widely adored Kelantan chief minister Tuan Guru Nik Aziz as an example of "proper" Islamic consumption (cf. Fischer 2008). Despite having been chief minister for twenty years, he still lived in the same kampong house he did before taking office. His long-term residence in a kampong house, a popular symbol evoking continuity with the Malay rural past, casts him as a common man rather than part of the "New Malay" elite (see Thompson 2007, 177, 183). They also proudly note that he still wears *baju melayu* (traditional Malay Muslim attire) with a turban like he did years ago, in stark contrast to the exquisite business suits and dress shirts of UMNO leaders. The Kelantan state government's "Developing with Islam" project, "anti-sinful-activities" campaign, and exemplary consumption practices remind and motivate people to live according to the straight path predicated on sharia rules and principles. Furthermore, the public absence of *maksiat*, such as alcohol consumption, prostitution, and gambling, and the simple, corruption-free lifestyle of the Kelantan chief minister, are embodied practices and symbols of the Islamic path to salvation.[18]

Interest-free banking was a national Muslim concern prior to the PAS electoral victory in 1990. Malaysian Muslim scholars shared a consensus that paying or receiving interest was prohibited according to sharia. The UMNO-led federal government had already embraced interest-free banking as part of its Islamization program establishing Malaysia's first Islamic bank, the Bank Islam Malaysia Berhad, in 1983. Nevertheless, PAS, galvanized by the UMI notions, propelled a further Islamization of banking institutions. State leaders in the early 1990s refused to store government funds in banks without interest-free counters, eventually spurring most banks to offer such services. They also established programs offering interest-free loans to civil servants and students, embodying their ethical cultural schema.

Furthermore, PAS, unlike UMNO-BN, established the principle of separating state funds into *halal* (permitted) and non-*halal* accounts based on their sources. If funds originated from interest, gambling, or alcohol, for instance, they were separated from funds made via "morally clean" sources (*halal*), such as agriculture and trade in permitted products. In 1991 the state government established an innovative fund called Tabung Serambi Mekah (TSM), which included money from *halal* and *haram* (forbidden) sources held in separate accounts and used for different purposes. PAS *ulama* explained that this fund provides an opportunity for people with money from *haram* sources to put it to good use in support of public works. According to the deputy chief minister's records, only *halal* funds were distributed to needy segments of the population—the poor and victims of natural disasters—whereas funds from *haram* sources were used for infrastructural projects or building non-Muslim religious institutions. These policies not only relieved pious Muslim fears that their *halal* money was being mixed with haram money but reaffirmed that untarnished good was being done with it through distribution to poor and needy Muslims. Arguing that this was the proper separation and allocation of these funds, PAS leaders enacted their ethical cultural schema and its extension through UMI. That is, state officials and civil servants were embodying pious Islamic ethics through their moral and responsible handling of funds. During the 2010 fiscal year through October, more than RM 2.5 million was spent from the TSM fund on fixing houses, medical care, help for fire and flood victims, and other forms of assistance.

In a fashion similar to that witnessed with the popular TSM fund, the state government has collected and centralized revenues, sometimes within the Kelantan Chief Minister's Corporation (Perbadanan Menteri Besar Kelantan; PMBK), and redistributed them to particular segments of the population. The state government collects funds from land, water, and forest concession taxes; leases; permits; service payments; low-cost housing rents; business profits; repayment of loans; and so forth. Officials and civil servants also encourage people who can afford it to donate money to the state. Cik Wan Azhar, a manager of a state agency, said that one of their main ideas in Kelantan is "to make money to help others." The ideas of *ubudiah* and *mas'uliah* come in, he stated, "when Tuan Guru agreed to pay people higher wages, but these people must pay *zakat* and must distribute the money, and these people with high pay brackets must remember that not all the money belongs to you. Some of it belongs to others."[19] PAS state leaders and officials not only try to embody the ethical cultural schema in their own policies and programs, but also call on individuals to do the same. The government emphasizes redistributing funds to the needy, including the elderly, disabled, women, and the poor, and to religious institutions, such as Islamic schools and colleges. One popular program is the Skim Takaful Kifaalah, which distributes money to the elderly population, aged sixty and above, from all ethnic and religious backgrounds. Thus, the state leaders integrate and embody pious Islamic ethics—mindful of the hereafter and performing good works—motivating responsible acts of justice for the needy and weak into redistribution processes. This serves to make Kelantan into a sort of Islamic social welfare state. Moreover, this "friendly and helpful style" of PAS leaders endears them with the rural poor and strengthens them against the constant attempts by UMNO to regain control of the state government.[20]

The Islamic social welfare character of the Kelantan state is also evident in the framing, discursive presentation, and pattern of redistribution of its 2011 state budget. Wan Nik, political secretary of the chief minister, explained that the budget is called "compassionate" and "friendly" because it focuses on improving the living conditions of the needy, a group that comprises the majority of people in Kelantan. He added that their use of the Kelantanese term *cakna* means "that the government and people as permanent friends work together to develop." Likewise, Wan Nik writes that the "compassionate budget implements the act of *sharing* and *giving* which will raise the future effectiveness of distribution efforts" (*Harakah* 2010a).

It should be noted that the infusion of Islamic notions and values into consumption and distribution processes is also used for proselytizing (*dakwah*) and political purposes, although we must be careful to avoid oversimplification (cf. Kessler 1978; Farish A. Noor 2003, 2004; Norani Othman

2005). For instance, PAS officials consider restrictions on "sinful" entertainment activities, avoidance of extravagant events, separation of non-*halal* and *halal* revenues, and redistribution of resources to lower social strata to be based in religious directives; however, they also use these practices to disseminate information about Islamic teachings and to point out the flaws in UMNO-BN practices. They severely attacked the federal government's 2011 budget for its mega construction projects, plan to expand Selangor's entertainment hub, and continued mixing of non-*halal* and *halal* revenues (*Harakah* 2010b). We can also note a similar, though variable, intertwining of pious, *dakwah*, and political motives concerning the launching of "sharia currency" and the Cheng Ho Expo. Moreover, state officials, PAS politicians, and their supporters consistently argue that the state government could accomplish much more for common people if it received the Petrolium Nasional Berhad royalties from offshore oil drilling that the federal government has denied them. They argue that Kelantan should receive 5 percent of the oil and gas revenues as required by legal agreements between the state, the federal government, and Petrolium Nasional Berhad. However, the federal government has interpreted the sites of drilling to be within the zones of other states, Sabah and Terengganu, rather than Kelantan. PAS officials' pious ethical schema is *pluripotent*, productive in multiple discourses and contexts. They use it to express and embody their religious virtue, argue for the correctness of the Islamic way of "enjoining good and forbidding wrong," and struggle for political and ideological victories over their Malay Muslim opponents in UMNO.

In August 2010 the Kelantan state government launched "sharia currency," the dinar and dirham (gold and silver coins) of Kelantan. Four years earlier, in 2006, they had minted their first gold coins, but this time both gold and silver coins were minted, in several denominations, with new standards and institutions. PMBK and the Kelantan Golden Trade Sdn. Bhd., its subsidiary, organized the sharia currency inauguration event (Qiadah 2010, 16). They had the World Islamic Mint in Dubai mint gold dinar and silver dirham according to the standards of the World Islamic Trade Organization. State officials found a basis for the position of gold and silver currency within an Islamic way of life and used the launching for *dakwah* and political purposes.

State leaders and PAS activists also perform *dakwah* by contrasting the benefits of sharia currency with the problems wrought through the contemporary dominance of the paper currency system. Proselytizers present gold and silver coins as an interest-free method of storing value and wealth, immune to inflation, speculation, and commodity manipulation and trick-ery. This message appeals to the sensibilities of Kelantan's large Malay peas-ant population, who are accustomed to storing wealth in their land. On the other hand, the paper money system is replete with defects and presented as at least partially culpable for the Asian economic crisis of the late 1990s and the US and European economic crisis of the mid-2000s. They viewed the commodity manipulation and financial investment scams, integral to these economic crises, as inherent shortcomings of a paper currency system. For these proselytizers, an Islamic monetary system offers the solution.

In addition, the launching of sharia currency was used for political and ideological ends. The state government presented itself as a leader of the Islamic revival and renewal, as an Islamic state led by an *alim* (religious scholar) picking up from where the fallen Uthmaniya Caliphate left off. Sharia cur-rency is a symbol of the return to this tradition. It also indexes the failure of the secular-oriented UMNO-BN federal government to fully implement Islamic principles. The chief minister's corporate magazine notes that even though Tun Mahathir called for gold coins in response to the monetary cri-sis, the federal government has failed to adopt the Islamic alternative. Fur-thermore, the currency is used discursively to express criticism of the effects of colonialism in Malaysia and opposition to dependence on pro-Israeli Western powers.

Given the practical difficulties with implementing gold and silver coins as an all-purpose currency—akin to problems with *hudud*—performing *dakwah* and the politics of sharia currency have taken on a greater signifi-cance. Initially, there appeared to be rather widespread uses promoted for gold and silver coins. Not only were they recommended for paying *zakat* (Islamic tithe) and marital exchanges, but hundreds of businesses were listed among those committed to accepting dinar and dirham for their trans-actions. However, after extensive criticism from the federal government, and perhaps from other opposition partners, chief minister Nik Aziz (2010, 41) clarified that the coins were only to be used as a matter of free choice by those engaging in "barter trade." State officials and local supporters were able to claim that sharia currency could not be fully implemented because the federal government blocked the state government's efforts.

Kelantan state officials organized the Cheng Ho Expo, which took place in the Kelantan Trade Centre and was opened by the sultan of Kelantan on November 21, 2010.[21] Over one thousand people attended the international event, including mayors from several areas in China, Uzbekistan, Turkistan,

Taiwan, and Thailand (*Harakah* 2010c). The event included official speeches, cultural arts, *halal* food festivities, Cheng Ho historical exhibits, and a Qur'anic recitation by a member of the Chinese delegation.

The main goal of the Cheng Ho Expo was to facilitate trade between China and Kelantan and to make the state into a distribution hub in the region. Cheng Ho City, a new trade center, is planned for Rantau Panjang in Pasir Mas. It will be built in a Chinese architectural style and include premises for *halal* Chinese food to be served to local Muslims. Indeed, Datuk Husam Musa, the state secretary of development, maintained that while the trade they are trying to develop with China will include several products, the most important are *halal* food products, since that industry is important for Malaysia's Muslim community (*Sinarharian* 2010b). Similarly, chief minister Nik Aziz (2010, 38) stated that it is hoped that following the Cheng Ho Expo Kelantan, given its geographical proximity to China, "will become a doorway for all sorts of products, especially halal products, which possess a high marketing potential in Malaysia these days."

Similar to spoken and written language pertaining to other forms of distribution, the discourse surrounding the Cheng Ho Expo and the development of Kelantan as a trade hub refers to core Muslim values, *dakwah*, and politics. Chief minister Tuan Guru Nik Aziz refers to Surah al-Quraish stressing the value of conducting trade and business enterprises and the significance of opening the door to trade on an international level. Kelantan state officials also performed *dakwah*, especially to Malays and Chinese, as they discussed the history of Cheng Ho, a Chinese Muslim, and the large population of Chinese Muslims in China. Through this discourse they lowered the "racial wages" or symbolic benefits often connected to Malay Muslim identity, making Chinese Malaysians feel more comfortable with Islam and motivating Malays to stress their Muslim rather than their ethnic identity. This mode of proselytizing directly feeds into ideological contests with UMNO, whom they often target as struggling over race more than they do for Islam.

Nevertheless, most important for our present discussion is the continued emphasis on instilling Islamic notions and values into distribution processes. In this case, the policy initiative behind the Cheng Ho Expo is the plan for turning Kelantan into a distribution hub for products made in China.

Unlike the extensive circulation of pious Islamic notions in distributive processes, I note quite a limited inoculation of such ideas into productive processes. However, chief minister Nik Aziz (2010, 37), has feinted at infusing Islamic notions into production processes. He refers to Ibn Khaldun's discussion of economic philosophy, noting the principles of justice, hard work, cooperation, and moderation, and immediately turns to criticize the federal government for unjustly denying Kelantan's rights to receiving oil royalties. He never returned to apply more fully these concepts to economic production. Here, this political tactic of blaming the UMNO-BN national government for partisan discrimination against Kelantan and its negative impact on economic development obscures the PAS-led state government's unpreparedness for instilling pious Islamic notions into production processes. Several political-economic and cultural factors impede them in this regard.

First, the federal government–linked agricultural, telecommunications, and energy monopolies dominate the local economy. They provide many local jobs and revenues for the state budget in the form of rents, fees, and taxes. In addition to facilitating the local operation of these monopolies, state agencies operate several smaller businesses both in these sectors and in other sectors where there is less competition with large, powerful corporations. None of these state enterprises is framed as part of an "Islamic economy." Thus, rather than trying to transform capitalist production processes, the state government actively participates in them.

The PAS-led state government's position is similar to what Ong (1987, 149–50) describes as the UMNO-led federal government's participation in global capitalist production in the early 1980s. UMNO *ulama* urged Muslims to emulate the work ethic of successful Asian "races"—namely, Japanese and Koreans—as part of the "Look East" policy validating transnational capital and new labor relations. Likewise, PAS state leaders relinquish internal corporate organization to the interests of capital while briefly citing Ibn Khaldun, a fourteenth-century Arab historian, to validate their potentially new economic model if only they were given the capital to manifest it. In contrast, Darul Arqam and later Global Ikhwan, and Muslim corporate leaders in some government-linked companies, instill sharia economic models into workplaces and production activities. Kelantan state leaders do not produce any cultural schema comparable to either of these. Instead, they leave internal corporate labor relations and organization to managers and evoke Muslim rather than non-Muslim cultural values. However, unlike these two cases, they have control of a state government that provides them with an opportunity to at least influence micro- and macro-economic principles impinging on the mode of industrial production.

Second, a large base of the PAS-led government's support consists of Malay peasants whose interests are opposed to widespread industrialization and mega projects usurping large tracts of land. The Kelantan State Economic Planning Unit (2009) finds agricultural, forestry, livestock, and fishery to be the main sectors of annual GDP growth. Add to this the fact that in Kelantan over 70 percent of the population is rural and that even in most towns, other than Kota Bharu, over 30 percent of the land is used for agricultural production, highlights the significance of the peasant population. When I asked state officials why they do not focus on bringing more industrial development to the state, other than citing problems related to the gender division, family disruption, and federal discrimination they also explain that the agricultural base of their economy is more stable and a hedge against economic crises. Nik Wan stated that it is better for the state and the country for local youth to leave Kelantan to work in industries in other states: the remittances they send back to families help the state, while their labor helps national economic development. Moreover, Dato' Dr. Zainuddin, the deputy state secretary of development, told me that although Kelantan has consistently been one of the poorest states, the residents hold lots of wealth in terms of land and property.[22]

Maintaining local Malay land ownership appears to be one of the mainstays of state government policy. Cik Hong, a local non-Muslim Chinese PAS supporter, stated that it is difficult even for Malays from other states to buy land in Kelantan. He also said that several economic development projects funded by outside investors were stalled at the state level when they were made to wait several years for permits. They eventually decided to invest elsewhere. For Cik Hong, it is not so much the federal government that blocks industrial and commercial development in the state, but rather the state government itself and the widespread orientation toward keeping land and property in the hands of local Kelantanese.[23] I think the official discourse and land policies reflect the importance of the Malay peasant political base.

Third, the PAS *ulama* appear unprepared in their social theory and economic-oriented religious interpretations to instill ethical cultural schema and pious Islamic notions into production processes.[24] They have applied the concept *itqan* to the work of civil servants, emphasizing the value of high-quality work. However, UMI is rarely applied to the relations between workers, managers, and plant owners. How should a sharia-based notion of justice play into salaries, benefits, and profits? Should private companies be allowed to concentrate control over natural resources? Rather than bringing sharia to bear on the mode of production through answering such questions, PAS leaders tend to target the UMNO-BN elites' bias and inclination toward corruption or point away from these worldly matters to the hereafter. The ethical cultural schema and pious Islamic notions here forestall and temper the pace of industrial growth rather than driving people to use it to accumulate divine merit for the cosmic long term.

For instance, Cik Wan Azhar, an employee of a state agency, recalled Nik Aziz speaking at a dinner sponsored by a successful Chinese gold-mining company. He reported being especially struck when Nik Aziz said, "I'm not that worried if my people are hungry, if my people are poor. But what I am worried about most is if they are rich and they tend to forget about religion." This made Cik Wan wonder, he said, how Kelantan would be able to develop economically and still be mindful of Islamic principles. It remains for PAS *ulama* to explain how Muslims can apply pious Islamic ethics, ever mindful of accruing *amalan soleh* for the afterlife, to their participation in economic production, including labor, management, and ownership in industrial and agricultural enterprises. Islamic scholars in the Middle East and South Asia have expressed a broad range of ideas on matters of economic production. Several have proposed forms of socialist production, while others posit Islamic forms of production as distinct from both socialism and capitalism (see Donohue and Esposito 2007, 78–113, 228–60). Operating with Screpanti's (1999) institutional definition of forms of capitalism, concentrating on private property regimes and accumulation governance structures, it is unclear whether sharia-oriented Islamic revival movements such as PAS, the Justice and Prosperity Party in Indonesia, and the Islamic Brotherhood in Egypt would establish a form of capitalism if given the opportunity to implement a full-fledged Islamic economic system. Although they embrace the concept of private property, they also propose significant limitations to accumulation governance structures, as does Sayyid Abul Aʻlā Mawdūdī (2011, 61–78), an influential figure for these movements. In terms of this Kelantan case, not only is there very limited implantation of Islamic notions and principles into productive processes in the broader society, including non-Muslim-owned corporations; there are also no state government-linked economic corporations framed as "Islamic corporations." PAS *ulama*, many trained in the Middle East and Pakistan, have not provided much help thinking through these matters within an Islamic worldview. Perhaps this is also partially due to the broader unpreparedness of contemporary Muslim scholars to address implementing sharia in modes of production that are not explicitly framed as part of an "Islamic economy" (see Muhammad Syukri 1994; Sloane-White 2011).

CONCLUSION

These different understandings of Islamic ethical imperatives within Malaysia can be compared with those in many countries throughout the Muslim world. For instance, the Middle Eastern Gulf States, Iran, Turkey, Pakistan, and Sudan have all moved to establish a sharia-compliant financial system. It is important to recognize that ethical schemas are diverse and multiple across and within societies, as they are shaped not only by core religious texts, written or oral, but also by ideas emphasized and elaborated on in communities of practice.[25] For instance, Daromir Rudnycykj (2009, 125) describes a group of Indonesian Islamic reformers that draw on pious Islamic ethics and their popular beliefs of cosmic accounting to motivate individual responsibility, transparency, and efficiency at work. He argues that in the ethnographic case of Krakatau Steel and ESQ (Emotional and Spiritual Quotient) reformers in post–New Order Indonesia, Islamic ethics and neoliberal norms converge to produce a "spiritual economy." However, generalizing this "spiritual economy" beyond its particular context is difficult. It is essential to realize that the spiritual economy Rudnycykj describes represents the articulation of core Islamic ethical beliefs with the notions and ideology of ESQ, a mystical, corporate-oriented new religious movement. ESQ religious guides and corporate managers worked together to merge pious Islamic ethics with neoliberal or capitalist, market-oriented norms in the context of post-Suharto economic transformation.[26] Thus, explicating cultural models allows us to account for both the similarities in higher-level goals and diversity in ideologically inflected subgoals across Islamic communities of practice. Moreover, "the global Islamic revival" is diverse and requires a theoretical framework capable of discerning multiple convergences with economic globalization (cf. Rudnycykj 2009, 107; see also Hirschkind 2006, 208).

The concept of religious ethical models elucidates how core religious beliefs and higher-level goals articulate with other notions and ideological formulations giving rise to various subgoals and motives. It provides us with a powerful analytical framework for examining prosperity and liberation theologies, spiritual economies, and alternative moral economies within and across belief systems. While the ESQ and PAS cultural models share core beliefs and higher-level goals of accruing good deeds for the afterlife, their subgoals and motives vary in accordance with their ideological formulations—those of a mystical, market-oriented new religious movement, or a normative, sharia-oriented Islamic political party. Moreover, these contrasting ideological formulations were forged in different sociopolitical contexts. ESQ emerged in late New Order secular nationalist Indonesia where Islam, playing an increasingly important role in the public sphere, still had no formal relationship with the state. PAS emerged from within UMNO during the transition to political independence and grew to adulthood in a Malaysia, with Islam constitutionally recognized as the religion of the federation, which was becoming increasingly Islamized.

Furthermore, this conceptualization of Islamic ethical models allows us to illuminate convergences between a variety of Islamic revival movements and economic globalization within Malaysia. First, UMNO-BN revival projects embody combinations of Islamic ethics with capitalist industrialization, consumerism, and corporate development. These projects largely instill Islamic ethics on a broad structural and bureaucratic level. Second, diverse pro-sharia Islamic NGO members and supporters participating in the "Islamic economy" embody combinations of Islamic ethics with ideas of individual and collective responsibility, and corporations as "miniature Islamic states" implementing sharia within personnel relations (Sloane-White 2011, 2017). Third, Darul Arqam's economic activities embody combinations of Islamic ethics with Sufi mystical notions of inner spiritual growth plus ideas of fulfilling collective religious obligations and performing *dakwah* aimed at establishing an all-embracing Islamic system. Fourth, PAS projects in Kelantan embody both Islamic ethics combined with UMI, and an activist ideology aimed at achieving political power to implement sharia in the broader society.

Although capitalist economic values remain dominant in Malaysian society, these diverse social forces infusing sharia economic models into consumption, distribution, and production serve to de-secularize these aspects of life in Malaysia. The Malaysian state has developed and organized a highly regulated system of Islamic banks and finance as an alternative to conventional banking services. Pushed by Darul Arqam and some other *dakwah* movements, the Malaysian state has promoted consumption of *halal* products as part of its nationalist and international strategies of development within the global capitalist system. It has also centralized state control over certification of *halal* goods industries. Kelantan state officials have initiated plans to turn Kelantan into a regional hub for the circulation of goods made in China, especially *halal* products, which bodes well for the interests of local traders. The PAS-led Kelantan state government has broadly instilled the ethical cultural model—notions of *ubudiah*, *ma'suliah*, and *itqan* and the pious worldly consciousness they constitute—into consumption and distribution processes. They have contributed to the explosion of interest-free banking and provided people with financial avenues to aid the general welfare while ridding themselves of *haram* money. Gold and silver coins (sharia currency) have been minted and put into partial circulation for barter trade and the storing of wealth. Darul Arqam's *ma-ash* system and the Kelantan government's innovative funds and "compassionate" state budgets have managed to construct modes of redistribution of resources to the needy segments of the population. This wide-ranging implantation of UMI and Darul Arqam's Sufi methods of self-purification indicates that pious Islamic ethics is stimulating a more equitable distribution of resources and commercial development.

Darul Arqam and the Kelantan state government's mode of redistribution offers a significant and viable alternative to neoliberal capitalist policies that are dominant in the United States and influential in many other parts of the world.[27] For instance, in the United States after the government bailed out banks in 2007–8 and prolonged tax breaks for the wealthiest Americans in 2010, workers' collective bargaining rights came under assault and national budgets were proposed that threatened to eliminate many programs for needy segments of the population. The wealthiest echelon of US society, the "super citizens" of neoliberal capitalism, would do well to be reminded of what Tuan Guru Nik Aziz said to the highly paid in Kelantan—that is, that some of the wealth they have accumulated is not for them, but for others.

In addition, corporate sharia elites and Darul Arqam / Global Ikhwan leaders implant Islamic ethics into economic production processes. Despite sharia advisors' directions of adjusting their moral concerns to the dictates of conducting profitable business in the broader environment, corporate sharia elites instill Islamic ethics into both the workplace and personnel rules and responsibilities. Darul Arqam's model entails the emplacement of pious ethics on macro and micro levels within a wholly Islamic economic system directed toward fulfilling religious aims and achieving movement goals. However, for the Kelantan state government, in stark contrast to distribution, economic production processes reflect a relatively limited infusion of UMI and the need for greater economic *ijtihad*—the interpretation and application of divine directives. PAS *ulama* appear theoretically unprepared and politically and economically constrained by the hegemony of federal monopolies and their dependence on the Malay peasant base. Rather than motivating industrial development, pious Islamic ethics, deflected by PAS scholars' fears of the deleterious effects of capital accumulation, tends to slow it down.

5 PRO-SHARIA DISCOURSES

Race, Religion, and Nation

DEMANDS FOR SOCIOPOLITICAL REFORMS—GOOD GOVERNANCE, fair elections, equality before the law, inclusive nation building, and religious freedom—have increased in Malaysia since the late 1990s. The sacking of charismatic deputy prime minister Anwar Ibrahim in 1998, the Asian economic crisis, and the reverberating effects of the Reformation Movement in neighboring Indonesia all contributed to the emerging intensity of calls for reform. These demands, emanating from political parties and civil society organizations, have increasingly challenged the hegemony of the electoral authoritarian government. This growing reform movement developed in the midst of several decades of Islamic resurgence that precipitated a stronger presence of Islam in the public and cultural spheres.[1] The ruling United Malays National Organization (UMNO)–led National Front coalition and the Anwar Ibrahim–led opposition coalition staged two highly competitive national elections in 2008 and 2013.[2] However, it is not the opposing coalition-based formations but, rather, the crosscutting commitments to civil liberties, minority rights, and Malay and Muslim preeminence that are most significant for understanding sociopolitical dynamics in Malaysian society (cf. Weiss 2006). That is, the constituent minority parties in both coalitions share an interest in civil liberties and equal rights, while UMNO and PAS (Parti Islam SeMalaysia; Islamic Party of Malaysia), members of opposing electoral coalitions, coalesce around Malay and/or Muslim hegemony. The cultural politics are more fundamental and not easily contained within electoral politics. A new political anthropology is well equipped to deal with cultural politics and transformations in power relations (Özyürek 2006, 22). Sharia dynamics in Malaysia are evident in the diverse ways in which political parties and nongovernmental organizations have engaged with the Islamic discursive tradition and created multiple mixtures of sharia conceptions with other ideas and practices.

MALAY AND ISLAMIC SOVEREIGNTY

The UMNO, a Malay nationalist political party, has led the multiracial and multireligious National Front (Barisan Nasional; BN) that has ruled the Malaysian federal government since political independence in 1957. UMNO has facilitated the implementation of traditional Sunni interpretations of sharia in family and personal law cases within state-level courts overseen by religious councils and ultimately by the sultans. UMNO political elites and affiliated *ulama* interpret sharia within a secular nationalist modernity project, linking Islamic notions to conceptions of the Malaysian nation, multiculturalism, development, and modernization. For instance, prime minister and UMNO president Najib Tun Abdul Razak stated in his keynote speech to the UMNO National Convention in October 2010: "What we struggle for today is not something new. To the contrary, this is the continuation of the aspirations of Malays together with the people of Malaysia at the time we decided to demand independence. Actually, ever since that time, we have consistently held on to three main principles, that is, first, Malay solidarity as the foundation of national unity; second, Islam as *dīn*; and third, a prosperous country based on social justice." The Malay category is set aside and prioritized as the foundation of the imagined national community, a cultural model sometimes referred to as *Ketuanan Melayu* or Malay sovereignty. Islam, long understood in precolonial and colonial contexts as an attribute of Malays, is here considered the *dīn* or way of life of Malays. After more than three decades of Islamic resurgence, this behavioral expectation of Malay-ness has risen in significance. In addition, this image of sovereign Malay Muslims living according to the norms of Islam is connected with the goals of economic and technological development and modernization.

After citing a poem lauding presumed Malay ancestral characteristics of flexibly accommodating customary principles with sharia and faithfully serving the Muslim community, UMNO President Najib, in his keynote speech, proceeds to further elaborate on their approach to sharia and its connection to Malay leadership of a diverse Malaysian society and economic modernity:

> In fact, in terms of those Malay ancestors, they have passed the test of time. This personality is also what has caused Malays to be received as leaders within a diverse society. This attitude is also a resource for a people who are trusted to carry national leadership. Even more beautiful again, the trait of

Malay leadership emphasized here, after being purified with the arrival of the teachings of Islam, proclaimed, taught, and supported the *wasaṭiyyah* approach. *Wasaṭiyyah* is a method of carrying out the life of an individual or society in a balanced and universal fashion within all areas, especially within challenges related to solidarity and nationality. . . . After that, from time to time, the teachings of Al-Quran together with the *Sunna* [was] neatly planted and woven into the tapestry of the everyday life of Malay people. Since then until now, Malay peoples' values are heavily colored with taking the *wasaṭiyyah* or middle course. Referring to the interpretations of *ulama*, it is explained that the *ummat wasaṭiyyah* overall is an *ummat* that is just and moreover has the energy to develop and work hard for a prosperous life in this world and in the hereafter.

Within this elite UMNO ideology, *wasaṭiyyah* fits with the already-present flexible and accommodating character of ancestral Malays who embraced Islam.[3] This particular formulation of the "middle path" appears to be a complex concept that organizes and provides a framework for understanding many domains in which Malays have adopted a position between two extremes.[4] Instead of extending equal citizenship to all Malaysians or restricting citizenship only to Malays, they negotiated a "social contract" whereby citizenship is extended to all Malaysians but full belonging or *Tuan* status is reserved for "indigenous" Malays. It also applies to adopting "Islam as the religion of the federation" together with "religious freedom" for non-Muslims. UMNO President Najib, following the framework laid out by former PM Mahathir Mohamad, underscores the importance of *wasaṭiyyah* for economic development and modernization. Not only is modernity compatible with Islam, but Muslims taking the "middle course" are especially well suited to modernity. Similarly, *wasaṭiyyah* navigates between the extremes of implementing *ḥudūd* punishments and treating serious violations of Islamic mores to the whims of individuals by establishing sharia criminal laws, including *ta'zir*. UMNO-led federal governments have continued the three-five-six limits set out in the Syariah Courts (Criminal Jurisdiction) Act of 1965 (as amended in 1984) that restricts sharia courts from imposing any punishments that exceed three years of imprisonment, a fine of RM 5,000, or six strokes of the rattan. Thus, in UMNO's sharia model, Islam and moderate implementation of Islamic laws are attributes of the Malay race, the sovereign "hosts" of multiracial and multireligious Malaysia.

Although UMNO's format for linking race, religion, and nation has persuaded many Malaysian Muslims and non-Muslims over the years, it has not achieved total hegemony. Following the race riots of 1969, the UMNO-led Barisan Nasional government co-opted and funded many Malay nationalist *silat* (martial arts) groups that promoted the racialized *agama, bangsa, dan negara* (religion, race, and nation) ideology of Malay political elites (Lawrence Ross 2013). These groups became organized on a national level and shifted their targets from non-Muslim opposition groups to PAS as electoral politics fluctuated over the last several decades. Similarly, Malay rights organizations, such as PERKASA (Pertubuhan Pribumi Perkasa; Organization of Empowering Indigenous Peoples of Malaysia) and GERTAK (Gerakan Kebangkitan Rakyat; People's Awakening Movement), have emerged, shoring up some support for *Ketuanan Melayu* and attacking detractors and opponents of UMNO. For instance, PERKASA arose in the aftermath of the twelfth general election of 2008, in which UMNO lost five states to the opposition and its two-thirds majority in the Parliament. In my interview with a few PERKASA leaders in Kedah, they blamed the electoral loss in that state on the "defection" of large numbers of Chinese and Indians from Barisan Nasional. Kedah is a northern state with a Malay majority of more than 75 percent, where PAS and UMNO have had hotly contested elections for several decades (see Daniels 2013a). This Malay rights organization lists its main goals as Islam, Malay, and *Bumiputera* rights, Malay sultans, and Malay language, all conventional symbols of Malay-ness evoking *Ketuanan Melayu*. Most of their public discourse concerns these issues, stressing the need to tighten Malay domination and to curtail the social forces they perceive to be threatening Malay unity. For instance, the head of PERKASA in Negeri Sembilan, addressing the topic of "strengthening requirements for citizenship," is quoted in their newspaper, *Suara Perkasa* (2010a), as stating that "Chinese and Indian people, and other minority ethnic groups within our country, are very easy to respond angrily whenever matters related to Malays come up, especially when religious issues and sultans are discussed." The article argues that applicants for citizenship must be required to acquire a better understanding of the history of *Tanah Melayu*, the land of Malays.

PERKASA and many other Malay rights organizations are quick to criticize PAS and PKR (Partai Keadilan Rakyat; People's Justice Party) for selling out the Malay race, and they occasionally use Islam or sharia as a metaphor for Malays. Another article in *Suara Perkasa* (2010b) complains of visible alcohol cans in the garbage next to a Selangor state government building: "This is proof the upper-level state leaders suffer from an extremely weak administration. . . . [N]ot more than four of the state Exco [Executive Council] members are Malay within the Parti Keadilan Rakyat's state administration.

It's as if they have no voice or power because the majority of Exco members are from non-Malay groups." Alcohol cans in garbage bins near the PKR-led state government's office building are symbols of the lack of Malay leadership. Thus, if Muslim opposition forces are shown to not be upholding sharia among their non-Muslim cohorts, then this is evidence of their failure to carry on the struggle for Malay rights. The way Malay rights organizations' public discourse emphasizes the racialized dimension of the hegemonic sharia model allows UMNO the latitude to appear as a "moderate" option, advocating racial harmony and national unity, in the eyes of the multiracial and multireligious supporters of the National Front.

On the other hand, PAS has mounted a significant ideological and political contest over the last three decades against both UMNO's and Malay rights organizations' manner of linking race, religion, and nation. The Islamic Party of Malaysia's long-range goal is the establishment of an Islamic state that will fully implement sharia, including *hudud* and *qisas* criminal punishments. Rather than the *Ketuanan Melayu* championed by UMNO and PERKASA, PAS proposes *Ketuanan Islam* or Islamic sovereignty. Tok Guru Nik Aziz, then governor of Kelantan and spiritual leader of PAS, told me, "In Malaysia, there are two courts. There is the civil court and the sharia court. Who said it is supposed to be this way? In the time of the Prophet Muhammad, in the time of the caliphs, there was only one court." He exclaimed that when they gain control of the state there would be only one court of law, the sharia court.[5] PAS rejects the "secular" arrangement of relegating sharia courts to handling Muslim family and personal criminal laws on the state-level, while the civil High Court handles all manner of cases on the state and federal levels. PAS has passed two *hudud* and *qisas* enactments—in Kelantan in 1993 and Terengganu in 1999—but was not able to implement them due to federal-level restrictions. They remain dedicated to the full implementation of sharia despite some fallout in the Anwar Ibrahim–led opposition coalition, Pakatan Rakyat, of which they were members together with PKR and DAP (Democratic Action Party). PAS leaders view the establishment of an Islamic state as a Muslim responsibility:

> Governing and administering the *negara* [country] is actually included
> with religious tasks. This is demonstrated by Rasulullah S.A.W. who
> himself served as the prime minister of the first *negara* Islam [Islamic state]
> in Madinah Al-Munawarrah and every day supervised the administration
> of the country's affairs. . . . Through the Constitution of the Sky called
> Al-Quran, Allah SWT delivered the revelation that is not just suitable for

commanding prayer and fasting, but instead covers criminal laws, jihad, distributing inheritance, proper treatment of prisoners of war, appointing workers, leading soldiers, resolving household problems and handling sexual and property crimes. (Nik Abdul Aziz 2010, 27–28)

According to PAS leaders, the obligation for Muslims to establish an Islamic state is rooted in the Holy Qur'an and the example of Prophet Muhammad, the *Rasul* or Messenger of Allah. Muslim leaders of the Islamic state must implement the laws and ethical norms provided by the sacred constitution, Al-Qur'an, and Prophetic Traditions. Combining their notion of a broad operationalization of sharia that extends into all domains of life with the contemporary idea of the "nation-state" does not pose any problem for them. They believe that the revealed *ḥukum* (laws) should be applied by, and provide the guiding principles of, whatever sort of polity (or *negara*) exists.[6] Islamic forces must attain political power to establish the Islamic state as a geographical entity that will comprehensively execute the laws of Allah (Muhammad Syukri 1999). The current problem from their perspective is not that Islam is connected with the state but that "secular" leaders are in control of the state. "Secular" here refers to UMNO leaders' basis in struggling for

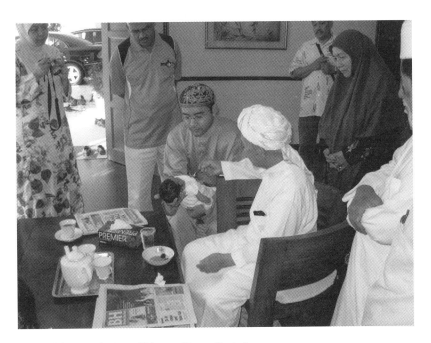

Nik *Abdul* Aziz Nik Mat in Kelantan House, Kuala Lumpur

Malay rights and their lack of commitment to fully implementing sharia, including, quite notably, the *hudud* penal code. Not only has PAS been campaigning for installing *hudud* laws for several decades, but they have also institutionalized a program called *Hari Hudud* (*Hudud* Day) in which they try to educate and raise public awareness about Islamic law. In fact, many of my interlocutors in Kelantan tended to respond to my general questions about sharia with statements about *hudud*. As a result of PAS political campaigning, the Islamic penal code has become magnified within many of their supporters' models of sharia.

In the process of challenging UMNO-BN hegemony, the *ulama* leaders of PAS formulated competing notions for imagining the Malaysian nation, multiculturalism, and economic development. Drawing on religious sources that emphasize piety over race or ethnic identities, they stressed virtuous Muslim identities over Malay-ness. In their model of *Ketuanan Islam*, Muslims rather than Malays would be the rightful leaders and full citizens of the Malaysian nation. However, they also promote the appointment of non-Muslim local leaders as well as criteria based on need and class rather than race for the allocation of goods and services. In addition, PAS leaders criticize the mega projects and elitism of the UMNO-BN modernity project and argue for a populist and class-conscious economic approach that infuses sharia into processes of consumption and distribution (see Daniels 2013a).

PAS leaders publicly contest UMNO and Malay rights organizations' formula of Islam-race-nation and their basis in struggling for Malay rights. The spiritual leader of PAS and governor of Kelantan, Nik Abdul Aziz, shocked many in the Malay community when he announced to a media gathering in September 2010 that he was not proud of being Malay. Race is something that comes automatically and in Islam there is no dominant race; if there were a dominant race in Islam, it would be the Arab race, he reportedly added. When invited to give a speech, he insisted that he would not do it in the name of Malays, but in the name of Islam. Chief minister Nik Aziz also informed the media that the PAS-led state government of Kelantan has spent as much as RM 7 million to build a Chinese-style *masjid* in Rantau Panjang and organized the Cheng Ho Expo in an effort to rid the society of racism. For several days his words reverberated in the media, and they elicited several scathing responses in the Malay-language newspapers (*Utusan* 2010a). In the *Sinarharian* newspaper, Mohd Zawawi, a state political official in Terengganu, called for Nik Aziz to clarify his statement, complaining that it could confuse the masses; in a place like Malaysia where Malays are Muslims, his words could be interpreted to mean he is not proud of being a

Muslim. Ramlan Husain, a director of a *Bumiputera* business association in Selangor, charged that this statement values politics to the detriment of Malay pride and appears to be part of a project to eliminate Malay special rights when Nik Aziz and his children have benefited from these privileges as Malays: "Islam does not forbid the Muslim community from being concerned about their racial origins as long as they are not held to be more important than Islam. . . . This Malay leader possibly has a racial identity crisis. . . . What is his problem? You would think that he would acknowledge and be proud of being Muslim and Malay because Malay and Islam cannot be divided in this country."[7] *Utusan*, a Malay-language newspaper closely tied to UMNO, and *The Star*, an English-language newspaper, reported that Datuk Alwi Che Ahmad, the leader of BN opposition in Kelantan, called on Nik Aziz to resign as chief minister of the state for making comments that could "cause unrest among Malays." He evoked the conventional "social contract" notion, stating that the "rights of Malays are enshrined in the Federal Constitution" and that "Malaysians of all races lived in harmony." Like other UMNO leaders, Datuk Alwi suggested Nik Aziz was "playing politics and is not a sincere Muslim because even Prophet Muhammad had stressed . . . the importance of race."[8] UMNO leaders' and supporters' public responses to Nik Aziz's downplaying of Malay racial identity exhibited a pattern of criticizing his political motivations and arguing for Malay rights, the indivisibility of Malay identity and Islam in Malaysia, and the permissibility of stressing on one's race in Islam. Some also interpreted that Nik Aziz was expressing his opposition to UMNO's overtures for unity talks with PAS.

In the context of late 2010 and early 2011, there was plenty of discussion of political divisions in the Malay community and calls for Malay unity. With the backdrop of major UMNO electoral losses in the general election of 2008, former prime minister Mahathir Mohamad made several public statements and speeches complaining about the current weakness of Malays, which he contended was the result of political divisions into UMNO, PKR, and PAS camps. The elder statesmen appeared at public events organized by PERKASA, and together they called for Malay unity to maintain their political leadership of the nation. While UMNO leaders were declaring their preparedness to work together with PAS for Malay and Muslim unity in the country, PAS leaders were reminding the public that the *dasar* (basic foundations and principles) of the parties were different. Nik Abdul Aziz responded to these calls by stating that the "Malay political strength depends on the preparedness of UMNO to change their *dasar* to Islam" (*Malaysiakini* 2010).

He called for principled unity based on struggling for Islam rather than struggling for Malay domination. Moreover, as UMNO ideologues continued to emphasize his downplaying of Malay-ness, Nik Aziz repeated his perspective, stating, "If I was born in a group from Orang Asli society or whatever it would not matter, my origins would be in Islam and having faith in Allah Subhaana Wa Ta'ala (SWT)." This was in response to Mahathir Mohamad publicly asking him to be thankful for being born Malay since Malays are definitely Muslims. Mahathir argued that the Malay race is unique because, according to the Constitution, they must speak Malay, perform Malay customs, and have Islam as their religion. In this exchange, Nik Aziz repeated that all races are the same and there are no special ones among them, including Arabs, except for Muslims believing in Allah. Besides, if race was important, he added, then surely Prophet Muhammad's fellow Arab, Abu Jahal, would enter heaven, but Allah already stated long ago that he would be among those sent to hell. Reiterating PAS ideals, the spiritual leader pronounced that the Islam they struggle for is "simple and situated in a high place and opposes past actions that contradict religion" (*Malaysiakini* 2011). Similarly, the head of the PAS Youth wing, Nasrudin, who has emerged as a prominent media figure, contested the accusations of the president of PERKASA, Datuk Ibrahim Ali, that since PAS began working together with PKR and DAP they no longer prioritize religion. He responded to this typical attack by stating, "Ibrahim's thickly racist attitude makes him unfit to struggle for Islam because religion does not allow things to be divided according to race" (*Sinarharian* 2011).

Although UMNO secular nationalist ideologues and Malay rights activists can adequately engage in public discursive skirmishes with PAS over matters relating to *bangsa* and the special position of Malays, they are not qualified to effectively debate the *ulama* leaders of PAS on *agama* or religious affairs. As part of the long-term contest with PAS over which party is "most Islamic," UMNO often draws on the expertise of government and party *ulama* to rebut PAS positions on many religious issues. Fathul Bari Mat Jahya, the director of UMNO's Young Ulama Secretariat, has even been argued for UMNO to establish its own council of *ulama* within the party. It would be UMNO's version of the Majlis Syura and Dewan Ulama in PAS. On July 19, 2012, a highly publicized debate between Fathul Bari and Nasrudin was televised, transmitted on the radio, and covered in other media during the run-up to the thirteenth general election. The title of the program featuring these two young *ulama* of opposing political parties was, in translation, "Who Will Young People Vote For?" Although UMNO has stopped short of organizing an *ulama* council within its party and fielding large numbers of *ulama* in elections, they have aggressively deployed government and party *ulama* to undermine PAS authority as a political party struggling for Islam. For instance, when deputy prime minister Tan Sri Muhyiddin Yassin demanded that Nik Abdul Aziz stop making statements like "the prayers of UMNO people are not accepted" and that "BN just thinks of contracts when building *masjids*," Fathul Bari came to his assistance and requested that the National Fatwa Council immediately investigate all of Nik Aziz's statements. The young UMNO religious scholar, trained in the Middle East and at the International Islamic University Malaysia, claimed that such statements uttered by the spiritual leader of PAS deviates from *aqidah* and divides the Muslim community. Verbally chastising the revered PAS leader, Fathul Bari said, "Don't be so busy judging the actions or *ibadat* of UMNO people because it is only Allah that determines those matters" (*Malaysiakini* 2013).

Similarly, Perak mufti Tan Sri Harussani Zakaria and Selangor mufti Datuk Mohd Tamyes Abd Wahid debated PAS *ulama* about the proper religious approach concerning the potential conflict of performing the obligatory *ibadah* of hajj with fulfilling responsibilities of participating in the upcoming Malaysian general election. These Islamic scholars along with some UMNO political elites wrangled over this matter in June 2012 when there was the possibility that the thirteenth general election would be called at the prerogative of the prime minister later that year, overlapping with the time Malaysian pilgrims would be departing for Mecca. Prime Minister Najib dropped hints that this might happen, and PAS leaders warned that it would deprive tens of thousands of Malaysians of their right to vote. While PAS leaders asked Prime Minister Najib to guarantee that the general election would not occur during the hajj season, they also announced that their party members directly involved in the election—including candidates, their representatives, and election directors—should postpone their plans to perform hajj. There was a flurry of media interviews and newspaper articles covering the ensuing debate. Dr. Abdul Rani, the PAS electoral officer in Selangor, said he supported this announcement made by the PAS information chief Datuk Tuan Ibrahim Tuan Man: "We study closely the principles of *fiqh awlawiyat* clarified by Dr. Yusuf al-Qaradawi, that is, whenever presented with two important matters, we need to select the matter that is of more importance. Performing the hajj is definitely important to the Muslim community but the right for determining the national leadership is more important" (*Sinarharian* 2012e). To the contrary, Selangor mufti Datuk Mohd Tamyes Abd Wahid expressed the legal opinion that performing hajj for the second or third time or more is *sunat* (recommended behavior), so the decision to proceed with the *niat* (intention) to make hajj or not devolves to the individual. Individuals receive a reward for performing *sunat*, but if they fail to do the act it is not a sin. However, if individuals are performing hajj for the first time and they and their families have enough provisions, then it is *wajib* (obligatory) for them to proceed with their intention to make hajj: "If they cancel their intention just for some worldly matter . . . and let's say the person dies before they have the opportunity to perform hajj they would die in the condition of ignorance" (*Sinarharian* 2012b).

Nik Abdul Aziz responded to scholarly criticism of the PAS announcement by stating that the hajj is not an *ibadat* that needs to be done immediately and that the *dalil* (evidence) for this lies in the *Sunna* of the Prophet. The PAS spiritual leader further clarified that *Rasulullah* himself performed hajj in the tenth year of Hijrah although the revelation that performing hajj is *wajib* came down in the sixth year of Hijrah. "This proves that *ibadat haji* does not have to be performed immediately," he said (*Sinarharian* 2012b). Moreover, this evidence, Nik Abdul Aziz asserted, demonstrates that Islam allows followers to postpone the hajj even if they are listed in a group prepared to perform this *ibadat*. Perak mufti Tan Sri Harussani Zakaria presented his rebuttal to the media the following day, declaring that *ibadat haji* is the fifth obligation of the Rukun Islam (Pillars of Islam) and that if one fulfills all the requirements of having enough resources, including *nafkah* for the family, then it cannot be delayed due to a general election. If one is sick or the situation is not safe, then that is sufficient reason to postpone making the hajj. Like the Selangor mufti, Harussani warned of the possible grave outcome if the individuals delaying their hajj die in the interim. He reported that there is a *hadith* that points out the death of such individuals would occur with them in the state of being a Jew or Christian, a major sin (*Sinarharian* 2012f). As it turned out, the thirteenth general election was not called in the last quarter of 2012; instead, it took place on May 5, 2013. Clearly, the advanced Islamic knowledge of these government *ulama* has allowed them to go far beyond the criticism of secular nationalist elites that PAS was just prioritizing politics over religious obligations. They were able to present opinions on the legal and ethical status of postponing performance of the hajj and warn of the dire consequences of delaying it for inadequate worldly reasons. It is important to note that they downplayed the obligation of participating in electoral politics, considering it a mundane matter. In contrast, in the PAS sharia model performing one's political responsibilities has religious significance; it is part of political jihad aimed at

attaining the political power to establish an Islamic state and to fully implement sharia laws. I found that this methodological and epistemological distinction between UMNO-oriented and PAS-oriented *ulama* carries over
into the *masjid* context.

The UMNO-led BN government attempts to control the expression of
ideological and political perspectives in *masjids* by having JAKIM administer the texts of *khutbah* (Friday sermons) and the Islamic religious departments regulate the *tauliah* of *ulama* permitted to give religious talks in the
mosque (*kuliah masjid*). These regulated speech events tend to focus on the
specific religious teachings on a topic and/or reflect the ideology of Malay
political elites. For instance, UMNO-oriented *ulama* present the details of
conventional interpretations of Qur'anic verses, *hadith*, and *fiqh* rulings on
particular topics without making analogies or connections to contemporary
political contexts. One *ulama* giving a religious talk following the evening
prayer (*kuliah maghrib*) at a large *masjid* in Selangor spoke extensively about
apostates in the days of *Rasulullah* and his *Sahabat* (companions) and how
these authorities responded to the matter of *murtad*. He shifted from the
texts to the present context, mentioning the case of a high school student who
committed *zina* with a religious figure in Malaysia, but he did not make any
connections to politics. Likewise, another *ulama* at a local *masjid* focused
on the details of Shāfi'ī rulings about the requirements for being an imam
leading collective ritual prayers and which types of people should take precedence over others in performing this important role in worship. The person should be the best at recitation, *fiqh*, and *akhlak* (ethical conduct), but
if several people are on the same level in these characteristics you select the
one who has *berhijrah* (migrated) for the longest period of time. This scholar
interpreted *berhijrah* as referring to "the longest in Islam" and declared that
this means that if there are "born Muslims" and "*mualaf*" (converts) on the
same level in terms of other valued features, the "born Muslim" must be the
imam regardless of age and length of time as a Muslim. This scholar's interpretation appeared to reinforce the racialized hierarchy of Malay Muslims
as the preferred group of Muslims over non-Malay converts. However, when
the *masjid* organizing committee falls under the influence of PAS-oriented
members, sermons and other religious talks expressing counter-hegemonic
models may take place in these venues.

During 2011 and 2012, many of the *masjids* and prayer halls I visited were
sites rife with contestation of dominant cultural frameworks, and their
kuliah masjid tended to make explicit analogies and metaphorical connections to contemporary politics. At one prayer hall I often attended in 2012,

the committee moved the evening *kuliah*, during the month of Ramadan, to
the time after we performed *Isyak* (late evening) or *Tarawih* and *Witr* (recommended prayers during the month of Ramadan). Because of strong local
values of performing *ibadat* and spending more time in the *masjids* and
prayer halls, there was always a large group of men and women staying late
at night for these religious talks. On one occasion, the scholar spoke extensively about how firm faith in Allah can bring assistance from Allah in the
believer's times of need, even in the form of miracles. Initially, he provided
examples from the histories of *Rasulullah* and his *Sahabat*, and then shifted
to make connections to recent events in Egypt, where Muhammad Morsi
had just won the presidential election; and then to Malaysia, where Muslims
are struggling for Islam. This scholar mentioned being with other *ulama*
protesting in support of the Selangor opposition government's project to provide free water for people, which the federal government is blocking. He
likened Morsi and other moral fighters for Islam to Prophet Yusuf, and cruel
oppressive leaders throughout the Muslim world, including Malaysia, to
Firaun (the Pharaoh). On another night during Ramadan, a scholar in his
thirties gave a *kuliah Isyak* focusing on the fact that we are not given much
time in our lives to worship Allah and wondered about how many years will
we have the opportunity to fast for Ramadan. Many of us wait until the end
of our lives to worship Allah and do the things that are most important in
this world. He spoke about the experience of different prophets when the
Angel of Death came to take their souls, and contrasted their behavior to
that of the *zalim*, or cruel and oppressive rulers, who seem to live for a long
time. Finally, the scholar made connections between the moral and immoral
figures of the past with contemporary Islamic movements and their foes in
Egypt and Malaysia. These sorts of talks went on for much of the month,
except for a few days when the *surau* (prayer hall not used for Friday congregational prayers) seemed to be under surveillance by government authorities. Around the same time, Malay-language newspapers were reporting that
the Islamic religious department in Selangor was investigating what it considered *masjid panas* (hot *masjids*). Sultan Sharafuddin Idris Shah, the sultan of Selangor, declared that he "did not want the people in his state to
make *masjids* and prayers halls political places or for people to gather there
forming political associations that don't bring development to Islam" (*Sinarharian* 2012d). A PAS member I interviewed in this neighborhood in Selangor told me that this prayer hall is now under the control of PAS, but around
1995 JAIS raided and seized control of it, terminating all *kuliah* there and
appointing new religious figures. Gradually PAS got stronger and was able

to take it back. These are the kinds of political and ideological skirmishes happening on the ground in many neighborhoods as UMNO and PAS forces vie for control of religious spaces, hearts, and minds. There is great interdependence between the discourses and approaches of these political camps, including attempts by PAS to fashion their own alternative multiculturalism and efforts by UMNO to organize and mobilize their own *ulama* corps. Although they continue to clash over which party presents the best approach to race and religion, UMNO and PAS often find themselves working together, along with many Islamic NGOs, when confronted with issues perceived to be threatening Islam and challenging its place in Malaysian society.

THE UMNO—ISLAMIC NGO—PAS DYNAMIC

There are many long-standing and recently formed Islamic nongovernmental organizations that share some aspects of both UMNO and PAS pro-sharia worldviews. These civil society organizations—such as ABIM (Angkatan Belia Islam Malaysia; Malaysian Islamic Youth Movement), JIM (Pertubuhan Jamaah Islah Malaysia; Malaysian Islamic Renewal Organization), the Malaysian IKRAM Organization (IKRAM),[9] PUM (Persatuan Ulama Malaysia; Malaysian Ulama Association), RICOI (Research and Information Centre on Islam), MACMA (Malaysian Chinese Muslim Association), and PERMIM (Persekutuan Pertubuhan Muslim India Malaysia, Malaysian Indian Muslim Association)—engage in a wide variety of *dakwah* and *tarbiah* activities trying to enhance and spread Islamic knowledge. Although these diverse Islamic NGOs operate with a variety of sharia models formed in their own communities of practice and sometimes in overlapping networks of activists, they are generally in support of stronger and more extensive implementation of sharia in criminal laws (including Islamic penal codes), Islamic economics, and everyday social life. However, they have a wide variety of ideas about how to arrive at the point where Malaysians would be ready for a more comprehensive operationalization of sharia laws and ethical norms. Most stress educating the Malaysian public first, Muslims and non-Muslims, about sharia and/or creating a positive ethical social environment before enacting *hudud* and *qisas* laws. These diverse organizations also promote the embodiment of sharia norms in social conduct, attire, and personal comportment. Some of them are critical of the way the Malaysian state has been moving to implement sharia economics and argue for stricter standards of sharia compliance. MACMA and PERMIM also must negotiate their Muslim identities in a society where Malay and Muslim categories are intertwined and Chinese and Indian groupings are heavily associated with non-Muslim religious identities. Furthermore, many of the Malay Muslim NGOs have not shifted away from equating Malay and Muslim identities as fully as PAS and remain committed to both *Ketuanan Melayu* and *Ketuanan Islam*. For instance, Zaid Kamaruddin, president of JIM, told me:

> Of course, from a principled point of view to us it is not the *Ketuanan Melayu* but a Muslim or Islamic system. Ours is beyond this small boundary of Malaysia, but the problem for the moment, from our point of view, is that as an *umma* from the world we are separated by nation-states. So the context of *Ketuanan Melayu* or the supremacy of the Malays is not the basis of our struggle. But they can justify it, because . . . according to one of the theories the Malays are the people of this area who accepted Islam. And also in the constitution it says a Malay, ideologically, it is not a racial term; Malays are defined as Muslims. So, in that case both approaches [those of UMNO and PAS] become very close, if you say that *Melayu* means Islam. But they [have] got to live up to it. . . . But we do argue technically [that] the constitution of a Malay should be Islam. So you should hold on to this correct understanding. Then there is a meeting point between what everyone says if *Melayu* means Islam.[10]

Even if they believe in the eventual transformation to an Islamic system, they still see value in having the current state led by Malay Muslims. Many members of these Islamic civil society organizations felt that the current tensions between Malaysian Muslims and non-Muslims were caused by anti-Muslim groups in Malaysia and global Christian forces unifying to attack Islam. For instance, Ustaz Zakaria, a member of ACCIN (Allied Coordinating Committee of Islamic NGOs) told me, in the aftermath of the public drama of contention discussed below, that "the IFC, or Inter-Faith Commission, was a way for non-Muslims, especially Christians, to seize power over Muslims."[11]

These diverse Islamic NGOs interact with UMNO and PAS forces and sharia projects in a variety of ways. As noted above, they often spur UMNO to attempt to move in front and lead on a number of Islamic campaigns, such as developing and regulating *halal* goods and services. Scholars and activists in these organizations also benefit from opportunities to fill the expanding Islamic bureaucracies and serve as government *ulama* and civil servants.[12] They use these political and economic positions not only to advance UMNO projects but also to further their own sharia projects, as we

Islamic NGOs in Selangor

have seen with members of Islamic NGOs playing the role of *khalifah* in some government-linked and -owned corporations. Many members of Islamic NGOs are also in social and organizational networks with PAS activists, participate in Islamic schools, and support the PAS-led Kelantan government programs. Some of them are recruited as members of PAS and others work together with PAS-controlled *masjid* and prayer hall committees giving PAS-oriented *khutbah* and *kuliah*. These civil society organizations tend to promote broad Malaysian Muslim unity and/or strengthening the global Muslim community.

The collision between UMNO's *Ketuanan Melayu* secular nationalist project and the PAS *Ketuanan Islam* extensive sharia religious project is mediated by the *dakwah* activism of numerous Islamic NGOs. What I would like to stress here is that these diverse Islamic NGOs play an important role in checking the UMNO-led state and PAS when they appear to be violating Islamic and/or Malay Muslim hegemony. To demonstrate this, I would like to briefly discuss two dramas of contention. The first surrounds the forming and naming of a multireligious council under the Prime Minister's Department of the federal government. In the wake of several highly publicized and contentious conversion and child custody cases, liberal rights organizations formed an Article 11 coalition calling for religious freedom and drafted legislation for the establishment of an Inter-Faith Commission for Malaysia (ICM).[13] In response, the federal government held two inter-religious dialogues involving the Malaysian Consultative Council on Buddhism, Christianity, Hinduism, and Sikhism (MCCBCHS), JAKIM, and IKIM before announcing that the conditions in Malaysia did not require the "Inter-Religious Council" (Martinez 2008, 133–34). Islamic NGOs and PAS were opposed to the call for an ICM, arguing that it was an attack on Islam and Muslim rights to practice their religion. The ACCIN coalition issued an alarmist pamphlet titled, in translation, "Islam Is Threatened: You Need to Act, Widely Distribute This Information: Abolish the IFC." It argued that the proposal for what they labeled an "Inter-Faith Commission" was an attack on "Allah's laws," which must take precedence over international human rights norms created by humans: "These international norms do not differentiate between Muslims and non-Muslims. For Muslims, regulations for their lives would no longer be Islam but rather these international norms that were created by humans. Is it just hoped that Islamic teachings that contradict these international norms would be eliminated. This means that Allah would have to bow down to international norms. This destroys the religious convictions of Muslims" (ACCIN 2005, 5–6). Subsequently, opposition to an Inter-Faith Commission grew among Islamic NGOs and in the broader Muslim community. The terms "interfaith" or "interreligious" were perceived as a symbol of this organized, non-Muslim attempt, with international support, to undermine the supreme position of Islam in Malaysia. When IKIM, the Islamic think tank within the Prime Minister's Department, restarted the process of forming a multireligious council for dialogue, one of the main issues was the name of the council. At the inaugural meeting, which I attended in 2010, the council was called the "Committee for the Promotion of Religious Understanding and Harmony" and ACCIN and the Malaysian Ulama Association were part of it. Thus, the UMNO-led state was perceived as caving in to influential non-Muslim minorities with global backing, and Islamic NGOs felt they had to check the state and bring it back to defending Islam.

The second drama involves the controversy over whether the Catholic Church should be allowed to the use the word "Allah" (*kalimat Allah*) in its weekly publication *The Herald*. The 2009 decision of the High Court that the Catholic Church had the constitutional right to use the word was met with some sporadic incidents of violence and attacks on houses of worship. The UMNO-led government filed an appeal against the High Court's decision and mobilized corps of government- and UMNO-affiliated *ulama* to research and write about how *kalimat Allah* should only be used by Muslims. Malay rights groups and Islamic NGOs were also galvanized into action opposing the court's decision. Many initially justified restricting Christian usage in the interest of not confusing the average Malay who may read Malay-language Catholic publications. However, PAS and PKR rejected this reasoning and publicly supported the court's decision and the right of Christians to use the word, noting that non-Muslims have used it to refer to God in Arabic-speaking societies for a long time and continue to do so. They interpreted the drive to restrict Christian usage as an expression of Malay chauvinism. This "cosmopolitan" position, not upholding the special position of Malay Muslims, did not convince much of the Malaysian Muslim community. Most Islamic NGOs and Muslim intellectuals were persuaded by the extensive literature *ulama* produced arguing that *kalimat Allah* is uniquely connected to *Tauhid* (Islamic monotheism). The PAS *ulama* council met not long before the thirteenth general election and changed their position to be in concert with most organized groups of the Malaysian Muslim community. On October 14, 2013, the Court of Appeals unanimously ruled "against allowing the Catholic Church to use the word 'Allah' in its weekly publication *The Herald*, saying that the government did not impugn on the Church's constitutional rights in banning the use of the word" (*Malay Mail Online* 2013). Thus, the swinging of Islamic NGOs in favor of the UMNO-led position checked the PAS attempt to practice its alternative, multiethnic approach and motivated them to reengage and reinterpret religious sources. This UMNO-Islamic / NGOs-PAS dynamic reinforces and reproduces the centrality and hegemony of *Ketuanan Melayu* and *Ketuanan Islam*.

CONCLUSION

The cultural politics of religion, race, and nation in Malaysia are central to understanding sociopolitical dynamics, including the fissures in electoral coalitions. In order to "defend Islam," PAS feels compelled to work together with UMNO, their chief political foe in the realm of electoral politics. Normative sharia projects—including UMNO secular nationalist, Malay rights, PAS traditional Islamic, and Islamic NGO *dakwah* projects—join together to uphold Malay and Muslim prerogatives and dominance. Moreover, when UMNO or PAS are perceived to be adopting public positions on controversies that do not properly defend the special position of Malays and Islam, mediating Islamic civil society organizations pressure them to reconsider.

Campaigns for liberal rights tend to strengthen the motivation for Malay and Muslim unity (Moustafa 2013). These challenges are often interpreted as threats to Islam and hegemonic images of the nation in which Malays and Muslims are located atop social hierarchies.

The growing polarization of liberal rights and normative sharia projects has intensified the drive of dominant Malay forces toward a pattern of increasing sharia-tization, a more enchanted modernity, and a heightened emphasis on the Malay-preferred hierarchical image of the nation. To be sure, the Islamic resurgence and the concomitant UMNO and PAS competition over Islamic credentials has been moving things in this direction for some time. However, it is important to note that the hesitant secular nationalist elites, masters of appropriating Islamic campaigns and symbols and feinting at greater substantive Islamization, are being more strongly pushed by numerous social forces in the face of perceived threats to the Malay Muslim–dominated sociopolitical order. Many recent developments indicate that the partially secular format long championed by UMNO is shifting toward greater sharia-tization. The Prime Minister's Department is formulating new federal policies on apostasy and a sharia court system that will supposedly be on par with the civil court system. In addition, the federal government and the PAS-led state government of Kelantan are currently deliberating a rollout of Islamic criminal laws, including *hudud* and *qisas*, in the east coast state. Although I think a full rollout of sharia criminal laws is unlikely under a Najib Razak Cabinet, the Malaysian state is expressing a commitment to implement stronger sharia-oriented policies.[14] Furthermore, the long-term pairing of a Malay Muslim–dominated hierarchical image of the nation with a horizontal image of diverse and equal citizens is being delinked, in favor of a Malay Muslim–led polity (see Daniels 2005). These changes are occurring, in part, due to growing pressure from liberal and human rights organizations.

6 CONTRA-SHARIA DISCOURSES

Islamic and Secular Human Rights

IMPLEMENTATION OF SHARIA FAMILY AND CRIMINAL LAWS IS FAR from unanimous in Malaysian society, as a significant array of social forces produce contra-sharia discourses and promote competing sociopolitical projects. Although the Malaysian Muslim political parties and NGOs that coalesce around the sharia projects evoked by the phrases *Ketuanan Melayu* and *Ketuanan Islam* remain dominant, they are increasingly challenged by liberal Muslim reformers and secular human rights organizations. Liberal Muslim reformers and secular human rights organizations, however, are not the only social forces speaking of "human rights." The UMNO-led Malaysian government is a signatory of many international human rights covenants and has adopted the position of formally accepting all the provisions of these statutes that do not conflict with traditional Islamic laws and ethics. Many Malaysian jurists in sharia courts and government departments as well as activists in Islamic NGOs also speak of "human rights" within an Islamic worldview, in which they are dependent on divine directives and subordinate to the "rights of God." In contrast, liberal Muslim reformers, whom I also refer to as "Islamic human rights" proponents, strive to reconcile Islamic ethical notions with a fuller embrace of dominant global conceptions of fundamental human rights. They often join with secular human rights activists to form a phalanx of social forces aimed at blocking and reversing the move toward greater sharia-tization. These secular human rights activists, unfettered by commitments to religious ideas, call for the upholding of secular, liberal, and pluralist principles in Malaysian society.

Of relevance here are the cultural ideas, sharia models, and sociopolitical projects of the liberal Muslim civil society organizations Sisters in Islam (SIS) and Islamic Renaissance Front (IRF), the political parties People's Justice Party (PKR) and Democratic Action Party (DAP), and some secular civil society organizations. These groups illustrate the interplay of sharia projects and the predicament of Malay political elites that are increasingly being driven toward realizing a more sharia-oriented state and enchanted modernity. There is much less interdependence and compromise concerning the liberal rights of ethnic and religious minorities than there is with gender. While Sisters in Islam and their supporters engage in some give-and-take with the Malaysian government and some Islamic NGOs about reforming sharia family laws along the axis of gender, Islamic and secular human rights groups and traditional Muslim forces tend to clash in a more uncompromising fashion over changes along the axes of race and religion.

SIS AND IRF: REFORMING MUSLIM THOUGHT AND PRACTICE

SIS is an Islamic feminist and human rights organization that combines Islamic concepts with the dominant global culture of "human rights," gender equality, and the "secular" individual. SIS and many international scholars in their network—such as Amina Wadud, an American academic who cofounded the group; Shad Saleem Faruqi, and Abdullahi Ahmed An-Na'im—promote a reinterpretation of the sources of sharia to bring them in line with the "liberal rights" of individuals, symmetrical gender equality, and a "secular" nation-state. In an issue of the SIS bulletin *Baraza!* Abdullahi Ahmed An-Na'im (2007, 3), an internationally recognized scholar of Islam and human rights, wrote, "Rather than viewing secular and religious foundations of human rights as incompatible rivals, I would emphasise the interdependence of Islam, human rights and secularism defined as the religious neutrality of the state. In fact, I need the state to be neutral regarding religion so that I can be Muslim by my own free conviction and not out of fear of the coercive powers of the state." In contrast to the Malaysian government *ulama*, PAS, and other Muslim organizations discussed above, Abdullahi considers the neutrality of a secular state to be congruent with the foundations of Islam. He arrives at this position through breaking strong hermeneutic links with the script-based sources of sharia and utilizing a methodology that escapes the traditional literalist approach by reading "human agency" into the early processes of revelation, interpretation, and practice. From this perspective, the lexical and technical meanings of the revealed texts were based in particular historical contexts in order to deal with specific situations. Hallaq (2004, 45–48) suggests that such new methodologies are required to remold traditional legal theory to fit with the "powerful values, institutions, and epistemologies" of a globally dominant modernity. Similarly, Universiti Teknologi MARA law professor Shad

Saleem Faruqi (2007, 6) argued for an "Inter-Faith Commission" and legal reforms in the direction of realizing freedom of religion in Malaysia:

> An Inter-Faith Commission must be set up which can assist to draw up some ground rules. Religious preachers need to be told that no religion has a monopoly on the truth; that there are many ways of finding salvation. . . . Just as with the right to propagate, the right to convert is part of the constitutional and international right to freedom of religion. However, though conversion is an intensely personal decision, its exercise must be regulated by the law if the conversion adversely affects the rights of others. The recent case of Sgt. Moorthy highlighted the pain and anguish a conversion can cause to the non-converting spouse.

Rather than advocating for Malay and Muslim hegemony, he promotes religious pluralism and religious freedom for believers of all faiths to propagate their religions. Moreover, he argues for reforms in laws governing conversion and apostasy cases to bring them into concert with international laws, constitutional guarantees, and "the spirit of Islam," which includes the principle that there should be no compulsion in matters of religion (ibid.).

SIS, like many of the international Muslim scholars in their network, forges a reformist path within the Islamic discursive tradition that diverges from classical legal theory and doctrine. They combine reformulated conceptions of sharia with modern, Western notions of "gender equality," individual civil liberties, and privatization of religion. SIS is opposed to the implementation and enforcement of sharia criminal laws they argue discriminate against women and encroach on individuals' civil liberties. SIS bulletin coeditor (and its first male associate member) Shanon Shah (2007, 15) criticized state-enforced sharia criminal laws by arguing, "In effect, turning personal sins into crimes against the state radically alters the relationship between the believer and his or her God from one of personal piety to one of duress. Furthermore, an individual's personal relationship with God is transformed into a matter of public policy. In any sensible democracy, when policies have such far-reaching implications, the public has the right to debate them extensively and offer as many divergent viewpoints as possible in a civil manner." Shanon frames Islamic ethical norms as personal and private matters that should be out of the purview of state and public policy. Moreover, what he considers the unwarranted intrusion of the state into issues of personal morality that adversely affects Muslims and non-Muslims should be the subject of open debate in civil society. As noted above, SIS opposes state-enforced sharia criminal laws. This articulation of Islamic ethical norms with the privatization of belief, participatory democracy and pluralism advocates for a more extensive secularization of Malaysian society.

SIS situates its feminism within a "religious secularist" perspective that reengages and reinterprets religious texts to be congruent with the dominant global culture of "human rights" and Western notions of symmetrical "gender equality." Many SIS scholars have argued that the patriarchal cultures of many traditional scholars influenced their readings of religious texts and shaped their gender-biased rulings, which have been adopted by jurists in both Malaysia and other Muslim societies. Thus, SIS actively challenges local interpretations of Islam that discriminate against women by violating their universal "human rights" as laid out in the Convention on the Elimination of All Forms of Discrimination against Women, and promotes reinterpretations of sharia compatible with such international human rights documents. They call for substantial reforms of sharia family laws and reformulations of gender and marriage in Islamic legal theory to enable contemporary Muslims "to attain the objectives of justice, equality and fairness that are central to Qur'anic principles, the social objectives of the Shari'ah (*maqasid al shari'ah*)" (Norani Othman 2005, 9). Like many other Muslim reformers, Norani Othman, another SIS cofounder, deploys the notion *maqāṣid al-sharī'ah* in combination with other ideas circulating in early twenty-first century Western versions of modernity. Cara Wallis (2013, 68) reminds us that modernities are *about* gender. Unlike the dominant local version of modernity championed by UMNO and many Islamic NGOs, SIS rejects the traditional asymmetrical model of gender relations in favor of the Western, feminist construct of symmetrical gender relations.[1] SIS contends that this notion of "gender equality" is pursuant of the objectives of sharia.

Although the Malay women I spoke with in the Prime Minister's Department criticized the feminist worldview of SIS, they also told me they engaged in dialogues with SIS on many legal matters pertaining to women. For instance, when I interviewed a group of female legal experts at JAKIM, Haryaty stated that although they view SIS as a feminist movement they do not ignore their perspectives. They invite them to discussions and listen to their opinions when working on sharia law provisions (cf. Azza Basarudin 2016, 154–57). Likewise, Dr. Zaleha binti Kamarudin, the deputy director of IKIM, informed me they often invited SIS to participate in their seminars and discussions. She noted that the SIS perspective is very different from the "traditionalist" perspective they adopt at IKIM, "in which we take into account the problems of society where sharia is being implemented and try to make the society fit with the laws." Dr. Zaleha contrasted the SIS model of gender relations with the model she interprets to be based in sharia; yet she also spoke of the concept of equality and the need for male heads (*khalifa*) of household to practice consultation with their wives in order to make good decisions.[2]

There has been considerable interaction and exchange between the Sisters in Islam and federal government Islamic institutions and some other Islamic civil society organizations, such as JIM. Salime (2011, xx) defines the interactions between the feminist and political Islamic women's movement in Morocco as "interdependencies," which "refers to the entanglement of the . . . movements . . . and the ways they have constituted each other's discourses, politics, and forms of organization." Similarly, I contend that there are interdependencies between the SIS feminist project and the UMNO-led sharia project in Malaysia. As Haryaty from JAKIM noted, the federal government listens to the opinions of SIS and responds to their concerns about gender discrimination. Dr. Zaleha's discourse also indicates interdependence in the way she merges a gender perspective that is concerned about the fair treatment of women and their participation in decision making *within* the traditional framework of asymmetrical gender relations under male leadership. During one of my visits to the Shariah Court of the Federal Territory of Kuala Lumpur, a sharia judge enthusiastically informed me that they had recently appointed their first two female sharia court judges.[3] Moreover, Norhafsah Hamid (2015) discusses some of the reforms the federal government made in sharia family laws in response to complaints from SIS, including changes in laws regulating polygamy, male pronouncements of divorce, and matrimonial property. On the other hand, SIS has been actively engaging with religious texts and suggesting changes in the way sharia family laws are applied (see also Azza Basarudin 2016). For instance, in my separate interviews with Norani Othman and Zainah Anwar, they both worked within prevailing traditional sharia frameworks to argue for reform rather than opposing such frameworks altogether. Dr. Norani criticized the manner in which polygamy was practiced in many states, and Zainah problematized the discrepancies between the way the traditional theory of gender rights is supposed to work and its actual practice. Rather than becoming locked into oppositional binaries, these contrasting reformist and normative sharia projects entangle and partially constitute each other's discourses when it comes to making gender-related reforms in sharia family laws.[4]

Similar to the Sisters in Islam, the Islamic Renaissance Front is a Muslim reformist organization that combines Islamic ethical notions with dominant global ideas of liberalism, pluralism, and inalienable human rights. IRF is an intellectual movement and think tank that aims to promote Islamic reform (*islah*) and renewal (*tajdid*) directed toward achieving a modern, pluralistic, inclusive, and just Malaysian nation. They stress the significance of engaging in dialogues and discursive exchanges to revive Islam in the modern age of pluralism and democratic nation-states. Tariq Ramadan, a popular European Muslim philosopher, officially launched the organization on December 12, 2009. His ideas and those of other Muslim reformers from around the world influence the discourse of IRF leaders and intellectuals. They have issued press releases stating their positions on a number of contentious issues, including PAS plans for amputations as criminal punishment, the banning of Shia teachings, religious freedom for Muslims, prohibitions of voting for DAP, and the banning of Irshad Manji's book *Allah, Liberty and Love*.

In 2014 Dr. Ahmad Farouk Musa, a cardiothoracic surgeon, university-based academic, and director of IRF, wrote a press release criticizing the proposed plan to have surgeons amputate the hands of thieves as part of the PAS Islamic criminal law bill. He argued that physicians and surgeons are "instruments of God on earth" for healing people of ailments and suffering, and to suggest that they inflict punishment is contrary to the Declaration of Geneva, which revised the Hippocratic oath in a modern way and clearly stated that doctors shall not use their medical knowledge to "violate human rights and civil liberties." He also rebuked the Islamic Medical Association of Malaysia and IKRAMHealth for their tacit or explicit support for having surgeons execute amputations, and suggested that the error rate in corporal punishments should militate against using amputations as a form of punishment. This IRF press release was published in *Malaysiakini* and the *Malaysian Insider*; following public outcry, the PAS altered the proposal to have a special group of executioners exact the *hudud* and *qisas* punishments, rather than surgeons, in their planned rollout of a sharia criminal law bill in Kelantan.

IRF is also an outspoken advocate for what they consider the inalienable rights of freedom of thought, conscience, and religion. A 2012 press release titled "End the Smear Campaign," also published in the *Malaysian Insider*

CONTRA-SHARIA DISCOURSES 169

and bearing the name of Ahmad Farouk Musa and six other members of
IRF, condemned the mischaracterization of Nurul Izzah Anwar's statement
on religious freedom (Islamic Renaissance Front 2012b). Nurul Izzah is the
daughter of Anwar Ibrahim, and they are both popular leaders of PKR and
the opposition coalition. IRF clarified that she was merely summarizing the
well-known Qur'anic verse, Sūra al-Baqarah 2:256, which declares, "Let there
be no compulsion in religion." They argued that this Qur'anic principle of
"freedom of conscience" should be applied to Malays and Muslim converts
and not just to non-Muslims. Moreover, they criticized the erroneous confusion of ethnicity with religion in the assumption that "Malays can only be
Muslims" and called for their supporters to speak out "against the rising tide
of religious chauvinism and speak truth to power." In a 2013 press release
titled "A Perverse Understanding of Human Rights," Dr. Ahmad slammed
the statement of Datuk Seri Jamil Khir Baharom, an official in the Prime
Minister's Department and director of IKIM, that "there was no violation of
human rights in the banning of Shia teaching." He asserted that this statement reflects a clear misunderstanding of the language of human rights, and
clarified that "human rights are inalienable fundamental rights to which any
human being is inherently entitled" and therefore cannot be taken away.
The IRF director proceeds to articulate the international culture of human
rights with interpretations of the divine will expressed in the Qur'an:

> From the perspective of the Qur'an, these rights came into existence when
> we did; they were created, as we were, by God in order that human
> potential could be actualized. No ruler or government could abolish the
> rights created and given by God. Eternal and immutable, they ought to be
> exercised since everything that God does is for a just purpose. Hence the
> greatest guarantee of personal freedom for a Muslim lies in the Qur'anic
> decree that no one other than God can limit human freedom and that
> judgment as to what is right and what is wrong rests with God alone. The
> state has no business to dictate what people should believe in and which
> denomination they chose to subscribe to.

Dr. Ahmad reconciles the ideas of inalienable human rights embedded in
international conventions with revealed knowledge through positing that
God created those rights simultaneously with his creation of humans. He
suggests that the "human rights" Western peoples discerned through using
their reason and intellects were the rights that God originally created. This

approach intertwines a version of Islamic natural law with Western Enlightenment thought and its emphasis on the use of reason to determine what is right and wrong. Dr. Ahmad contends that banning, outlawing, and harassing Shias unjustly violates their "basic fundamental human rights" of religious freedom, dignity, and the opportunity for developing human capacities. IRF called for the Malaysian government as a member of the United Nations Human Rights Council to protect the human rights of Shia Muslims equally and without discrimination. Their discourse and combination of ideas suggests a form of religious secularity akin to that of SIS and PKR's Muslim leadership.

IRF contests the hegemony of race and religion and incorporates ideas of pluralism, justice, and democracy in their vision of the Malaysian nation. In a 2012 press release titled "Lesson from the On-going Demonization of DAP," the Islamic Renaissance Front (2012c) challenged recent claims by UMNO politicians and *ulama* that voting for DAP is *haram*. To the contrary, IRF asserted that voting for a just non-Muslim rather than an unjust Muslim is more in keeping with the Islamic principle of supporting justice. They drew on the opinions of Tariq Ramadan and a nineteenth-century Syrian reformer to buttress their position in support of DAP: "The great Muslim reformer from Syria, Abd al-Rahman al-Kawakibi (1854–1902), held the opinion that since oppression and despotism are contrary to Islam, a just non-Muslim ruler is preferred to a tyrannical Muslim leader. In particular, we find DAP's vision of Middle Malaysia, wherein dignity, opportunity and prosperity is promised to *all* Malaysians regardless of ethnicity, gender and religion, wherein the welfare of the poor and oppressed are secured, as in no way in contradiction with Islam's own aspirations for a just society in a modern globalized age." They also stated that they adopt the position of Tariq Ramadan, who downplays the significance of aiming to establish an Islamic state and implementing the *hudud* penal code and instead stresses the need for Muslims to deal with pluralism and focus on "objectives and values of justice." IRF noted the inconsistency in UMNO political leaders' expressed commitment to *wasaṭiyyah*, or a moderate approach to religion, and the "extremism" propagated by UMNO sympathizers and members such as Fathul Bari Mat Jahya and other scholars in their organization of *ulama*. Likewise, IRF and fourteen other civil society organizations, including SIS, SUARAM, Aliran, All Women's Action Society, and Women's Aid Organisation, issued a joint statement on June 6, 2012, titled "Agree to Disagree: Book Banning Frenzy Must End," calling on Malaysian authorities to stop banning books "as the first step towards promoting diversity and respect" (Islamic Renaissance

Front 2012a). They mentioned the recent uproar against Irshad Manji's *Allah, Liberty and Love* but underscored how the larger trend of banning works contradicts the *wasaṭiyyah* stand on diversity and tolerance and stifles the open discourse necessary to develop a healthy democracy. IRF's sociopolitical project involves striving for a modern, inclusive, democratic Malaysia through activism and dialogue.

Although the Sisters in Islam developed some traction with dominant pro-sharia projects in terms of gender, SIS and IRF have been the targets of severe criticism for their liberal positions on many other issues. In the seminar "Liberalism and Pragmatism: Truth and Reality," attended by representatives of mufti departments, government departments, NGOs, and religious teachers in July 2012, Datuk Marzuki, the director of the Selangor Department of Islamic Religion, mentioned IRF's support for Irshad Manji's book as evidence that liberalism has already made an impact on Malaysian society. He warned that these movements, with their "upside-down ideologies," pose the danger of fomenting confusion, divisions, and hostilities within the Muslim community (*Sinarharian* 2012c). Furthermore, the persistent alliance of SIS with secular liberal rights organizations has made them the subject of a recent fatwa of the Selangor Fatwa Council, which declared that SIS has deviated from Islamic teachings by subscribing to liberalism and religious pluralism.[5] This suggests that while contention over the existing gender norms can be tolerated, a challenge to the underpinnings of the racial and religious hierarchy cannot.

PKR LEADERSHIP: STRUGGLING FOR MALAYSIAN PEOPLE'S SOVEREIGNTY

Anwar Ibrahim, the leader of PKR and the opposition coalition (Pakatan Rakyat), has argued strongly for the compatibility of Islam and democracy, drawing on Islamic ethical notions as well as ideas from Western intellectual history (Allers 2013, 2017). The Islamic studies scholar Charles Allers demonstrates that over the course of his political career, Anwar has consistently recognized the resemblance between, and merged, Islamic theological and legal notions with Western ideas of freedom, civil society, and democracy. Similar to SIS, Anwar Ibrahim creatively interprets and applies the notion of *maqāṣid al-sharī'ah* to support his liberal democratic and pluralist model of *Ketuanan Rakyat* (People's Sovereignty). In a PKR press release, Anwar stated, "I believe that the *Maqasid al-Shariah* (the higher objectives of the Shariah) are important principles of governance and are not inconsistent with the precepts of democracy. In this regard, Pakatan Rakyat will remain guided by the principles of universal justice, good governance, accountability, transparency and competency in order to achieve public good for the people" (Anwar Ibrahim 2012). He interprets that the *maqāṣid al-sharīʿah* are "principles of governance" directed toward achieving the *maṣlaḥa* or public good. This usage of the concept "higher objectives of sharia," as with SIS, differs from Abū Ḥamid Muḥammad al-Ghazālī's (d. 1111) classic conception of a limited list of objectives: faith, life, intellect, lineage, and property. The Egyptian scholar Yusuf al-Qaradawi, Anwar Ibrahim, and many other contemporary scholars of various religious and ideological orientations accept Taqī al-Dīn Ibn Taymiyyah's (d. 1328) revision of the *maqāṣid* to an open-ended list of values (Kamali 2006, 116–19). Al-Qaradawi argues that certain elements of democracy are obligatory for Muslims because they are the necessary means to the ends of sharia as derived from the revealed text (Feldman 2007, 112). In contrast, Anwar suggests that to apply these principles of governance, derived from the revealed text and foreign sources, within a liberal democracy instantiates the ends of sharia.

In Anwar Ibrahim's second public statement on the Lina Joy case, he claimed that freedom of conscience is one of the main elements of the *maqāṣid al-sharīʿah*. His position in support of a Muslim's right to freedom of religion placed him in unison with many other liberal Muslim reformers and secular human rights organizations. However, his media statement was rather nuanced and exhibited a compromising stand, no doubt informed by his previous experiences as a leader of the Islamic civil society organization ABIM and as an UMNO ideologue and government official. After noting that Islam is designated as the religion of the federation and that other religions "can be practiced in peace and harmony throughout the country," he addressed the polarizing passions on the topic of freedom of conscience and gave the UMNO-led government this advice:

> The authorities must strive to strengthen the public confidence towards the Shariah court, and assure the Muslims that there is no attempt to belittle the importance of the existing system. As for the non-Muslims, they must be assured that the fundamental guarantees enshrined in the Constitution [are] protected. In essence, while we should preserve the current procedure via the Shariah court with regards to cases of freedom of conscience, there should be no recrimination involved. After all, freedom of conscience is one of the key elements of the higher objectives of the Shariah, the Maqasid Shariah. (Anwar Ibrahim 2007)

Anwar astutely recommends that the government adopt a compromising posture, assuring Muslims and non-Muslims that their respective concerns and interests will be respected. Moreover, he continues with this conciliatory stance, advising that the current sharia procedures be continued—in the example of counseling a Muslim who wants to change her religion, if she persists in her desire to convert out of Islam it should be allowed without accusation or punishment. In contrast to government *ulama*, sharia court officials, and many Muslim activists who tend to interpret prohibiting Muslims from leaving Islam as fulfilling the major objective of sharia—that is, preservation of religion—Anwar interprets that protecting freedom of conscience is also a key objective of sharia. The leader of the opposition coalition proceeds to chastise the UMNO-led government for their failure to achieve a broad consensus on this issue, which could have been done by promoting more "dialogue, discussion, and deliberation." This posture of negotiation and give-and-take on divisive issues was rarely adopted by other parties in these debates and was difficult for Anwar and PKR to sustain.

In particular, PKR leaders were unable to navigate a conciliatory position with Malay and Islamic models of the Malaysian nation. Anwar and other PKR leaders' concept of universal justice envision a transformation of UMNO's model of a nation in which Malay Muslims reign supreme. Their idea of *Ketuanan Rakyat* projects a cosmopolitan image of the nation, delinking any racial or religious supremacy from the state and extending equal citizenship rights to all Malaysians. It seeks to replace the special position of Malays and Islam with a secular, pluralist political system. Unlike most other political parties, PKR comprises multiple races and religions, though it remains under Malay leadership. The party held a tenuous position between a democratic socialist, primarily Chinese DAP (Democratic Action Party) and the political Islamic party, PAS, in the opposing coalition, which had Anwar Ibrahim serving as its general head. Anwar Ibrahim's background as a Muslim youth activist and a former deputy prime minister, and his present commitment to moving the political system away from the authoritarian, UMNO-led ruling coalition government and toward a liberal democratic vision, facilitates his role as a mediating force holding together the two divergent opposition parties (see Allers 2013). However, his version of "religious secularity"—combining broad Islamic principles, aims, and objectives with pluralism, liberal democracy, and a vision of inclusive nation building—is seriously challenged by the growing push for Malay and Muslim forces to unite in order to preserve and solidify their dominant position. There was a firestorm of controversy stoked by the media following PKR president Datin Seri Dr. Wan Azizah Wan Ismail's statement at the Seventh PKR National Congress ridiculing the concept of *Ketuanan Melayu*. The PKR president and wife of Anwar Ibrahim said, "The concept of *Ketuanan Melayu* has to be eliminated because it is just a slogan of a small elite group of Malays that have the power to cheat Malays as a whole for their own interests. . . . This small group of Malays are the ones that commit acts of bribery and corruption and betray our trust and do all sorts of crimes without paying attention to the fate of their own race" (*Sinarharian* 2010c). For several days, Malay-language newspapers reported vociferous responses from UMNO politicians, UMNO-affiliated NGOs, and leaders of Malay rights organizations. Many demanded that Wan Azizah apologize for her comments. They claimed that PKR wanted to put an end to the special rights for Malays and the special position of the Malay rulers inscribed in the Federal Constitution. The sultan of Selangor expressed disappointment in Wan Azizah's statement and claimed it undermined the role of the institutions of the Malay Rajas and the special rights of the Malay race. On the other hand, Anwar Ibrahim and Azmin Ali, the deputy president of PKR, articulated strong support for her statement and announced that PKR needed to elevate and disseminate their concept of *Ketuanan Rakyat*. While this event was still being circulated in media reports a related controversy emerged. Anwar Ibrahim had reportedly stated that if PR were to win in the upcoming election, they would appoint Lim Kit Siang, a prominent Chinese leader of DAP, as the deputy prime minister of Malaysia. Nik Abdul Aziz, the spiritual leader of PAS, told reporters that he did not think race should be such an important issue in a democratic country, and declared that he did not have a problem with Lim Kit Siang being appointed to this position. UMNO ideologues and the Malays rights groups saw this as a prime opportunity to substantiate their claims that Malays and Muslims would lose out if the opposition coalition were to win the general election and take control of Putrajaya. The president of PAS, Abdul Hadi Awang, and Nasrudin were quick to announce that they did not agree with Anwar's statement and declared that the leaders of an Islamic state must be Muslim. These events demonstrate the widespread opposition of social forces, including PAS, their own coalition partner, to PKR's efforts to realize a transformed, liberal, pluralist vision of the Malaysian nation. Nevertheless, they do have support from some other social forces that share many of their sociopolitical ideals.

DAP AND SECULAR NGOS: LIBERAL RIGHTS AND
SECULAR FUNDAMENTALISM

Sisters in Islam, Islamic Renaissance Front, and the Anwar Ibrahim–led PKR find strong support for their ideas of limiting the extent of state implementation of sharia laws, and encouraging pluralism and secularism, within DAP and non-Muslim liberal rights organizations. It is important for an anthropologist of Islam to be concerned with the roles Muslims *and* non-Muslims play in dynamic processes of power (Asad 1986, 105). Although DAP and these non-Muslim NGOs are not speaking from within the Islamic discursive tradition, their sociopolitical projects interact with proponents of various sharia projects. In Malaysia, where non-Muslims constitute about 35 percent of the population, their discourses about sharia play a significant role in politics. Lim Kit Siang and Karpal Singh, longtime veteran leaders of DAP, have consistently opposed PAS campaigns for an Islamic state and more extensive implementation of Islam law. In 1990, Karpal Singh notoriously declared that there would only be "an Islamic state over my dead body." DAP's democratic socialist ideology entails a vision of a secular Malaysia in which civil rather than religious laws would be paramount. They feel that the Malaysian Muslim drive for a greater standing and scope for sharia deviates from the intent and nature of the original 1957 Federal Constitution. In my interview with Dr. Ramasamy, a deputy chief minister of the DAP-led state government of Penang, he stated:

So the party [DAP], we talk about secular Malaysia, a Malaysia for Malaysians. We don't subscribe to the *hudud* law or the Islamic state. Because we still believe that the constitution is fundamentally a secular constitution. Islam is our official religion, and the practice of other religions is allowed in this country. So, even though PAS is in this coalition . . . we oppose the implementation of *hudud* law based on the sharia. . . . We are not going to agree on that. There is no question of us compromising on that. . . . See, Barisan Nasional plays also the Islamic game. On the one hand, they say we are open but then at the same time . . . if I am a Muslim . . . see, [if] I want to leave Islam, now I have to go to the sharia court. And we feel that non-Muslims have been told to go to the sharia court. For example, there is the case of a family where the father converted the children. Then the mother took up this case and then they said, "Okay, for that you have to go to the sharia court." Why would she have to go to the sharia court? The sharia court only applies to the Muslims. These are some of the areas in which we are not very happy . . . Then there was the case of someone who was converted at the age of seven. How can you convert someone at the age of seven? Again, it is not constitutional. Then the civil court says you have to go to the sharia court. I mean, do you expect justice at the sharia court?[6]

Although Dr. Ramasamy noted that Karpal Singh's declaration was rather harsh in its opposition to *hudud* and the Islamic state, he felt that it was the correct position. DAP's perspective is that the recognition of "Islam as the religion of the federation" in the constitution was intended, and should remain, within a secular format. They view the numerous cases of non-Muslims being sent to sharia courts when their spouses convert to Islam and subsequently convert their children to be contravening the secularism embedded in the Federal Constitution.

Secular NGOs such as SUARAM (Suara Rakyat Malaysia; Voice of the Malaysian People), Aliran Kesedaran Negara (National Consciousness Movement), and All Women's Action Society actively advocate for liberal rights

The DAP Penang office

that are often at odds with current government policies and the views of Muslim activists. International studies scholar Meredith L. Weiss (2006, 17–18) points out that many of these civil society agents have formed a multiethnic coalition for political protest and reform in a context where racial and religious fears and racialized communalism remain salient. In my interview with P. Ramakrishnan, the president of Aliran, he expressed strong commitments to secularism and religious freedom as well as fears about the encroachment of sharia courts into non-Muslim lives. During my visit to their Penang office, he stated:

> Well, we are for a secular state. That's how Malaysia came into being. That constitution supports that kind of government. We support that. We also feel that there should be freedom of choice when you embrace a faith, and you should also have freedom of association if you want to move out. This comes into direct conflict with the sharia. In Ipoh, there is a kindergarten teacher whose husband just converted without her knowledge and converted the children. The court had given her the custody of the children but the husband has taken away an infant girl and is keeping her in hiding. . . . But when you go to the civil court they tell you this is sharia jurisdiction. So you have to go. But if you are not a Muslim, why would you want to go there? This guy has taken away the child. If they wanted they could have apprehended him at any time. But just because he is a Muslim, they are not doing anything that may be seen as going against Islam. They won't push the issue.[7]

Like DAP, these liberal rights NGOs want to see greater secularization of Malaysian society and view the growing influence of Islam on the state as a threat to their liberal rights as guaranteed in the Federal Constitution. They oppose any rise in the jurisdiction of sharia courts and have mixed feelings about supporting the opposition coalition because of the persistent PAS commitment to establishing an Islamic state. P. Ramakrishnan told me that they have to set their disagreement aside on that issue for the time being in order to form a political coalition. According to Anil Netto (2007, 100), an Indian intellectual in Aliran:

> In 1988, the administration of then Prime Minister Tun Dr. Mahathir Mohamad introduced controversial constitutional amendments to include Article 121(1A), which states that the civil courts (despite being federal level courts) shall have no jurisdiction in respect of any matter within the

jurisdiction of the *Syariah* Courts (state-level Islamic courts that have jurisdiction over Muslims in specific personal law matters). Since then, a crisis has emerged because of a conflict of laws and what appears to be a lack of clarity regarding the jurisdictions between the civil and Islamic systems. . . . [I]t does not address the predicament of citizens who have changed their religion and no longer consider themselves Muslim; or that of non-Muslim married couples who later find that one of the partners is converting to Islam.

In concert with SIS, IRF, and the intellectuals in their respective networks, Aliran advocates for a secular and neutral state that would extend equal rights to all citizens of the nation-state and not adopt policies slanted toward the laws and ethical norms of any religious group, including the Muslim majority. They consider the slight tweaking of the jurisdiction of sharia courts under Tun Mahathir Mohamad as a move away from the proper elevation of the civil courts in the original 1957 Federal Constitution. Moreover, there remained conflicting areas in which both civil and sharia courts had jurisdiction, notably in relation to matters involving Muslim and non-Muslim parties.

Liberal rights NGOs' anti-sharia projects stress liberal secularism and what they view to be the violations of "human rights" under current implementations of Islamic laws. Tan Seng, a young activist I interviewed in the SUARAM office in Petaling Jaya, told me that "freedom of religion is a fundamental human right for everyone and the state should not step into personal beliefs."[8] They also argue for the elimination of sharia criminal laws and highlight the violations of the principles of liberal secularism and multiculturalism in the current string of controversies over sharia family laws. They argue these cases reflect Malay and Islamic hegemony that must be transformed into a more "cosmopolitan" multiculturalism. In 2009 SUARAM (119–27), in its annual human rights report, criticized the impact of state implementation of sharia laws and ethical norms on the lives of Muslims and non-Muslims:

The codification of Islamic "norms," "values" and "morals" into state legislation imposes restrictions directly on Muslims and indirectly on non-Muslims. The Syariah criminal laws are enforced throughout the country and govern a wide sphere of the lives of Muslims. Muslims are subject to restrictions on "immorality" though prohibition of alcohol consumption, gambling, and *khalwat*. . . . As in the previous year, 2009 saw numerous manifestations of Malay-Muslim groups who propagate the supremacy of Islam and Syariah laws over other religions and laws in the country and those who promote freedom of religion and equality among religions.

Likewise, in their 2014 human rights report overview, SUARAM cited continuing legal battles over the right to use the term "Allah," the JAIS confiscation of Bibles, the Penang Department of Islamic Religion's seizing a woman's body at a Taoist funeral, the custody of children in conversion cases, the arrests of Shia for participating in banned religious activities, and the Kelantan state government's fining of female traders not wearing *tudung* as some of the violations of religious freedom. These non-Muslim NGOs—embracing the dominant global culture of human rights with its emphasis on secular notions of the individual and personal freedom from state-enforced moral codes—interpret state enforcement of Islamic ethical norms and the special position of Islam as violations of human rights. Thus, these organizations are major nodes for the circulation of hegemonic global values of Western modernity, including a supposedly neutral secular nation-state, privatization of religion, and liberal pluralism.

Given the numerous and highly publicized conversion, child custody, and apostasy cases, as well as the *kalimat Allah* and "Inter-Faith Commission" controversies, there has been extensive interaction between liberal rights organizations and the UMNO-led government (and other proponents of sharia projects). However, this interaction has been more antagonistic and uncompromising than have those between the Muslim feminist and UMNO-led sharia projects. Rather than reflecting entangled and interpenetrating discourses, the debates between secular NGOs and Islamic agencies, parties, and organizations indicate rigid and hardening ideological positions. Tamir Moustafa (2013, 797) notes that "the liberal rights versus shariah binary [has] clearly exacerbated cleavages in Malaysia and, to some degree, shifted the principal cleavage from race to religion." In addition, he argues that the intervention of outside agents and the perceptions of "threats" to Islam or minority communities have contributed to both sides becoming further entrenched in oppositional stances. To some extent these dueling binaries of liberal rights and normative sharia projects are hardening into diametrically opposed fundamentalisms: secular and religious. The liberal rights camp holds fast to their convictions that the original 1957 constitution is secular and provides a blueprint for a secular Malaysia, that the civil courts should have jurisdiction over the sharia courts, and that the state must be neutral in terms of religion and race. On the other hand, the normative sharia project camp embraces their certainty that Malay natives and Islam enjoyed a special position in the constitution and that as Malays or Muslims they are the rightful rulers of Malaysia and therefore are free to refashion the legal structures to defend Islam and/or their race.

CONCLUSION

Delineating the diversity of pro-sharia and contra-sharia cultural models is crucial to understanding the interplay of sociopolitical projects. PAS often finds its Pakatan Rakyat opposition coalition partners, DAP and PKR, uniting with secular human rights NGOs, SIS, and IRF in liberal rights campaigns. The persistent stream of controversies involving the opposing binaries of liberal rights versus sharia, pluralism versus the special position of Islam and Malays, and secularism versus political Islam demonstrate the interplay of sharia and other sociopolitical projects.

The interdependence between the feminist SIS project and the UMNO-led sharia project contrasts with the antagonism between the liberal rights project and the broad range of normative sharia projects. Muslim feminists make arguments for reform within prevailing social practices, while government Islamic agencies incorporate a gender perspective into their normative Islamic model of gender relations. Interplay between these reformist and normative sharia projects also entail interaction between their versions of modernity. Secular SIS modernity, with its Western, feminist-style model of gender equality, has inflected UMNO's partially enchanted modernity with greater concern for the position and treatment of women. However, their activism alongside other civil society organizations around issues that challenge the underpinnings of the Malay- and Muslim-dominated sociopolitical order has met with censure from political and religious authorities.

As noted above, the growing polarization of liberal rights and normative sharia projects has only added impetus to the move of dominant Malay forces toward a more sharia-oriented state and Malay-dominated hierarchical image of the nation. Delving deeper into the cultural models and sociopolitical projects of the social forces arraying in a phalanx against proponents of normative sharia projects, this chapter helps to explain why this repositioning is occurring. With few exceptions, these liberal rights projects directly challenge equally staunch normative sharia projects, leaving little room for conciliatory postures and interdependent discourses. Both younger and elder generations of the Islamic resurgence, Malay secular nationalist and political Islamic parties, and nongovernmental organizations are uniting around the cultural politics of preserving and strengthening a Malay- and Muslim-dominated sociopolitical order. Globally dominant versions of Western modernity, promoted by SIS, IRF, PKR, DAP, and secular human rights organizations, are being eclipsed by the move toward a more stringently Islamic modernity with expanded public space for normative Islam.

On the other hand, increased interdependence between liberal rights and normative sharia projects would create new possibilities. To facilitate the emergence of new forms of citizenship and statecraft, hegemonic Malaysian Muslims must envision more space for minority and individual rights within their normative Islamic worldviews, and Malaysian secular humanist activists must be able to admit more linking of the state with Islam in their notions of secularism.

7 INDIVIDUALS

Views, Voices, and Practices

THE MALAYSIAN STATE, *ULAMA*, POLITICAL PARTIES, ISLAMIC NGOs, liberal Muslim reformers, and Malay rights organizations produce discourses about sharia family, criminal, and economic laws and ethics that circulate through society. Sharia laws and ethics—institutionalized in sharia courts, fatwa councils, and government religious departments—have a powerful effect on Muslim lives. Reports and seminars on existing and proposed sharia laws, Friday sermons, Islamic religious classes, newspaper articles, and televised religious talks disseminate the UMNO-led Malaysian state's normative Islamic views. However, these are complemented and/or contested by many social forces that create alternative discourses, models, and projects. These alternative views are circulated in mass media, seminars, *kuliah masjid*, political rallies, bulletins, and the activities of a variety of communities of practice. Many of these discourses, both hegemonic and alternative, constitute disciplinary practices that influence the cultivation of Muslim selves and their everyday practices (Mahmood 2005; Hirschkind 2006). The anthropologist Talal Asad (1993, 2003), taking a cue from Mauss (1973), stresses the top-down influence of institutionalized social authorities on the practices of subordinates. However, it is also necessary to consider the effects of changes in individuals' practices on the programs for cultivating body techniques and virtue promoted by social authorities. In addition, there is significant influence from various secular disciplinary practices, local and global, on individual behaviors of body comportment and expression of emotion. Most important, there is a theoretical need to oscillate from analysis of practices to embodied knowledge and relations of power and other aspects of context in order to provide more comprehensive analysis (see Daniels 2017).

PUBLIC PRACTICES AND EMBODIED KNOWLEDGE

The public behavior of Muslims across the states of peninsular Malaysia embody diverse forms of knowledge and often express shifting and merging senses of self. Attire is one important form of patterned body techniques. Most Malaysian Muslim men wear pants and shirts. I have rarely seen a Muslim man in public wearing shorts cut above his knees; for men to cover the *aurat* (i.e., the parts of the body that are not to be exposed), slacks must fall below the knees. Although dressing indecently in public would bring censure, merely dressing modestly in this manner does not embody a sense of virtue. Some men add an Islamic headdress—*kopiah* or *songkok* (fez-like cap)—reflecting Malay and/or Muslim attire. The sharia court judges I interacted with usually wore dress slacks, shirts, or suits with *pici hitam* or black conical headdresses, which are Malay Muslim and nationalist symbols. One judge in the Federal Territories Shariah Court told me that many in PAS circles do not respect this form of dress and view them as lesser than traditional scholars wearing robes and *serban* (turbans). He expressed the feeling that this common form of attire for sharia court judges embodied their Islamic modernity. Malaysian Muslim men also wear *baju melayu* in the streets, at work, and in the *masjids*. These colorful two-piece outfits, often accompanied by a sarong and headdress, embed and perform both Malay and Muslim identities. In many *masjids* and *suraus* affiliated with PAS around Kuala Lumpur, Kota Bharu, and Alor Setar I have observed a large number of men wearing *jubah* (long robes) and *serban*. For men wearing these forms of clothing, they embody a stricter sense of piety, adherence to the *Sunna*, and Islamic identity. Moreover, for some in Islamic NGOs, PAS, and Sufi movements, *baju melayu* expresses a conflation of Malay and Muslim identities from which they want to distance themselves. They seek to dress themselves in a fashion that expresses and embeds their unambiguously Muslim identities and commitment to Islamic virtue.

Similarly, Malaysian Muslim women often wear *baju kurung* that embody Malay and Muslim identities. Most women wear these two-piece outfits together with *tudung*, but some women wear them without head covering. Moreover, some of the fashionable new styles of *baju kurung* are shape-fitting and tight, and some *tudung* are short or sheer, which flout stricter notions of proper body covering. However, these stylish outfits embed modern Malay Muslim identities. Young Malay women on college campuses, at work, and in the streets often wear jeans, a long T-shirt, and a short head-scarf, embodying a liberal Islamic identity. Several of my Malaysian Muslim contacts have informed me that some of their Malay friends that wear *baju melayu* or *baju kurung* and *tudung* are doing so as public performances of Malay identity but lack Islamic knowledge and do not practice their five daily prayers. Conversely, some of my close Malay friends often did not wear

Islamic style clothing expressing their piety, but they did perform their daily prayers and other practices that embodied their religious convictions and commitment to virtue. As Lara Deeb (2006, 220–28) noted in her study of Shia Muslim women in Lebanon, personal piety is not always unambiguously expressed in public piety. Nadiah, a twenty-three-year-old college student, told me that transformations in her personal piety were not yet reflected in her choice of attire in public. On the occasion she shared this self-reflection with me, she was dressed in stylish black jeans and a tight, bright purple sweater with her long black hair uncovered. A few years later, she was regularly wearing longer garments and headscarves.[1] In fact, I observed many other Malay women wearing more loose-fitting *baju kurung* with *tudung*, and some donned *abaya* (long robes) and long *tudung*, which covered the shoulders and breast and fell around the waist, and even added socks or stockings when wearing sandals. This latter form of dress, similar to *jubah* and *serban* for men, embodies a strong sense of obedience, piety, and Islamic identity. Women in *dakwah* movements usually wore this form of attire, and some students on campuses also practiced this body technique in public. I have seen more Middle Eastern women visiting Malaysia as

Devout Muslim women in
Alor Setar, Kedah

tourists wearing *niqab* (facial veil) than I have seen local women dressed in such a manner.

On the other hand, some Malay youth appear to embody secular ethics and perform secular body techniques. I observed large groups of Malay teenagers and young men around malls and shopping centers wearing jeans, T-shirts with colorful designs, and occasionally jackets. Some of the young men in these groups even wore shorts. They did not appear to be doing much shopping, but rather congregating to socialize with their friends and fraternize with young women. I watched one group of young Malay men standing in a circle and performing break-dancing beside the entrance to a mall in Alor Setar, Kedah. Not far from the mall entrance, down one of the alleys, I saw some Malay teenagers selling and buying drugs. Malay juvenile delinquents, popularly known as *mat rempit*, are often depicted in mass media as a social problem and moral challenge for the Malay Muslim community. These groups of Malay youth tend to embody a racialized Malay identity and perform secular body techniques aimed at having fun and seeking worldly pleasures. As such, they are a base for chauvinistic campaigns and mobilizations led by Malay rights organizations and *silat* groups. There appears to have been a group of this sort that slung racial slurs at an African international student on his way home from morning prayers before killing him (Daniels 2014a, 864). Likewise, I have seen many young Malay women in Melaka and Kuala Lumpur wearing chic, tight-fitting jeans with short T-shirts or blouses, without headscarves. During my visits to the large shopping centers in Kota Raya, Melaka, and Bukit Bintang, Kuala Lumpur, I observed many young Malay women dressed in similar clothing styles as many of the Chinese non-Muslim women, except that some of them would add a short headscarf as an accessory to otherwise immodest dress. In some of these cases, the headscarf may primarily be a conventional symbol of their racial identity as Malays, thereby distinguishing them from young women of other racial categories dressed in similar popular fashions. Many of the body styles they exhibit reflect the influence of popular culture images flowing in from the West and Asian countries such as Taiwan and South Korea. In particular, Korean popular culture is prevalent among Malay youth.[2] Whereas some Malay youth wearing *baju kurung* or *baju melayu* embody both racial and religious identities, these Malay youth sporting some of the latest fads personify modern and secular body techniques occasionally alongside symbols of Malay-ness.

Public comportment with members of the opposite sex is another area of practice that exemplifies normative and liberal Islamic, as well as secular,

Secular Muslim youth in Bukit Bintang, Kuala Lumpur

body techniques and cultivation of the self. Most of the Malaysian Muslims I observed on university campuses, restaurants, and other public places were alone or with a friend of the same gender when not accompanied by their families. There were often groups of two or more Malay youth of the same gender walking or sitting together in restaurants and cafeterias serving *halal* food. They sat separately from groups of the opposite gender and sometimes in different parts of the restaurant. Such practice embodies the pious ethics of normative Islamic authorities that advise against the mixing and interactions of unmarried men and women, even in public places. On the other hand, some observant Malaysian Muslims do date members of the opposite sex, going out together to dining and entertainment establishments. However, they avoid inappropriate touching and seclusion with their prospective partners. Unlike more traditional youth, they want to fall in love with the person of interest before marriage. These young people generally strive to operate within the limits of sharia and embody a combination of liberal Islamic and modern secular ethics. They attempt to perform a sense of secular modernity, manifesting in their individual autonomy in choice of mate, while also adhering to the moral and legal norms of avoiding any prohibited and indecent sexual actions.

On the other hand, some Malay youth transgress normative and liberal Islamic limits in their public conduct with members of the opposite sex. For instance, during June 2012, I saw two teenage Malays engaging in public displays of affection on a public train. The young girl seemed to be around sixteen years old and wore a short *tudung* that covered her head and came down just below her neck but far above her bosom. She wore tight jeans and a blouse. The boy seemed to be around seventeen, wore jeans and a T-shirt, and sported a punky hairstyle. They playfully tussled with each other. Then they stood close together, leaning against the side of the train, and the boy began to caress the girl's face and hair. A Chinese family, several adult women, and children occasionally looked at them. Similarly, in June 2012, I observed a young Malay couple sitting together in an intimate fashion and engaging in body contact in a McDonald's restaurant in Bukit Bintang. The girl wore a short, light blue *tudung* with jeans and a blouse, and the boy wore jeans and a casual shirt. She was sitting in her seat, facing straight ahead, and the boy was sitting facing her with his legs open, with one knee around her buttocks and the other in front of her knee. He rubbed and caressed her, stroking her head, face, and shoulders. One of the young Malay female employees, sweeping and mopping in that area, smiled and seemed to tell him to calm down. But he continued to sit as he was, and the worker continued doing her job. Other Malays in the restaurant did not say anything to the couple. When I left, they were still sitting together in the same fashion and the boy was still caressing her. These practices, which I occasionally noticed around Melaka and Kuala Lumpur, explicitly violate sharia laws and ethics and embody secular senses of self, pleasure, and individual freedom.

In addition to attire and public comportment, activities surrounding the performance of daily prayers and opening the fast during the month of Ramadan embody piety and cultivate humility, obedience, and remembrance of Allah. *Masjids* and prayer halls in neighborhoods establish the five daily prayers, but most local residents are in other areas of town during the morning and afternoon, working and performing household chores. However, there are prayer halls in government buildings, shopping centers, and transportation hubs. These *suraus* distributed throughout society are active centers for worship during the day, especially for the early afternoon and late afternoon prayers, *Zohor* and *Asr*, and sometimes for evening prayers (*Maghrib*) while people are in transit, returning home after work. In Malaysia, *masjids* and *suraus* generally have separate sections or rooms for men and women to perform their obligatory daily prayers. I often saw men and women scurrying into prayer halls in shopping centers and transportation hubs. At times they had to stand in long lines to perform their ritual ablution (*wuduh*) at faucets and pack into rows to perform prayers collectively or stand in the back and make prayers individually. Likewise, during the month of Ramadan, when Muslims are fasting from before sunrise to just after sunset, special Ramadan markets are erected across town that are popular with Muslims and non-Muslims. They begin selling food a few hours before the daily fast is set to end. Many Muslims will purchase their meals at these markets and take them home in order to open fasting (M. *buka puasa*) together with their families. In fact, I found that most middle-class Malaysian Muslims preferred to have their fast-opening meals (*ifṭhār*) at home. *Masjids* and prayer halls offer free meals during the month of Ramadan to all worshipers, but most of those in attendance tend to be lower-class and poor Muslims. I participated in *ifṭhār* at *masjids* and prayer halls on several occasions. Around thirty minutes prior to the time for the evening prayer, Muslim men and women, in separate sections, will form rows sitting on the floor, and attendants place small containers with dates, cakes, and fruit along with bottles of water in front of each worshiper. An *ustaz* (learned Muslim) can usually be heard reciting the Qur'an over loudspeakers, and worshipers engage in individual prayers as the time for the daily fast winds down. At the moment people hear the call to prayer (*adhān*) being recited, they can begin to eat and drink. Following this snack, evening prayers are performed, people reform rows on the floor, and larger meals are distributed to the congregation.

Many working- and middle-class people prefer to open their fasts with friends and relatives at restaurants if they are not having *ifṭhār* at home. On several occasions I opened my daily fast together with scores or hundreds of Muslims at restaurants. In these sites, Muslim stand in line to purchase their meals and drinks and then find seats at tables, where they set their food until the call of prayer, which can be heard from a nearby *masjid* or *surau* in the case of outdoor venues or over public communication systems or from someone's telephone at indoor restaurants. For instance, in August 2011, I sat at a McDonald's in Kuala Lumpur Sentral, a transportation hub, waiting to open my daily fast together with scores of Malays who filled most of the tables and counters. There were fewer Malays there on this occasion than earlier in the month because many had already returned home for Hari Raya Aidifitri, the celebration at the end of the fasting month. At some tables were young, seemingly unmarried Malay couples who appeared to be taking this special time to spend with their romantic partners. At one table sat a middle-aged woman with five young Malay women. At the counter sat several young Malay men. We heard *adhān*, perhaps from someone's phone, and began to make our supplications (*doa*) to Allah and open fasting. These public performances of piety, enacted either in religious institutions or in restaurants, embody Islamic ethics and virtues.

These and other public practices illustrate that ethical notions are integral to broader processes of Islamic resurgence and increasing implantation of religious values and norms throughout society. The authoritative discourses of government *ulama*, Islamic NGOs, Muslim political parties, and global Islamic revitalization movements have clearly affected the daily practices of many Malaysian Muslims. On the other hand, the widespread cultivation of pious dispositions creates an upward pressure on authorities to formulate discourses and policies that are more sharia-compliant. Indeed, growing numbers of youth fostering and exemplifying virtuous selves cry out for a greater institutionalization of religion that would more closely reflect their inner feelings and experiences.

SURVEYS OF THE VIEWS OF THE YOUNGER AND OLDER GENERATIONS

I conducted a survey of Muslim youth and adults, males and females, asking them a structured set of questions aimed at eliciting their views about sharia laws and ethical norms. I approached my respondents in public places—such as transportation hubs, indoor and outdoor restaurants, mall cafeterias, newspaper stands, *masjids*, and *suraus*—introduced myself as a social science researcher, and asked for permission to ask them a series of questions and to record their responses on my digital recorder. I interviewed 101 respondents for this structured survey: fifty-four youth versus forty-seven adults, fifty-eight females versus forty-three males. I met them all randomly, out in public, but later found out that a few of them were affiliated with political parties and nongovernmental organizations. Nonetheless, most of them were not directly affiliated with political parties, NGOs, or government offices. I tried to alternate my clothing and appearance from casual slacks, T-shirts, and baseball caps to more Islamic-style attire to minimize my influence on their responses. They knew I was also a Muslim, but I tried to elicit their responses without guiding them to answers they may have thought I wanted to hear. Subsequently, I conducted secondary interviews collecting the sharia personal narratives of a subset of these respondents.

My interlocutors were overwhelmingly in favor of having sharia family and criminal laws institutionalized and implemented in society (see table 7.1). Only one young woman, Lila, a twenty-three-year-old recent business college graduate from Kelantan, told me she felt that other people should not get involved in the "private matters" of individuals who decide to go to nightclubs, drink alcohol, and commit *khalwat*. She agreed with the liberal notion that these moral issues should be treated as personal matters between individuals and God. In contrast, 99 percent of my respondents disagreed with this idea, arguing that the state must get involved for the sake of society and religion. Most of them supported the dual court system and held that it is better to apply sharia laws to Muslims. They also generally stated that human rights were more protected under sharia laws, but even those few that maintained that human rights were stronger under civil courts and law still expressed the opinion that sharia courts are better for Muslims in order to strengthen and uphold Islam. One of them also questioned the motives of human rights campaigns, stating they are often used for political objectives.

Nearly 90 percent of my respondents were in favor of strengthening existing sharia criminal laws. They felt that many Muslims are not deterred from violating sharia ethical norms because of the low level of punishment under current sharia law, and expressed the view that the level of fines, prison terms, and canings should be increased. Most of them were in favor of a gradual increase implemented together with more Islamic education and *dakwah* aimed at making Muslims more knowledgeable and observant practitioners of the faith. Some asserted that this gradual increase in the level of punishment should eventually arrive at full implementation of the *hudud* penal code, while others expressed the view that *hudud* does not fit with Malaysia's ethnic and religious diversity. Zaidah, a twenty-two-year-old recent college graduate from Sabah, told me that she preferred the

TABLE 7.1. General views on sharia laws

	Females	Males	Youth (16–34)	Adults (35+)	Overall
In favor of sharia family and criminal laws	98.3%	100.0%	98.1%	100.0%	99.0%
In favor of strengthening existing sharia criminal laws	86.2%	90.6%	85.2%	93.6%	89.1%
In favor of applying *hudud* penal code to Muslims and non-Muslims	5.2%	2.3%	5.5%	2.1%	4.0%

"balanced" approach of UMNO, gradually applying Islamic laws and continuing with economic development. To the contrary, there were several that opined that full *hudud* should be implemented as soon as possible, or even immediately, and argued that it fits with Malaysia's diverse society just as it did with the diverse society of Medina under the leadership of Prophet Muhammad. Some also stressed the idea of applying sharia law to rich and poor alike as integral to the process of making sharia laws stricter. For instance, Ishmael, a working-class Malay man in his mid-fifties, suggested that the problem of how to punish crimes of *rasuah* (bribery) must be studied before *hudud* laws are applied.

Only 4 percent of respondents were in favor of applying the *hudud* code to both Muslims and non-Muslims. Most of those in support of the idea of immediately or eventually implementing *hudud* and *qisas* punishments argued that they should be applied only to Muslims. Some added that these punishments could also be applied to non-Muslims who choose to be punished according to *hudud* rather than civil laws. This has been the PAS position for many years. Nevertheless, three respondents expressed the view that *hudud* laws should fall on both Muslims and non-Muslims. Nor Arushah, a young married woman, told me that *hudud* is good for everyone, and since Malaysia is one nation and Islam is universal it should be applied to Muslims and non-Muslims equally. Likewise, Siti Aini, a twenty-five-year-old college student from Kuala Terengganu, contended that because sharia is definitely just, there is no problem applying it to both Muslims and non-Muslims. Rohaya, a twenty-year-old student at an Islamic school in Kota Bharu, to support her position, gave me the example of a mixed non-Muslim and Muslim couple committing *zina*. She felt that for the non-Muslim partner to not be punished according to *hudud* while the Muslim would be was not an acceptable policy. As a supporter of PAS, she was surprised when I told her that the PAS position is to give the non-Muslim person in the couple the option of having *hudud* punishment applied or not. She concluded that more study is needed of how *Rasulullah* applied *hudud* in Medina.[3]

Only 8.9 percent of my respondents were in support of using only advice and counseling as the institutionalized treatment of apostates (see table 7.2). More females (13.8 percent) and youth (13 percent) were opposed to any penal punishment of *murtad* than were males (4.7 percent) and adults (4.3 percent). Again, most respondents called for more widespread and organized education and proselytization of Muslims to enhance their religious convictions and commitment to the Islamic faith. Suzanna, a thirty-three-year-old investment consultant, stated that even when people want to renounce Islam, it is another opportunity to speak to them and find out why they would want to do such a thing. If they are meant to be out of Islam, she added, then that is it, they will be outside of Islam. Lila, who was opposed to sharia criminal punishments in general, spoke of the influence of the Internet and popular music on youth. Three Malay female teenagers I interviewed in a mall in Negeri Sembilan told me they thought this state's policy of advising and counseling apostates and eventually issuing declarations that they are outside of Islam should be adopted as the national approach for handling *murtad*. Faridah, a twenty-seven-year-old employee of a conventional bank, expressed the opinion that apostates should be given advice but allowed to leave Islam if that is still what they want. They cannot be forced to remain Muslims, she added, and besides, the Muslim community would be better without them if they do not want to be Muslims. On the other hand, my respondents were overwhelmingly in favor of institutionalizing some form of penal punishment for Muslims that persist in their desire to leave Islam even after receiving scholarly advice and counseling. They felt that apostates should be arrested and imprisoned for a period of time or beheaded if they do not repent. For instance, Roslan, a twenty-year-old college student I interviewed in the Kuala Lumpur Sentral transportation hub, declared that apostasy is not allowed in Islam and that many Shāfiʿī *ulama* say *murtad* should be put to death. Many Malay elites say that nothing can be done about this problem, but PAS has the best approach for implementing sharia, he added. Most respondents opined that this sort of penal punishment should be meted out equally to people "born as Muslims" and to converts, and argued that this must be done to uphold Islam and to make the general public develop greater respect for the faith. Several spoke of the problem of non-Muslims that convert to marry a Muslim, and how they need to be instructed in Islamic knowledge and internalize a commitment to the religion before marriage. Conversely, some Malay

TABLE 7.2. Handling of apostates (*murtad*)

	Females	Males	Youth (16–34)	Adults (35+)	Overall
Advice/counseling	13.8%	4.7%	13.0%	4.3%	8.9%
Penal punishment	86.2%	95.3%	87.0%	95.7%	91.1%

adults told me they know of non-Malay converts that do study Islam and develop strong faith after converting for marriage.

The notion that men should be the leaders of the nation, perform the role of imam in religious contexts, and be the heads of households is widespread in Malaysian Muslim society. Over 98 percent of women and 100 percent of men I interviewed held these views (see table 7.3). Only one young woman, Suzanna, expressed the opinion that men and women should both be leaders of the nation and of households. She said she feels that the Sisters in Islam are a bit "extreme," but that she agreed with them that gender equality is based in the Qur'an and *Sunna*. Suzanna told me that during the Prophet's time there was a *shūrā* (collective deliberation) council, implying that Muslim men and women today should form this sort of consultative organization in the home and in society at large. Gender inequality is based in culture, not religion, she added. However, she did not challenge the leadership of male religious figures in terms of performance of *ibadah* in collective, mixed-gender religious contexts. Yet, all of my other respondents held the traditional Islamic view, propagated widely in Malaysian society, that according to revealed knowledge men should be leaders in homes, *masjids*, and polities. For example, Julianna, a twenty-five-year-old executive for a private telecommunications company, told me that men should be the *ketua* (heads) of families and society and that she totally disagrees with Muslims who promote the notion of "total gender equality" in the sense of men and women being on the same level throughout society. She declared that Muslims of this sort must relearn the basics of Islam, including *'aqidah* (religious belief) and *Tauhid* (Islamic monotheism).

Julianna and the vast majority of my interlocutors were in favor of polygyny being allowed in sharia family laws. Over 96 percent of women and 100 percent of men expressed the view that men should be permitted to marry more than one wife, up to the limit of four decreed in the Qur'an. Rosmawati, a twenty-two-year-old diploma graduate of a civil engineering program, informed me that she agreed with the opposition of SIS to polygamy and their drive for reform of current provisions on *nusyuz* (disobedience) in family sharia laws. She went on to express the view that husbands should be sympathetic with their wives. Similarly, Siti Zubaidah, a twenty-year-old student from Perak, stated that she disagreed with allowing polygamy overall but thought it was acceptable in cases where the first wife accepted it. Although practically all of my contacts thought men should be permitted to marry more than one wife, they did not feel that this permission should be given without conditions. Several young men and women

TABLE 7.3. Women's views of gender relations and sharia family laws

	Young women (16–34)	Women (35+)	All Women
Pro male leaders of nation	97.8%	100.0%	98.3%
Pro male imam	100.0%	100.0%	100.0%
Pro male head of household	97.8%	100.0%	98.3%
Pro polygyny	95.7%	100.0%	96.6%
Pro reform of *nusyuz* provisions	11.0%	0.0%	8.6%
Pro gender equality at work	100.0%	100.0%	100.0%

expressed the view that men must be able to provide sufficient financial support for their wives and families and be able to treat each wife fairly. For instance, Azrul, a twenty-year-old student from Melaka, stated that practicing polygamy is a lot of responsibility and that only men with the ability to provide for their wives should be allowed to practice it.

While no men or adult women were in favor of reforming current *nusyuz* provisions, 11 percent of young women felt that reform of these provisions is necessary. For the five women who were critical of current provisions requiring wives to be obedient to the lawful demands of their husbands, these laws contradicted their ideas about fair, flexible, and complementary social relations between men and women in families. For example, Ruzita, a twenty-five-year-old university student from Kedah, stated that in Islam men are leaders but below the leader there are women, and *qualified* male leaders should treat women justly. Emilia, a twenty-year-old chemistry student, similar to Suzanna, argued that flexible gender roles in which women work outside the home and men perform domestic chores are based in the *Sunna* of Prophet Muhammad.

Although young women overwhelmingly supported current provisions and traditional understandings of *nusyuz*, many of them held ideas that placed checks and ethical limitations on male behavior. Hamidah, a twenty-eight-year-old married woman, stated that she learned in Islamic institutions that the man should be the leader of the family, but if he is brutal or abusive there is a process to correct his behavior. She said that "women should follow their husbands in general as long as they don't order something that is contrary to Allah's orders." In addition, some young women viewed sharia regulations prohibiting men from engaging in sexual relations outside of marriage as corresponding to *nusyuz* for wives; men must be obedient and not betray their wives, just as wives are not to betray their husbands. They argued that both sides of these ethical norms are based in the Qur'an. All of my male interlocutors, both young and adult men, were in full support of *nusyuz* provisions, viewing them as part of the rights and responsibilities Allah bestowed on them. A few young men stressed the obligatory nature of the requirement for a wife to "submit" to the lawful demands of her husband by reciting the popular aphorism *Syurga isteri di bawah kaki suami* (A wife's heaven is under the feet of her husband). For Azrul, the young man from Melaka, this saying meant that a wife must follow the desires of her husband even if she is not in the mood or tired after a long day of work.[4]

Even though they generally thought women had to follow the leadership of, and be obedient to, their husbands at home, all of the men and women I interviewed were in favor of gender equality at work or in the broader economic life of society. Nur, a twenty-six-year-old university graduate, expressed the widespread view that it is all right for women to lead on the job, but when they come home they still must follow the leadership of their husbands. Likewise, Siti Zubaidah told me that men must be the heads of families and the country, but in the economy it is good for men and women to be on the same level. Ruzita, Rosmawati, and others stated that women should play prominent roles in society, including positions in business and government. My findings with Malaysian Muslims is comparable to Christel Manning's (1999) research with conservative Catholic, Evangelical Protestant, and Orthodox Jewish women in the United States, in which she found that many believed it appropriate to have male leadership at home and in religious institutions but supported gender equality at work. Manning concludes that the conservative religious women in these three communities take on a "feminist" self-conception in the secular context of work and a "traditionalist" self-conception in religious institutions. In contrast, I infer that Malaysian Muslims learn and share a cultural model they use to reason about and organize gender relations across the contexts of home, *masjid*, and work. Whereas their cultural framework raises a patriarchal gender hierarchy at home and in the *masjid*, it reduces gender stratification and constructs more of an equal playing field in the domain of work.

These surveys indicate that the disciplinary practices of government *ulama*, Muslim political parties, Islamic schoolteachers, and *dakwah* movements have had a strong influence on the views of Malaysian Muslims, who have internalized normative sharia models and use them to construe the need to implement the laws and ethical norms sent down from Allah to regulate Muslim lives and benefit society. As these sharia models entail representations of Malaysia's ethnically and religiously diverse citizenry, many are concerned about the effects such institutionalization of *hudud* and *qisas* criminal laws in Malaysia will have on the lives of non-Muslims. Thus, they generally either want to strengthen existing sharia laws falling short of *hudud* or want to only make *hudud* mandatory for Muslims. Likewise, my interlocutors utilize normative sharia models to reason about the proper handling of apostates, concluding that they must be given advice and an opportunity to repent, but that they be punished if they fail to reform themselves. They believe that Muslims, through birth or conversion, cannot be permitted to move from belief to unbelief. However, liberal Islamic models, entailing a reformed emphasis on the objectives of sharia and religious freedom, have had some impact on the views of Malaysian Muslims. Similarly, the sharia models of SIS scholars and activists have influenced the views of my respondents. Although they tend to consider SIS "extreme" or lacking in Islamic knowledge, their discourses still reflect the impact of this NGO's reformist campaigns. While they internalize and operate with the normative sharia model of proper Islamic gender relations projecting male leadership in political, religious, and domestic contexts, they also claim gender equality in work contexts and inclusion and consultation in other settings with male leadership. They tend to search for a basis in sacred rather than secular sources for their efforts to tweak the normative sharia model in the direction of leveling patriarchal gender hierarchies.

SHARIA PERSONAL NARRATIVES AND PRACTICE

I asked some of my interlocutors to respond to more open-ended questions about the role of sharia in their personal lives. These interviews aimed to elicit information about how their communities of practice, including family and educational backgrounds, have shaped their ideas and feelings about sharia. I also tried to have them speak about how they implement sharia in their everyday lives, as well as how sharia affects the mass media they normally intake and the political and/or religious movements they support. Below I present segments of their personal narratives about the role of sharia in their lives in their own words, followed by my analysis. I think these individual sharia stories reflect aspects of their psychological conditions and of the broader social and cultural context, as well as their own performances of self (Luttrell 2005).

*   *   *

The first sharia personal narrative I present is from Lili Zohail, a thirty-one-year-old unmarried Malay woman, who lives and works in Kuala Lumpur. She was born into a working-class family in Kedah and moved to Kuala Lumpur thirteen years ago. I met her for this interview, with her friend Marianne, a young Indian woman that converted from Hinduism to Christianity but who now considers herself a "free thinker." We discussed sharia in her personal story for over three hours at a restaurant near the Bangsar Village shopping mall. She wore a tight pair of jeans that accentuated her shapely body, with a short button-down blouse and no *tudung*.

TRYING TO SOFTEN MY TONGUE AGAIN

Yes, of course, when you finish your school and studies, you want to enjoy your social life and to try something with men. But at the same time, my mother teaches Al-Quran in Kedah. Even if I am in Kuala Lumpur and even though I am social, in my mind I am still afraid of my mom. She just passed away last January. I think, just maybe, because I am in Kuala Lumpur and no parents [are] here, I just follow my friends. But I think if given another chance and I could turn back time I don't think I would do this. I am sorry I enjoyed these things. . . . I think it was just temporary or maybe culture shock. I enjoyed the music but I had no intention to change my religion. When people think about changing their religion it is often about the relation between one woman and one man. It is not about dancing or drinking in the clubs. Some people say they are thinking of changing their religion. I disagree. It is about enjoying . . . the club. We do not talk much about religion. We are enjoying the music and dancing and that is it. . . . I am always thinking about my mom. I don't stay with a guy like a husband and wife because I was also thinking about my mom. I think some of the people in Kuala Lumpur do *khalwat* and things, but some of them are still thinking about religion and about their parents. . . . In their minds, they still have an idea of what religion is about. . . . I see people around me, my friends, and they are still scared. . . . I was going to nightclubs for around five or six years. I realized what I did was wrong. But I was surrounded by my friends. . . . I had no bad experience at all going to the nightclubs. . . . I had a few boyfriends during that time period. . . . I agree with what they say about alcohol, it is a pathway to *zina*. The connection is there. Alcohol is one of the most serious sins. From drinking alcohol, it is where things often start. . . . Social problems started there and then things moved on to the next level. . . . "You know me, you know me, and you have free time, can I come to your house?" and you see things go from there. . . . I did that for around five years. I began to limit my time for doing these things. It was hard to get myself out. I had no parents here and my friends were doing these things. Sometimes, I have to go out because of my friends. I don't blame my friends. You also feel that you are alone and want to go out. I'm looking mostly for music. For me, my intention is to get drunk and dance. . . . I like rock, house, techno music. . . . You can enjoy every music actually without alcohol and drugs. . . .

I don't really like clubs much anymore, maybe once in three or four months. I just drink alcohol when I am at the clubs. Some people can drink it at their home, but not for me. . . . At my home, I am a Muslim, so alcohol is not at my home. . . . My entertainment now is some karaoke and that is it. It is better that I concentrate on education now and not to spend so much time in those things. I won't say that I have 100 percent quit, because I still can go to the club with my friends sometimes. But not like before, [when] I was more excited about it than the kids. Last time, I drank alcohol because one of my friends posted me and said you are in Kuala Lumpur and you have not drunk or had sex yet, and he sort of pushed me. . . .

Now, sometimes, I wake up at night and read *Ayatul Kursi* [the Throne Verse, Q. 2:255] and recite it 179 times to protect me from evil. Last time I tried for one week and it really helped me. I was really in despair and trauma. The effects were very good for myself and I was very satisfied with what I did . . . because I have left behind my praying and now I think it is time to get it back. . . . Sometimes I want to study and be better now, but I am not sure how to start. Because once you are lost, you know you need to get back to one way but you don't know how to get back to the right way. . . . After I asked my friend and my friend asked me to do this 179 times and I did and he said *Alhamdulillah*. I was not dizzy. . . . I know what to do but I am lost in myself. . . . I know how to read Qur'an, read slow, and I admit that last time I drank alcohol, so my tongue is not soft like other people. So, last time I was reading with my mouth, and my mom was teaching me that it is not right. But now since my mom is not around, I just use the Roman translation. If my mom were around she would not allow me to just read the Roman script. . . . Sometimes, I search in myself and I want to get back now. I found a place to learn Al-Qur'an and I will go to this place. . . . Now, she is not around, it is so sad. Last time, I was crying around in the morning, so sad. . . .

Every other day I recite *Ayatul Kursi* 179 times. I am starting little by little, but continuously now I read some Qur'an and recite *selawat* [praises of Prophet Muhammad]. . . . I went to *sekolah kebangsaan* [public school] when I grew up. . . . But the community in Kedah, the neighbors will be talking about *ugama* [religion]. In terms of general knowledge about the Qur'an, I have to say I am the most knowledgeable among my friends. I would often talk with my mom about *ugama*. She knew almost all of the *ayat* [verses] of Qur'an and so did her father. . . .

Please pray that I marry my boyfriend from the UK. He is a Muslim. I've been waiting for so long to get a Muslim. All of my previous boyfriends were non-Muslims. A few boyfriends wanted to marry me, but at the time my mother was still alive and she would not accept it. So I was just patient and I did not want to do what my mom disliked. So if God bless[es] me, even though my mom is not around, I still want to do what she wants. I will not convert to another religion, and she didn't want someone to convert just to marry me. She had the instinct that they wanted to convert just to marry me. . . . I think he is my real love, my true love.

I asked my boyfriend, the convert man, about practicing Islam in the UK. He said there are so many places to learn about Islam and there are lots of *halal* restaurants, even KFCs. . . . I thought it may be difficult for me to practice sharia in Europe if I marry a man that just converted to Islam, but this man already converted and he knows about Islam. He converted around seven years ago.[5]

Lili's story reflects some of the broader social and cultural conditions surrounding the movement of rural or small-town Malays into cities such as the sprawling cosmopolitan capital, Kuala Lumpur. Lili, like many other Malay migrants, moved from a highly homogeneous environment in the northern state of Kedah to a diverse urban context in which she became part of a social network of Malaysians from different ethnic and religious backgrounds. Although she attended a national public school rather than one of the numerous Islamic schools in Kedah, she received a foundation in Islamic knowledge from her mother, who taught local people to recite Qur'an and often attended religious talks, and from neighbors who discussed religious topics. Her mother and three elder sisters always embodied public piety by wearing *baju kurung* and *tudung*. At the age of eighteen, Lili went to the metropolis and was confronted with the psychological challenge of reconciling her Islamic background and the ethical norms she had learned with the interests and practices of her youthful, more secular cohort. The secular discourses of her friends, emphasizing the fun to be had in drinking and having sex, motivated her to join them on their outings to nightclubs. Presenting herself as a responsible person, she admits her own personal desires to not be "alone" and to relieve stress. As the secular discourses excited her imagination, like they do to many youth, she felt it was better not to miss out on the opportunity to have fun. Lili joined her friends and began to engage in the body practices of dancing to popular music, singing karaoke, drinking alcoholic beverages, and interacting intimately with men. Nevertheless, Lili contended that she often remembered what her mother taught her and maintained a fear of the cosmic outcomes of her sinful behaviors more than other Muslims in her social network did. Many of them appeared to be no longer "afraid," while she kept some of her religious sense of self, even though it became engulfed by her secular self and its practices of self-indulgence. Performing for Marianne and me, she presents an image of herself as being in control of her limited use of alcoholic drinks, not being boy crazy, and not going to the extent of sharing an apartment with a boyfriend. In addition, she considers herself the most knowledgeable Muslim among their social group. She was clearly contrasting herself with Liza, one of their Malay girlfriends, who lives with her Chinese boyfriend she is trying to convert to Islam so that they can get married. Lili continues to uphold her mother's conviction that she should marry a man that has a sincere belief in the Islamic faith rather than a man that converts for marriage.

After many years of frequenting nightclubs and enacting related body techniques, Lili laments her past actions and wants to turn her life around. In many ways, her story mirrors the popular theme in Islamic TV dramas of a sinful Muslim going through a personal transformation to return to a life of piety (see Daniels 2013b). However, Lili has to face the all too real problem of cultivating a pious self in a body that has been trained with secular desires and experiences. She moaned that she knows *what* needs to be done but does not know *how* to do it. Her secular body has dispositions that are contrary to the required qualities of a pious self. Even though she presents herself as having lost some interest in clubbing and regrets past actions, she continues to attend nightclubs, revel in dancing, and enjoy drinking beer and wine. Nevertheless, she is struggling to "soften her tongue again" so that she can return to reciting the Qur'an the way her mother instructed her, with slow and precise recitation of Arabic. Following the advice of one of her Muslim friends, she has begun to recite *Ayatul Kursi* numerous times every other night and intends to revive her practice of performing the five daily prayers. She hopes to marry her first Muslim boyfriend, a Muslim convert from the UK, and to continue along this course of personal transformation.

*   *   *

The next sharia personal narrative is from Aliza Abu Bakar, a fifty-six-year-old married woman, who was born into a working-class Malay Muslim family in Singapore. Her father worked as a police officer. She married a man from Negeri Sembilan and lived and worked in Melaka and Negeri Sembilan for much of her life. I interviewed Aliza in her office, located on the thirty-sixth floor of a high-rise office building in the heart of Kuala Lumpur, where she and her husband, Datuk Latt, ran a construction firm and several other enterprises. She wore a *baju kurung* and *tudung* on the three occasions I interviewed her. On one occasion, she was wearing a long white prayer cloak (*telekung*) and performing her evening prayers in her office when I arrived. I also had the opportunity to engage in long discussions with Aliza and her husband when we went out for late evening meals following a few of our interviews.

I ONLY NEED BLESSINGS FROM ALLAH, THAT'S ALL

My father sent me to religious education when I was young. In Singapore, we only learned in the *surau*. It was like a *pondok* [traditional Islamic boarding school] but it was in a *surau*. We learned to recite Qur'an, Arabic language, and all the Islamic topics. I was one of the Qur'an contestants. That time, I was around twelve or eleven years old, something like that. . . . At the age of five or six I started at the *surau*. My main course in Singapore schools was English. Actually, I learned more about Islam from readings and . . . also from my father's advice. My father and me are like friends. This relation is very important. Anything to do with family, it must go to the relations of a family, father and son, father and daughter, mother and daughter. These relations are very important; they are priceless. . . . My father was a policeman, a hardcore worker. . . . I was very social at that age. Honestly, I was not [a] pious person. I did not pray. Imagine that! I went for my religious classes, but once I finished those and I went for my primary English school I [didn't] pray. . . . I had a misunderstanding a bit with my mom. So my mom is against me all the time. First thing, I am not as educated as my sister. So I was a bit down, you see, so I will always rebel. . . . But somehow or other . . . my late father motivated me, all the days of my life. He is concerned about whatever I do, and his concern had no restrictions. That is why I am very brave and I am daring, and I can go anywhere and I mix with anybody. I mix with all races, even though my English was not so good at that time. He always told me [that] "as long as you take care of my family's name and your name, as a woman, as a girl, as a lady, and you know what you do is wrong . . . You have to think. You can be as sociable as much as you want, but at the same time you have to think whether that is the right way or it is wrong. If you are still not certain than you can ask me."

When I got married to my husband, I was still social. I still [didn't] pray. Because at that moment, I'm so sorry, I had this kind of . . . I wanted to know more about what social life is. I did not need to do bad things, but I wanted to entertain myself. I was from a family where only my father took care of me. My mom was different. She always told me that "if you don't know how to take care, you go to hell." . . . As I grew up, I wanted to socialize myself, to make myself easy. I did not want to strain myself, because I am scared that I may not be able to control . . . I may do worse than this. So what I did was just explore; I just mixed with anybody, any races, but less with Malays. Muslims were just a small portion, but mostly non-Muslims, English, Indians, any races. Then from there I learned. I was gifted in such a way that I liked to learn the characteristics of a person. When I go to my friend's home, their family is like this. And myself, I liked to go with groups of friends, whether they are Muslims or non-Muslims. Even though I was social, I would take non-*halal* food, but I always would take my father's advice in my head. I would say, oh, by myself, this is wrong. I used to do the talking to myself, my father say this. I don't care what people say. Everybody was like, last time, they put on *baju kurung*, but I put on miniskirts. I put on anything, I put on all tight-fitting clothes, until [I] was eighteen or twenty, until I got married. So I don't care, I put on miniskirts. But somehow or other, because of my late father's teachings, he always told me, "You can put on any dress you want as long as you know where to go. If you go to the party this is your dress; if you go to the *surau* this is your coverage; if you go to *kenduri* [a traditional feast] this is what you should wear." . . . That is where I noted to myself every time. So my father did not control me. This where I begin to take what I initially need to learn. I did not feel tense. If you want to bring your friend, you can. I bring my Christian friend, whatever friend, to the house. He said, "If they want to bring you out, they have to come to meet me." . . . But sometimes I lied to him also, because you have three or four friends that put on these tight-fitting skirts and all this kind of thing. He said, "Where are you going?" I tell him that we are just going around Singapore. "Why are your friends not coming?" I tell him we just meet outside. He [said], "You sure?" and asked, "What time are you coming back?" I will be a bit late. "It's okay but just let me know when." At that time, I could not come back after six at night. A few times I lied to him. I slept at my friend's house and I was slapped by him. . . . I was carried away I think. I was at a family house. . . . Actually if I want to stay over night I have to inform him earlier. . . . He told me he whacked me because what I did was wrong. . . . He felt the guilt but he didn't spoil me. . . . Sometimes when I go with my friends they eat soup with pork. . . . *Alhamdulillah*, at the end, I become a better person.

So when I got married, my mom was against the marriage. . . . But his father and my father both gave their blessings. Because they are the head of the family, whether you like it or not, they make the decisions. They are the best motivator[s], rather than . . . the ladies. . . . I wanted to make myself a good housewife. I never thought of education at that time. I wanted to prove that I was a good housewife; I'm a good mother with responsibility . . . but unfortunately when I married my husband, his mother treated me bad. So nothing is granted in life. I had to drag myself a second time, what my mother did to me now his mother did it. . . . I have gone through a lot of hurdles in my life. . . .

What I do for my mother-in-law, the feelings I have with my mind are all the same. I tell my friend and tell myself, when we are with Allah, we pray to Allah. What is our main intention? It is because it is our duty as *hamba* [servants of] Allah . . . Whatever you do to Allah it is our duty. When we do to my husband and my mother-in-law, I train myself to be faithful to my husband and children and it goes to my mother-in-law; it is responsibility. When I think of responsibility that is when I do more in the family. But if I think I want gratitude or compliments from my mother-in-law . . . if I want that then I don't think I can perform that well, because you see I [have taken] care of her for twenty-six years. She [doesn't] give me anything and I know I don't get anything from her. First thing is I am not her flesh and blood. I'm totally out from her family. I am nothing, so of course I don't expect anything from her. But it is just because of the duty and responsibility that I have, and that is why I got married, and this is what I have to perform. . . . I do this as a responsibility, because when I am aged I know I have already done my part. Only Allah knows when to give and when not to give. It is a blessing that I will get from Allah. . . . When I think of Allah, Allah [gives] us the right decision for our feelings. . . . Several times my mother-in-law told me that I will get *pahala* [blessings] from Allah if I take care of the elder person. She told me this because none of her children [wants] to take care of her. . . . So I told her, I was sitting like this having drinks with her, and said, "Mak, since I have been grown and married, whatever I do in this world for you and my family, or for whoever, I don't need anything. I only need blessings from Allah, that's all. If Allah says I don't give you anything, then I don't mind, because I know that Allah has always chosen the right time, the right person for me." . . . Allah has given me so much courage and strong feelings . . . I can work and my husband, at last, realized that he has to work. He realized that he is the leader of the family and he has to give me money and that he has to give shelter to the family. These are the *pahala* that I get. . . . I need to establish myself because I belong to Allah and Allah belongs to me. Nothing can separate us. Allah cannot be separated from me. . . .

When my father passed away . . . I was at a loss because I really needed guidance from my father. But some way or other I had to go on my own. . . . Every time that experience happened I look at my surroundings, my friend[s] tell me this and my friend[s] tell me that. So from them I began to go to the mosque by myself. . . . Every time I sleep or something, I wondered if I was in the grave and all these things I left behind. After my friend passed away . . . all of a sudden . . . slowly it develops my mind. God want[s] to take, you don't know when. . . . So at the same time, I began to realize that I have done a lot of wrong things, so why not I be by myself first and go to the mosque. . . . I come back from the mosque at night. . . . Anybody who comes to me, Allah will give me the feeling . . . maybe they need something to eat or whatever. . . . My feeling began to grow toward Allah. . . . But somehow or other, I told my husband, *Alhamdulillah*, from the day . . . I started maybe a thousand times already that is why I feel the strength and the clearance of my heart. Whether I have money or I don't, I feel the clearance of my heart. This particular feeling, *ikhlas* [inner sincerity], I don't think anybody can get if they really don't mean it. . . .

I wanted to wear miniskirts and tight clothes because I wanted to be stylish. . . . Many people looked at me and said, "You are over thirty and still putting on skirts." . . . I was brought up that way, even my father did not stop me. Certain things he would let me know. When I got married to my husband, the same thing. After I got married, I tried to respect my mother-in-law. Then no more skirts. I began to wear *baju kurung* and *kebaya* or long pants. That is the time, when I go into the married life, then I respect the in-laws' family. . . . I have to look out for my husband's reputation and I have to obey. . . . So I try my level best to be a good wife, a good mother, a good daughter-in-law. . . . So it has to do with my reputation of my image of putting on physical dressing. When I thought about it I had done [everything]. If you already start putting on *baju kurung*, the miniskirts are already gone, the tight-fitting clothes are already gone. . . . First, I have to consider the size and fit for my body structure, and then [it] comes to whatever patterns. As I go through, my family does not stop me, as long it is not low-cut or too tight. The skirt becomes long pants. You know, the short sleeves become long sleeves. These are just the beginnings, and the scarf is the last one and is difficult to put on my head. Nobody can stop me and no one can ask me to do what they want, because I want to do what I want. Because to me when I put everything on to fit, I want to make sure physically whatever I have already done that my internal features are already done with all [spiritual things in good order]. And I think I have already gone that far. And to me I think it is good, *amanah*. At the end of the day, then, I will feel satisfied, because [these are] my pieces of life. . . . I make sure that whenever I do something that it is good physically and internally. Only Allah knows as judgment goes. That is why when I read all of my characteristics [i.e., reflect on myself], as I go along, I think I can get along with most people, Muslims and non-Muslims. So that is why I started to put on my scarf. Because [in regard to] the time of the corrections, I think I have already made my corrections. Only I don't have the right person to lead me [to] the right way, to the *hukum* [law] of the things as a Muslim. Actually, I have to do all, for example, I still need to perform my *umrah* [shortened pilgrimage] and *hajj*.[6]

Aliza's early experiences in 1960s and 1970s Singapore reflect the experiences of many Malays in the majority Chinese non-Muslim urban context of this newly independent city-state with a colonial heritage of being tied directly to British rule. The Malay Muslim minority in postcolonial Singapore was subject to the top-down multiculturalism of the Chinese-dominated state. Aliza's father sent her to study Islam in a prayer hall for her younger years, but then she attended English-medium public schools (i.e., schools where education was conducted in English) and developed friendships with youth from mostly non-Muslim and non-Malay backgrounds. She began to learn and embody popular styles and performed secular body techniques, donning miniskirts and short blouses and engaging in social activities with diverse members of Singaporean society. Her father, with whom she developed a strong relationship, instructed her in liberal Islamic teachings that facilitated her openness for social interactions but reminded her of limitations and the need to respect their family's reputation. She often thought of her father's moral teachings when she dressed for different contexts and socialized with her non-Muslim friends. On the other hand, being held in lower esteem than her siblings by her mother fueled her desire to explore and learn the characteristics of other social groups. She did not perform daily prayers or other forms of public piety while attending primary and secondary schools. As other Muslim women began to wear *baju kurung* and *tudung* under the influence of the Islamic resurgence of the 1970s and 1980s, Aliza continued to wear popular secular styles criticized as contrary to proper public comportment.

It was not until after she married her boyfriend from Negeri Sembilan that she began to wear somewhat more modest clothing, in order to uphold the reputation of her husband and his family. Nevertheless, she did not undergo a personal transformation and begin to wear clothing that expressed her personal piety until much later. Aliza stated that it was after her father passed away and she began to think more of death and the meaning of life that she made some personal changes. She started performing her daily prayers and going to the *masjid*, practices that honed her inner qualities and cultivated a religious self that felt humility and gratitude for blessings from Allah. From there she developed the patience and inner sincerity, feelings of *sabar* (patience) and *ikhlas*, to take care of her mother and mother-in-law, both of whom mistreated her, looking only for the rewards from Allah. She also began to regularly perform acts of *amalan soleh* (good works), providing direct assistance to poor Muslims that asked her for help with food or money, and mobilizing those around her to join in her campaigns to help uplift poor families struggling to survive. Aliza was critical of PAS for not promoting more economic development and for exhibiting a somewhat "backward" mentality, and of UMNO for staging campaigns to assist poor people for photo opportunities and other political benefits. She charged that after the media spotlight moved on, UMNO left most of these needy people in the same state that they found them. Eventually, after developing and cultivating inner religious features, she added a headscarf to her long-sleeved blouses and long skirts, placing her public embodiment of piety in accord with her personal piety. To be sure, Aliza's discourse constructs and performs the religious identity of a Muslim that has corrected sinful and negative personal characteristics and attained a heightened spiritual level of remembering Allah, performing selfless acts of righteousness, and feeling *ikhlas*. She presented the image that the only thing left to complete her life of devotion to Allah is to find the "right leader," an *ulama* no doubt, to instruct her in the laws of performing the pilgrimage to Mecca.

This leader is clearly not her husband, Datuk Latt, who has not undergone the same transformation of personal and public piety that she has. Although he is not the personal religious guide she seeks, he has been her husband for all these years and is the leader of her family. This fact accounts for some of the tension I perceived in her sharia personal narrative. As she has gone through personal changes, learning and embodying Islamic knowledge, her husband has finally developed the ability to provide more reliable financial support for his family. While Aliza took the responsibility of caring for her children and elder family members, she also worked several jobs in the private sector. On one job, which she held for many years, the Chinese company executives passed her over many times for bonuses, raises, and promotions. Now, she feels it is a "blessing" that she can work with her husband, who is accruing more wealth for them. However, it is largely through UMNO-affiliated *Bumiputera* business connections and their corrupt practices of giving and taking bribes and patronage money that he has been able to advance as a construction contractor. From one perspective, we can interpret that it is the gendered nature of their relationship as husband and obedient wife that underscores her inability to overrule him when it comes to his business dealings. However, from another angle, we can construe her interpretation that Datuk Latt's newfound ability to earn material wealth is a "blessing" as rooted in a sense of relief from a long life of socioeconomic challenges. After all, as Ustaz Ibrahim, a sixty-five-year-old working-class PAS member from Kedah, explained to me, applying the principles of *ubudiah*, *mas'uliah*, and *itqan* in one's economic life can be highly problematic.

*   *   *

The next sharia personal narrative is from Mohamad Zuhaidi, a twenty-seven-year-old University of Malaya graduate student, whom I met on campus. Hailing originally from Penang, for our interview he wore casual slacks and a shirt. Before I approached him he was speaking to a Malay woman in her late thirties with whom he seemed to be acquainted. Perhaps she was a fellow graduate student in his program. They were sitting at separate tables and speaking from a distance.

MY FATHER OFTEN CHASTISED ME IF I DID NOT GO FOR CONGREGATIONAL PRAYERS

In regard to Islam in my life, my father, from when I was young, around five or six years old, he already took me to the *masjid* and at the same time I studied to read Al-Qur'an. [At] five or six years of age, before I went to school, he had me instructed in religion, reciting Arabic, *alif ba ta* [characters in Arabic language], Sūrah Al-Fātiha, and other usual verses . . . I grew up in a *kampung* [village] in Pulau Pinang. After that, when I entered primary school, on the second floor there was an Islamic school, and there I studied *tajwid* [pronunciation of Arabic characters], *akidah*, fundamentals of religion that fit with my age. This was primary school. The normal primary school had more limited religious instruction. Only the village primary school had more religious instruction. We studied *hadith* and everyday supplications, prayers for entering the bathroom, [the] house, and other prayers that children could learn. . . . When I returned home, my father often chastised me if I did not go to the *masjid* for congregational prayers. Always in the middle of my time at home we would go to the *masjid* to pray *Zohor, Asr, Maghrib*, and *Ishak*. And at the *masjid* we would have religious studies, organized on the part of the *masjid*, advanced religious talks given by teachers on texts, *hadiths*, given by certain teachers. This is my life with my family. Then when I went to secondary school, I could help other students study religious topics, help them understand Arabic characters . . . and I take my younger relatives, when they reach the age of five or so, to the *masjid*. And sometimes at night, I can teach them to read Arabic, *alif ba ta*, at home. . . .

One matter that we have to consider today is the mixing of men and women in school and in many other places. I think that the interaction of men and women at school is good for us to understand the method of communication with other people and to know what women are like. We do not know that women are like this because we don't know automatically. We are instructed from when we are young about the fundamentals of relationships between men and women, so that we can know that these are the rights of women and this is the way to respect women. In case this knowledge is not acquired from a young age, knowing the limits of mixing with girls, then the boys may not understand how to respect women. I don't think there is a problem from a religious perspective of men and women mixing in an educational setting. Then, when you return home, we have mothers and fathers that can instruct us on the proper way to interact with boys and girls. Yet, it is still a problem when they don't have control and things are seen in public that are not supposed to happen. From my perspective, a strong religious basis [should be] at the level of schooling about the mingling of boys and girls, then when we grow up we understand and know the limits and know better than to do something that violates the limits of religion such as acts of *zina*. . . . But I think that today the level of religious education on the part of schools and families is low. They view religion, religious fundamentals, and religious lessons as if it is just for passing examinations and not to be put into practice. That is the problem nowadays.[7]

Mohamad Zuhaidi's narrative, and Wan Hafizi's below, reflect the lives and experiences of many born in the 1980s and later, in the midst of the Islamic resurgence, during which appeals for enhancing Islamic knowledge, practice, and institutionalization spread widely in Malaysian society. The environment in which this generation grew up was becoming increasingly Islamized—in the sense of greater promotion and adoption of normative Islamic disciplinary practices in public life—and conducive to the cultivation of virtuous Muslim selves. Mohamad learned first basic and then more advanced Islamic knowledge at home, schools, and *masjids*. His father facilitated his instruction and motivated him to practice and embody piety in his consistent performance of congregational prayers in the masjid and proper comportment with girls and young women. Mohamad, in turn, has become a socializing agent for his younger siblings and the next generation by transmitting Islamic knowledge to them. He does not view the mingling of young women and men in educational and social settings as contrary to sharia as long as the moral limits are not violated, such as through inappropriate physical contact or proximity in private settings. He argues for strengthening Islamic education in home and school contexts with the definite aim of putting this knowledge into practice.

*   *   *

Wan Hafizi's sharia personal narrative also presents an image of a consistently pious life from an early age. After meeting Wan Hafizi on a previous occasion, I scheduled an appointment to interview her at a KFC on the upper level of Kuala Lumpur Sentral. She brought a friend with her, Siti, a fellow finance student at the International Islamic University, Malaysia (UIA). They were off from classes for the weekend but still had some assignments to complete. They both wore polite clothing, closing their *aurat*. Wan Hafizi wore a black robe with a colorful *tudung*, and her friend wore a long top and *tudung* with a long, loose skirt. Wan Hafizi, from Kelantan, is twenty-two, and her friend twenty-one years old.

I ASKED MY MOTHER TO BUY ME A SCARF WHEN I WAS EIGHT

My father, from when I was small, invited me to read Al-Qur'an, and we prayed together in congregation, and we always made sure we had time together. My father's father was a very religious person, and also my father, and so I am definitely like them. From when I was small they instructed me in reciting Qur'an, and during primary school there was a religious school also, and then in secondary school I went to an Islamic school in Kelantan . . . and then I went to UIA because of the Islamic environment in UIA. . . . We have to wear loose clothing covering our *aurat*, and all students have to attend Islamic study groups, and they are trying to implement a regulation in which brothers and sisters sit separately in the library and cafeteria. But some students are not in favor of it. In the library, as far as we can see, students sit separately between genders. But in the cafeteria they may be doing discussion sometimes and work on the projects together but still sit separately, boys and girls . . .

I asked my mother to buy me a scarf when I was eight. When I was small, I liked to see people covering up. . . . I have some male friends, but if they saw me without my *tudung* I would feel miserable and that something is not right. I would feel ashamed because covering our *aurat* is an *amanah*; it's our responsibility. It is not forced. Actually, when I was young, I always liked to read books, especially Islamic historical stories. My father would always buy me books for my birthday present. I don't know if it is because of *iman* [Islamic faith] or not, but I always loved reading about the lives of Prophet Muhammad and his wives, about the women during those times, like Sūmayya, and I always admired them, and 'Āisha and Khadīja. Maybe that's why, because I already read those things, since I was small. . . . They were so scared of Allah, so much love for Allah. . . .

We also apply sharia in decisions in our lives according to the objectives of sharia. For example, if you want to buy something, which one do you prefer . . . so we have to give priorities to the thing to buy first . . . because we have the teenage feeling that we want to buy all those things. But we are here to learn and to gain knowledge and not to do other things . . . so when I make a decision between my desire, the things I like, or to just take the money for myself. . . . For example, in buying clothes, I accompany my friends and I really want to buy clothes, too, because all my clothes are the same and I have been wearing them for three or four years. . . . I have an interest in buying new clothes, but I keep thinking that I can buy new clothes in the future and I can still wear my clothes. They are still nice so I don't need to be wasteful and just to spend for those things, so I just keep it. . . . Many youth buy clothes to show that they are rich and for status, but this is just wastefulness and we would rather use it for studying or something.

I normally will spend some time to pray *Tahajjud* some nights, and another night I may pray *Hajat* or *Istikhārah*.[8] Some nights I will pray all three. But sometimes I just choose one and recite Al-Qur'an and wait for *subuh* [prayer time before sunrise]. And then after *subuh*, I will stay up and not sleep. According to Islam it is best to stay up after *subuh*. I stay up and recite prayers. I recite *Sunna* supplications every morning and also every late afternoon. . . . Sometimes I pray *Istikhārah* because every day we have to make decisions and I fear that I may make the wrong decision . . . Sometimes Allah will answer much later, so I perform this prayer three times. . . . Also one of my routines is to always recite *Sūrah Al-Wāqi'a* after *Maghrib* prayers because during my secondary school I read this one book that said that reciting *Al-Wāqi'a* opens up the *rezeki* [sustenance] and *Alhamdulillah* I can feel that I get lots of *rezeki*. There are lots of different kinds of *rezeki*. My friend, [Siti's brother], wanted to marry this girl and he recited *Al-Wāqi'a* every night. And he has already married her.[9]

Similar to Mohamad Zuhaidi, Wan grew up in a normative Islamic community of practice. Her father and late grandfather were religious people that socialized her with a strong emphasis on Islamic values and norms. She studied at Islamic schools in Kelantan from a young age and participated in congregational prayers and Qur'anic recitation with elders in her family. Wan's father also sparked her interest in reading Islamic books on various topics, including stories about the lives of virtuous Muslim women in early Islamic history. Wan and Siti both spoke about how these women are exemplary models for them to cultivate within themselves intense fear and love for Allah. Wan, at the young age of eight, asked her mother for a *tudung*. She and her friend expressed the feelings of shame and discomfort they would have around friends without their properly modest clothing covering their bodies. In contrast to Mohamad's views about the permissibility of men and women mingling in educational settings, these two young women agreed on the correctness of religious regulations at the International Islamic University that included the public performance of normative piety in the separation of students according to gender in libraries and cafeterias. Furthermore, Wan and others in her moral community often perform optional prayers, such as *Tahajjud*, *Hajat*, and *Istikhārah*, worshiping Allah in the middle of the night and asking for divine guidance and blessings. She also cultivates and embodies piety by staying up after morning prayers to recite *Sunna* supplications and after evening prayers to recite *Sūrah Al-Wāqi'a* (Q. 56). After the conclusion of this interview, I bought them both a chicken dinner and left them to eat it alone out of respect for their religious dispositions to not mingle unnecessarily with a man.

*   *   *

The final sharia narrative I will present here is from Cik Firdaus Koh, a fifty-two-year-old man, who converted (or "reverted") to Islam twenty years ago in order to marry a Malay woman. This was the third time we met. After returning from visiting his wife's family in a northern state, Firdaus asked me and my wife, Rachida, to attend a Hari Raya Aidilfitri open house with them at the home of a University of Malaya professor. They picked us up from a local train station near the event and drove us to their friend's house. Firdaus wore a *kopiah* with slacks and a dress shirt, and his wife, Nurul, wore a *baju kurung* and *tudung*. Following two hours of delicious Malaysian Raya cuisine and intense conversations with the host and other guests, they drove us back to the train station. I asked Firdaus if we could stop somewhere en route where I could interview him. He drove to a *masjid* in the area, we performed our evening prayers, after which we found a small room in the back where I asked him to share his personal sharia story.

THERE IS SOME WISDOM IN WHY IT HAPPENED TO ME

It was not easy for me as a "revert" to Islam, especially for the Chinese people. These converts, sometimes we call them reverts to Islam. It was mainly for marriage purpose[s], between Muslim and non-Muslim, twenty years ago. At that time, I was thirty-two years old. Of course, I married a Malay woman. I went through a lot of problems right from the beginning with my parents. My parents were old-fashioned. They came from China, and they were traditional Buddhists or mixed already. There [are] no longer any real pure Buddhists or Taoists; they have all become mixed already. They are all mixed together, that is why they have become like what Malays call *rojak*. . . . So, born into that family and being Chinese-educated for the first ten years of my school life, of course, I was brought up in Chinese ethics— that is, Confucius teachings, you know. It was a very good thing that we had one subject in Chinese school right from primary school called civic studies. Actually, it is moral studies; the proper term in English is moral studies, mostly Confucian values and some Taoism. It was good for me and I thought this knowledge of morality was good enough for me, when I was beginning, to carry on living as a Muslim. So, at that time, also there were not classes available everywhere for Islamic studies. The only place you want to learn probably is in the *masjid*, and when you are a new revert to Islam you are very skeptical, at least myself, and a bit afraid to go into a mosque. This morbid fear, you can call it an unfounded fear, something that is blocking; you cannot get to the *masjid*. And if I, at that time, went to the *masjid*, I would probably be the only one Chinese in the *masjid*. It is not so easily accessible to enter the Islamic classes; that was probably one of the reasons why I never got started in Islamic studies. So I was mostly on my own, on my moral values, and I went about my family life and career life with no major problems.

I did very well in my career actually as an electrical engineer at Telekom Malaysia. For nineteen years I was there. As I look back, the strange thing is that Telekom is a government-based company, mostly Muslims, maybe 80 or 90 percent of the employees are Muslims, and nobody at all spoke to me about Islam, you know, close friends, Muslim converts. A strange thing, you know. I cannot put the blame on people, you see, it was my own fault not to expose myself to classes. They were available [at] PERKIM; I was in Kuala Lumpur [and felt their classes were a] quite faraway kind of thing.[10] So I cannot totally put the blame on my fellow Muslims for not telling me about Islam. Actually, the main thing is my own fault for not [getting] involved in the classes or even just [reading] books about Islam. At the time, I was thirty plus, so the focus was on developing the career and trying to get promotions and so on. So I spent all my time in pursuit of career. And I must say I did, for a Chinese, quite well. I got a promotion fast, and even after only ten years I was a manager already. I even got a company car after fifteen years. But for *ibadah* I must say I neglected. Basic things, yes, simple *solat*, I was not regular. Fasting okay, somehow fasting attracted me. Other things, no major sins, I don't drink or smoke, no bad habits. So I thought that was good as a Muslim.

And I was quite ambitious in pursuing wealth. . . . Around 1985, when the company became privatized, we were given shares. This is the time I got exposed in stocks, and when I got deeper into it, in 1997, came the market crash, and I lost everything. And that was the time my wife decided to say goodbye. That was the worse thing to happen to my life. I could never have envisioned that I could have divorce in my life. So, in 2000, it happened officially. In 1999 was the time that I started to think very deeply, what is this religion about? Does it really place so much importance on wealth or on other things? So I started to learn Islam seriously in 1999 and, from that time, I never went back. Everyday I would be in religious classes and I found this Islamic NGO, which helped me really pursue the studies in Islam. I had a few very good Islamic teachers that really guided me. I found out so many things about Islam. All these perceptions that people blame on Islam, actually it is the Muslims themselves that portray a bad image of Islam. *Alhamdulillah.* That is my story from then until now. From 1999 until now I am still attending Islamic classes. . . . Well, it is something we call the grace of Allah, which we cannot really explain. I have come to realize it is something we call *hidayah* [divine guidance]. Some people may learn Islam their whole life but still don't get the *hidayah* and they still remain as non-Muslims. There are some people like that. I guess [the] first, immediate reaction is that I needed spiritual comfort. When you are in disaster, somehow you feel that there is a super being that you must get some comfort from . . . so when you are in trouble, you ask God is this something that should happen to me? . . . That was my initial reaction, but as I got deeper into getting Islamic knowledge I came to understand that there is a super being that is controlling everything, and the more I got in touch with good Muslims the more I found consolation and comfort. I also came to realize that this disaster is something that is good for me. There is some wisdom in why it happened to me. That was wonderful, very wonderful, and this is actually the teaching of Islam: when there is a *musibah* [misfortune] then there is something lying behind it. . . . There is something else better in store for me.

When you are really into it and seriously looking for the answer, Allah gives it to you. Allah gives you the solution. Like the saying goes, when you try to reach out to Allah and you just make the move, you run, and He will fly to you. It depended on my sincerity in looking for the answer and looking for the comfort; they both came together. The *ibadah* and the implementation of sharia just came naturally. . . . First thing, you must have the knowledge and I have been involved for so many years after learning, what are the obligations, what things are *haram* and *halal*, not just in terms of food, but also in terms of actions, in terms of thoughts, in terms of relations with Allah and with human beings. We really have to have the knowledge; without it you cannot differentiate between *haram* and *halal*. Once you have the knowledge and with the guidance of your teachers, you will become conscious of your thoughts and actions, your deeds. That is the whole Islamic life, and to put that into practice, at least myself, you are brave enough to step into the *masjid* and then everything else comes very naturally. You become brave and you are concerned about your dos and don'ts and you are no longer afraid of people in the *masjid* even if you are the only Chinese there. This is all through the grace of Allah. You put everything step by step, and as long as you have the intention to be a good Muslim, He will guide you. So there is no more looking back. . . . Three years later, by chance, I met my present wife. We were both attending a class in Islamic studies. Because Allah willed it my next marriage turned out to be much better. She was searching for Islamic knowledge, too, and she doesn't mind that I was poor. That was a beautiful thing. . . . This was a blessing. From then on, 2005, with Allah's will, someone just sponsored me to make my *hajj*. It was the environment I was in and I was working around a lot of people and it was Allah's way to touch their heart to help me back, which I never asked for anything like that. I got the news. You never ask for it but it came as a blessing. I had the intention to make my repentance in the Holy Land and it just came like that. No one can explain it.[11]

Cik Firdaus Koh grew up in a Chinese Buddhist-Taoist family that sent him to Chinese schools. The civics or moral classes, which instructed students in Confucian values and norms, appeared to have a lasting impact on his practice even after he converted to Islam in order to marry a Malay woman, much to the chagrin of his traditional Chinese family. These values continued to direct his actions in his family and work life, and were not displaced by Islamic ethics in the eight years from the time he converted in 1992 to 1999, when his first wife initiated divorce proceedings. During this period, Firdaus did not receive any religious instruction from his Muslim friends and coworkers and he did not seek out religious studies from Islamic institutions. His narrative reflects the experiences of many Chinese converts that are shunned by their families and marginalized in the majority Malay Muslim community (see Daniels 2005, 197–208). It was not until he experienced the twin disasters of losing his material wealth and suffering divorce that normative Islamic discourses began to influence his views and practices. Unlike some converts that look to officially return to their original religions when their marriage to a Muslim falls apart, Firdaus sought out Islamic knowledge and made a personal transformation to a life of piety. He continues to attend organized Islamic studies classes and puts this knowledge into practice, which he feels comes naturally when motivated by a sincere desire and intention to be a good Muslim. Firdaus founded an Islamic NGO and became part of a broad network of Chinese, Indians, and Malays involved in *dakwah* activities. In the midst of his studies and organizational work he met Nurul, his present wife, who accepted him despite his material poverty, and someone unexpectedly sponsored his trip to Mecca to fulfill his *ibadah* of *hajj*. Cik Firdaus Koh casts his experiences of finally acquiring Islamic knowledge after several years of legal conversion and receiving unexpected "blessings" after misfortune, as resulting from *hidayah* and *hikmah* lying behind the *musibah*. Moreover, Haji Firdaus has come to a place in his self-reflections of not blaming his fellow Malay Muslims for not sharing Islamic knowledge with him, but rather taking responsibility for his lack of personal initiative in seeking religious instruction. He performs an inspirational story of spiritual transformation that calls Muslims to actively search for deeper knowledge of their religion and to correct their misplaced priorities and materialistic orientation.

CONCLUSION

Public behavior, responses to surveys, and sharia personal narratives clearly indicate the strong influence of religious disciplinary practices on the lives, views, and voices of Malaysian Muslims. Widespread body techniques of modest public attire, restrained comportment, performance of obligatory ritual prayers, and fast-opening meals embody sharia ethical notions stressed in authoritative discourses of religious institutions and *ulama*. While normative Islamic forces are in general agreement about the requirement for men and women to cover their *aurat*, including the heads of women and the knees of men, there is some disagreement over the most appropriate Islamic style of dress. Some members of Islamic NGOs, *dakwah* organizations, and political Islamic movements prefer long robes for men and women, *kopiah* and turbans for men, and long *tudung* and socks or stockings covering the feet for women. On the other hand, UMNO, Malay rights organizations, and some Islamic NGOs promote *baju melayu* and *baju kurung* as Malay "traditional" dress, which also fulfills the religious necessity of properly covering the body. For them, these forms of attire are both Malay and Islamic, thus reflecting and reinforcing their conflation of Malay and Muslim identities. Some government religious officials and *ulama* also contrast their embodiment of Islamic modernity with the "backwardness" of PAS *ulama*, while the latter, in turn, consider the former's body techniques to be more about secular modernity than Islam. Likewise, there is consensus among normative Islamic forces about prohibiting the physical contact and secluded proximity of unmarried men and women, but some disagree over the permissibility of the mingling of genders without any improper contact and in public spaces. These diverse views were reflected in public practices as well as in the sharia personal narratives of Mohamad and Wan. Overall, the sharia personal narratives—whether the storyteller was consistently instilled with piety from an early age or on a path of personal transformation—revealed the increasingly Islamized social and cultural milieu constructed through the efforts of a variety of resurgent religious forces over the last four decades. Surveys of views about the general implementation of sharia, the handling of apostates, and the gendered dimensions of sharia also exhibited the hegemonic influence of normative religious discourses, although some liberal reformist discourses, especially those issued from the Sisters in Islam, have made an impact.

Nevertheless, these observations, surveys, and interviews also show that secular disciplinary practices have influenced the body techniques and outlook of many Malaysian Muslims. Aliza's and Lili's sharia personal narratives speak of the ways secular ideas and body techniques have been important aspects of their lives in diverse urban settings and communities of practice. While Aliza has transformed her secular body into a religious body, Lili was still in the midst of trying to recondition her secular body to perform acts of piety. In addition, my observations of the public attire and comportment of some Muslim youth suggest that secular discourses and ideas have instilled in them a fun-loving and pleasure-seeking sense of self. They violate sharia laws and ethical norms about public decency, alcohol consumption, *khalwat*, and related sexual infractions. However, some youth combine a secular, modern dose of personal autonomy with liberal Islamic ethics as they socialize with their romantic interests without transgressing the clear moral limits. A few of my interlocutors maintained that human rights are more effectively upheld in civil courts rather than in sharia courts, and one of them argued for privatization of religion and for the state to stay out of regulating personal violations of the precepts of Islam.

On the other hand, my research also indicates that individual practices have an impact on socially authoritative discourses. Many of the Muslim youth and adults habituated to performing public acts of piety also want to see more extensive implementation of sharia throughout society and want to de-secularize the broader politico-legal and constitutional structures. For instance, Mohamad calls for more emphasis on enhancing religious understandings in home and school, with the goal of putting Islamic knowledge more heavily into practice in society. Likewise, Wan and Siti were in favor of sharia regulations on their university campus and *hudud* and *qisas* throughout the country. My interlocutors going through personal transformations, such as Aliza and Firdaus, develop new ideas and insights that comment on or critique some aspects of authoritative discourses. As Aliza began to visit the *masjid*, performed her obligatory ritual prayers, and corrected features of her inner self, new insights emerged about the shortcomings of the UMNO and PAS political approaches vis-à-vis the needs of poor Malays. Her individually initiated campaigns to assist poverty-stricken families have the potential of influencing the discourses and policies of these two key players in Malaysian Muslim politics. Similarly, Firdaus's experiences—as a Chinese "revert" to Islam who founded an Islamic NGO and speaks of his personal spiritual journey—makes an impact on the socially authoritative discourses about converts, race and religion, and Islamic economics. These individual practices contain the potential of generating conciliatory ideas and approaches to clashes among Malay, Islamic, and people's sovereignties and between those involving sharia and liberal rights.

CONCLUSION

Sharia Cultural Models and Sociopolitical Projects

SHAPING THE DISCOURSES ABOUT SHARIA ARE THREE MAJOR aspects of the broader context—all occurring in Malaysia and, in some ways, spanning the globe—that are symptomatic of the transformations of our contemporary era. In Malaysia, for over five decades, people have experienced political independence, modern constitutionalism, nation building, and the lingering institutional and cultural effects of colonialism. Malaysians' experiences with these changes are comparable to those of other newly emergent postcolonial nation-states of the twentieth century and also to many "creole" nation-states of the Western Hemisphere or British Commonwealth of early historical periods. They have all been confronted with the modern concepts of nation-state, citizenship, civil liberties and, eventually, international human rights. Second, Malaysia has experienced four decades of Islamic resurgence that has more widely disseminated religious knowledge and organized institutions throughout society. The Malaysian government has built numerous *masjids*, established Islamic educational institutions, heightened implementation of sharia family and criminal laws, and organized a national system of *halal* certification and a highly regulated system of Islamic finance. PAS and several Islamic NGOs have established and supported an extensive network of Islamic schools; institutionalized small religious study groups and large religious talks, seminars, and forums; and promoted the embodiment of piety. Government, PAS-affiliated, and independent *ulama* have also distributed books and articles in various media on religious topics. This Islamic resurgence has been a global phenomenon, and the flow of its diverse ideas has crossed national borders. Islamic revitalization movements brought the intensified notions of Muslim community, returning to Qur'an and *Sunna*, and establishing an Islamic state into contact with ideas related to modern nation-states. In Malaysia, as in many other parts of the Muslim world, the idea of restoring sharia to a level of precolonial prominence has been integral to the frameworks of these resurgent movements.

Third, for over two decades, overlapping with the processes of nation building and Islamic resurgence, there has been a development and organization of cross-communal, multiethnic, multireligious political coalitions to contest the domination of the UMNO-led National Front, which has ruled the Federation of Malaysia since the advent of political independence in 1957. These cross-communal coalitions have served the ruling front its first major electoral losses in the general elections of 2008 and 2013. They have also brought intensified conceptions of liberalism, pluralism, and democracy into close contact with ideas of the nation-state and Islamic resurgence. As a political movement for transformation of the authoritarian Malaysian state, these cross-communal coalitions may be viewed as comparable to a wave of movements around the world striving to replace long-standing postcolonial political elites with new political forces. Grounded in a notion of cultural knowledge as lying behind spoken and written discourse and embodied in practice, this study has offered a multisited ethnographic exploration of both various conceptions of sharia distributed among Muslims and non-Muslims and the way they articulate with other ideas circulating in Malaysian society.

Much contemporary research on politics and culture in Muslim societies continues to adopt the interpretative approach that inappropriately utilizes a semantic theory designed for the lexical meanings of words to provide "intelligible" interpretations of cultural understandings. In recent years, this interpretative approach has been combined with social theories of power, producing interesting, but often flawed, interpretations due to their basis on faulty representations of cultural knowledge. The anthropology of knowledge approach employed in this study is useful for describing and analyzing conceptual structures, practice, and context, and thereby for discerning the links between politics and culture. Diverse cultural models or schemas, which local people used to reason about the role of sharia in everyday life and society and to direct various forms of social and political practice, may thus be inferred from discourse and behavior.[1]

Social forces across Malaysian society, comprising Muslims and non-Muslims alike, combine notions of sharia with other forms of cultural knowledge. Among Malay political elites, government religious officials, civil servants and *ulama*, Malay rights organizations, Islamic NGOs and PAS, and Muslim leaders of PKR, conceptions of sharia articulate with a range of other ideas to constitute cultural models. In addition, the leaders and members of DAP, liberal rights activists, and secular human rights organizations use cultural models to reason about the role of sharia and to direct their social and political activities. However, in the bulk of research about sharia, studies focus on only one of these social forces—for instance, only the state or piety movements, or Islamic or secular NGOs. While these studies provide important insights into the ideas and practices of these particular groups and, at times, their attendant sociopolitical orientations and projects, they generally fail to examine the interactions between a broad field of social forces and therefore are unable to illuminate the sociopolitical processes these interactions produce. We have observed in this study the diverse cultural models and sociopolitical projects of a wide range of social forces, and the form of interactions and social dynamics between them. Debates over implementation of sharia laws and ethics and surrounding public dramas of contention have illustrated the dynamic processes involving these diverse social forces. Many of these interactions and sharia dynamics pertain to civil liberties, international human rights, liberal pluralism, gender, secularism, modernity, political Islam, and Malay and Islamic sovereignty.

CIVIL LIBERTIES, INTERNATIONAL HUMAN RIGHTS, AND SHARIA

Although the Federal Constitution bestows jurisdiction on sharia courts to punish Muslim violators of the precepts of Islam, there has been a lively public debate over whether the state *should* be involved in these aspects of personal behavior. Secular human rights organizations, SIS, and many liberal Muslim intellectuals in their networks have argued for the state to not interject itself into individual issues of morality. From their perspective, Muslims should have the liberty to decide on whether to adhere to Islamic ethical norms of their own free will, without any threats of coercion from the state. Moreover, they view these personal liberties for Muslims and non-Muslims to be a fundamental human right to exercise their freedom of conscience. Civil and human rights activists from secular NGOs use cultural models that construe religious ethical matters as personal affairs, not public affairs for legal and political authorities to enforce. Liberal Muslim reformers also share this view, adding that it is best for Muslim believers to have the opportunity to exercise their faith and to follow Islamic ethical norms of their own accord, based on their moral convictions rather than state compulsion. These secular and liberal Muslim organizations are major nodes in Malaysian society for the circulation of hegemonic global ideas about civil liberties and fundamental human rights. Rather than viewing transnational flows of ideas as if they are deterritorialized, we have seen local social forces here within the broader national field of Malaysian society. In contrast to comparable forces in many other societies, these groups are subordinate forces, offering alternative perspectives that contest hegemonic views. However, these local proponents of human rights have the authority of powerful international forces behind their discourses, a fact that contributes to local sharia dynamics. On the other hand, Malay political elites, government religious officials and *ulama*, Malay rights organizations, PAS, and Islamic NGOs, operating with a variety of pro-sharia cultural models, argue that it is the Muslim government's responsibility to enforce the precepts of Islam, which are understood to be Allah's laws sent via the Qur'an and the Traditions of His Final Messenger, Prophet Muhammad. Respondents to at-large sharia surveys also were overwhelmingly in favor of the state implementing sharia family and criminal laws.

The Lina Joy case and others related to religious freedom have been the focus of many contentious debates between these social forces. SIS, IRF, and PKR leaders joined with secular human rights forces to support Lina Joy's and other Muslims' right to convert out of Islam without any form of sharia criminal punishment. Although there is much overlap in the ideas of these liberal Muslim reformist forces, there are some differences in their sharia cultural models and sociopolitical projects. SIS is a Muslim feminist organization that combines reinterpretations of sacred sources and liberal notions of the objectives of sharia with hegemonic Western conceptions of secular modernity and gender equality. Similarly, IRF is a Muslim reformist organization that intertwines liberal versions of Islamic ethics with conceptions of liberalism, pluralism, human rights, and a secular nation-state. Muslim PKR leaders draw on reformist notions of the objectives of sharia mixed with visions of an inclusive, multiethnic, multireligious liberal pluralist nation-state to unify a cross-communal coalition to contest the UMNO-led National Front. These Muslim human rights forces united with the social democratic DAP and secular human rights NGOs with whom they share a consensus on religious freedom for all Malaysians. In contrast, a broad array of conservative Muslim forces contend that Muslims must not be allowed to commit apostasy, moving from Islamic belief to non-Islamic belief. UMNO and PERKASA, both operating with Malay sovereignty cultural models—the former mixed with a version of the Islamic notion of moderation and the latter with more explicitly chauvinistic attitudes—stress that Malays possess a special impediment to becoming apostates: the fact that they are defined as Muslims in the Federal Constitution. UMNO is generally in favor of civil liberties and international human rights, except in areas that clearly contradict traditional Islamic law and principles. Apostasy is one area in which they take a firm position for limiting individual liberties. PAS and Islamic NGOs, operating with less racialized Islamic sovereignty cultural models, argue that all Muslims must be punished according to the sacred sources—or, as Nik Aziz (2010, 27) put it, "the Constitution of the Sky"—and that the punishment should be death. Islamic NGOs generally promote more widespread education and *dakwah* before such a *hudud* penalty is implemented, but PAS is currently striving to operationalize a version of their 1993 *hudud* bill in Kelantan. Many sharia court officials and other government *ulama* are in favor of implementing *hudud* as well, but they are working under the auspices of secular nationalist Malay political elites that are committed to lesser discretionary punishments. Government think tanks have formulated an apostasy provision that distinguishes between Muslims and the variety of Malaysian citizens that have mistakenly become registered and/or recognized as Muslims. The former would be punished with discretionary punishment if they try to depart from Islam, while the latter would be able to apply for a declaration of their religious status as non-Muslims. Government *ulama* hope that this one modern Islamic law will eventually replace the three forms of laws pertaining to apostasy-related cases across the states of Malaysia.

There has also been a series of telling disputes over underage marriage and child custody in conversion cases. Secular and Muslim human rights organizations have called for an end to sharia courts allowing youth under the age of eighteen to get married and permitting Muslim converts to unilaterally convert their non-Muslim children and subsequently to be given custody of them. They consider the current sharia family laws that set the youngest age for marriage as eighteen for men and sixteen for women as discriminatory, arguing that young women need more time to develop and to seek education. These social forces are also opposed to the provisions that give sharia court judges the discretionary authority to permit marriages at even younger ages. Moreover, they invoke international human rights laws pertaining to the rights of children. Conservative Muslim forces assert that there is no minimum age of marriage according to sacred sources. However, propelled by continued public debates over underage marriage cases, the National Fatwa Council issued a ruling that maintained the current ages and authority of the judges to permit younger children to marry but argued for greater restrictions on allowing these underage marriages, citing research that indicates that such marriages are detrimental to the well-being and benefit of girls and society. In contrast, only the Perlis State Fatwa Committee issued a ruling responding to the widespread controversies over child custody in conversion cases within a marriage of two non-Muslims. Most state-level sharia courts continued to allow the Muslim parties to convert children of civil marriages and to be favored for custody. The exceptional Perlis state fatwa stresses the benefit of the children, rather than the Muslim religious status of one of the parents, to determine child custody. This contrasting treatment of underage marriage of girls and child custody in conversion cases is part of a broader pattern of greater interaction and interdependence between Muslim feminist and UMNO-led sociopolitical projects than between the latter and secular liberal rights projects.

LIBERAL PLURALISM AND MALAY AND ISLAMIC SOVEREIGNTY

There are numerous cases that indicate the sociopolitical tensions over liberal pluralism and Malay and/or Islamic sovereignty. Similar to public skirmishes over child custody, there has been long-standing public controversy over the requirement of non-Muslims to convert to Islam in order to marry Muslims. Many secular human rights organizations and non-Muslims at large argue for eliminating any state-enforced requirements for these marriage-related conversions, in favor of facilitating greater national integration of Malaysia's diverse social groups. Some even nostalgically invoke past historical epochs when local indigenous women "followed" their Chinese and Indian husbands in practicing the Buddhist-Taoist or Hindu religions of their ancestors. Non-Muslims also disagree with the intervention of Muslim religious authorities in the marriages and funerals of non-Malays registered as Muslims. However, normative Muslim forces are squarely opposed to any such contraventions of sharia family laws and some even resent non-Muslims fondly recalling past times in which Muslims were not attendant to the norms of their own faith, Islam.

Likewise, disputes over the formation of an "Inter-Faith Commission," the raid of a Methodist church in Selangor, and the use of the word "Allah" by a Catholic weekly publication indicate the interplay of sociopolitical projects over issues related to liberal pluralism and Malay and Islamic sovereignty. Malaysians from various non-Muslim religious backgrounds viewed the establishment of an Inter-Faith Commission as a vehicle for dialogue with political authorities in order to facilitate greater integration and mutual respect. Moreover, secular and Muslim human rights activists were in support of such an institution to negotiate inclusive resolutions to issues of religious freedom, Muslim conversion, and child custody in previously non-Muslim families. The fact that many Malaysian Muslims, reasoning with various normative sharia models, interpreted Muslim reformers involved with the Article 11 movement for religious freedom to be "deviant" Muslims holding heterodox beliefs reflects the lack of interdependence between these opposing discourses. Furthermore, many Malaysian Muslims felt threatened by the perceived international support from foreign Christian organizations for these liberal rights forces. The initial move of Malay political elites to organize such a commission was reversed after a coalition of Islamic NGOs vehemently criticized this proposed institution as undermining the special position of Islam in Malaysia and threatening the faith altogether.

Similarly, mediating Islamic NGOs pressured PAS to shift its initial "cosmopolitan" positions on the raid of a Methodist church event attended by several Muslims and the use of the word "Allah" by a Catholic weekly publication. In both cases, PAS joined the chorus of normative Muslim voices, ranging from UMNO and Malay rights organizations to Islamic NGOs, calling for an end to Christian proselytizing among Muslims and for the immediate passage of an apostasy bill. These skirmishes indicate that mediating Islamic NGOs, operating with a combination of Malay and Islamic sovereignty sharia cultural models, can check secular nationalist Malay political elites and the political Islamic party when they perceive them to be taking positions that weaken the dominant stature of Islam in the body politic. Thus, although UMNO and PAS often find themselves in conflict over control of religious institutions and the contrasting basis of their political parties, they are consistently pulled to unite with each other and Islamic NGOs to uphold the supremacy of Islam against the increasingly intense challenges from a phalanx of secular and Muslim human rights activists attempting to forward sociopolitical projects for civil liberties, liberal pluralism, and secular modernity. Analysis of the discourse of interacting sociopolitical projects related to several public debates and controversies facilitates elucidation of the character of discursive engagement, which is highly contentious, uncompromising, and lacking in significant interdependence.

GENDER EQUALITY AND REFORM

The Sisters in Islam actively debate government *ulama*, conservative nongovernmental forces, and the Malay political elites over many aspects of sharia family laws that relate to gender. They criticize the standardized family law provisions pertaining to underage marriage, male marriage and family guardians, limited marriage contract stipulations, disobedient wives, polygamy, and divorce. From their perspective, these provisions discriminate against women, reinforce patriarchal norms, and do not fit with everyday experiences of women in contemporary families. SIS argues for reform of these laws, moving them in the direction of their conception of gender equality and justice and thereby fulfilling the overarching objectives of sharia. Their ideas of husbands and wives being partners or coheads of households is integral to their overall sociopolitical project advocating a form of secular modernity. Conservative nongovernmental forces, government *ulama*, and Malay political elites operate with traditional sharia models that understand properly organized Islamic families as consisting of male heads, providers, and protectors and female nurturers and caregivers. If family members are not playing these roles in everyday practice, then conservatives think the families need to be changed to better fit with the laws based on traditional interpretations of sacred texts. Although Malay political elites and government *ulama* acknowledge that their framework differs from that of the Sisters in Islam, they still invite SIS representatives to seminars and dialogues about sharia family laws. Furthermore, they have reformed sharia family laws by standardizing the requirement that both prospective husband and wife consent to a marriage, regulating male pronouncements of divorce, placing permission for polygamy in the hands of the sharia court judge, including domestic violence as grounds for stipulated and at-fault divorces, and adopting Mālikī legal positions that make it easier to provide evidence of domestic violence. While these reforms are not directly adopting the SIS proposals, they are responding to the concerns of Muslim feminists within an otherwise traditional framework.

My sharia surveys also demonstrate that although the SIS perspective is marginalized, considered lacking in Islamic knowledge, and even "extremist," the Sisters in Islam are still having an impact on the discourses of young women. Indeed, the normative Islamic cultural model is widely disseminated and internalized by Malaysian Muslims young and old, male and female, but a small segment of them are critical of the provisions on disobedient wives and polygamy and the idea of a male head of household. Most of my respondents believe that men should be leaders of the nation, family, and *masjid*, but all of them expressed support for gender equality at work.

In the sharia economic models of Malay political elites operationalized in the growing Malaysian-state-regulated Islamic financial sector, women serve at comparatively high rates as sharia experts. Intercultural studies scholar Laura Elder (2017) demonstrates that Malaysian women play a significant role in interpreting sharia compliance and creating new products in the Islamic finance industry. However, in the sharia economic models of "corporate caliphs," Kelantan state officials, and Global Ikhwan more gender stratification is likely, given their use of political and domestic analogies that stress male leadership and female subordination and obedience. The Malaysian state's emphasis on combining Islamic ethics with notions of development and economic growth in an Islamic modernity project appears to facilitate a lessening of gender stratification. In contrast to the nature of interplay between liberal rights and normative Islamic projects, the quality of discursive engagement of Muslim feminists with Malay political elites tends to be more compromising and interdependent.

POLITICAL ISLAM, SECULARISM, AND MODERNITY

There are several forms of political Islam, secularism, and modernity interacting in Malaysian society. As we have seen, Malay political elites have established sharia family and criminal laws and infused Islamic ethics into the economy and other social institutions within the secular format inherited from the British colonial era. They remain committed to political Islam, even strengthening implementation of sharia laws and ethics and expanding the space of Islam in public life, within overarching secular legal, political, and constitutional structures. Recall that prime minister Najib Razak directed couples involved in conversion cases, caught between lower level civil and sharia courts, to turn to the Federal Court. This constrained, "moderate" political Islam is integral to their project of producing an Islamic modernity. Participant observation, interviews, and discussions with government *ulama*, religious officials, and civil servants has allowed me to shed some light on how their sharia cultural models vary from those of Malay political elites. Many of these respondents are part of generations of the Islamic resurgence that were heavily influenced by the ideas, emotions, and experiences related to political and piety movements of the last four decades. Malay political elites have filled the expanding religious bureaucracies and Islamic economy with these youth and adults of the Islamic resurgence as part of their Islamic modernity projects. Indeed, these religious scholars and officials operate with a sharia cultural model that entails combining many notions of modern development and administration within a traditional Islamic worldview. However, in contrast to Malay political elites, many of them are less committed to maintaining the secular format and want to see at least gradual progression toward a sociopolitical system that returns sharia to prominence beyond the bounds of secular legal, political, and constitutional structures. Islamic NGOs also devise their own educational and proselytizing projects to prepare the population for a shift in this direction, and some of them also establish miniature "Islamic states" throughout society.

The Islamic Party of Malaysia promotes another variety of political Islam that explicitly rejects the secular structural format and aims to attain power in order to establish an Islamic state and fully implement sharia laws and ethics throughout society. They are critical of the limited institutionalization of sharia criminal laws and economic ethics under the UMNO-led Malaysian state and castigate UMNO's sociopolitical project as secular. In addition, many PAS members consider UMNO-affiliated and government *ulama* as being co-opted and corrupted by positions and money. From their perspective, these social forces are not struggling for Islam and will not arrive at the full implementation of Allah's *hukum* because they are reveling in worldly pleasures and materialism. Integral to their ongoing ideological and political competition, the discursive engagements of UMNO and PAS entail considerable accommodation and interdependence as they both strive to convince the electorate and Malaysian Muslim community that their version of political Islam is the best. Nevertheless, they often are pushed to set aside their differences to unite against the perceived rising tide of foreign-inspired and -supported secularism and liberal-pluralist modernity.

Secular and Muslim human rights activists from DAP, PKR, IRF, SIS, and a host of nongovernmental organizations are clamoring in electoral campaigns, Parliament, state assemblies, seminars, social media, and on the streets for sociopolitical reform. These social forces struggle for various forms of secularism and modernity in Malaysia, all of which entail a diminishing of the racial and religious hierarchies. In addition, many Malaysian Muslim youth are influenced by secular discourses and cultural models, and some of them perform secular body techniques in public. As noted above, the interaction of these secular modernity projects with normative Islamic pro-sharia projects tend to be highly oppositional and lacking in conciliatory engagements. There appears to be an uncompromising clash of secular and political Islamic fundamentalisms. This study demonstrates that a close examination of the interplay between these various sociopolitical projects and the quality of their discursive engagements allows one to discern the direction of change. The ongoing Islamic resurgence, the competition between PAS and UMNO over Islamic credentials, and from the up and coming generations of pious Muslim youth were already pushing for greater shariatization. However, the direct and inflexible public challenging of the Malay Muslim–led sociopolitical order and the concomitant escalating polarization of liberal rights and normative sharia projects, has added incentive for dominant Malay political forces to move toward a more sharia-oriented state, lay greater stress on the Malay-preferred hierarchical image of the nation, and further infuse Islam into their versions of modernity. On the other hand, proponents of secular and liberal rights projects are digging in and intensifying their criticism of Malaysian Muslim leaders' efforts to infuse more sharia laws and ethics into public life and to buttress their control over the political system.

Conversely, if social forces from these two opposing camps were to begin discursive engagements with more accommodative, compromising, and interdependent positioning, new possibilities would emerge. To this end, I recommend that politically dominant Malay Muslims envision and produce more space for minority and individual rights within their normative Islamic worldviews and try to practice more *adab* (good manners) in relation to their neighbors and fellow Malaysians from non-Malay and non-Muslim backgrounds. Likewise, I recommend that subaltern secular and Muslim human rights activists adopt more flexible postures, allowing for more linking of Islam with the state and the infusion of sharia laws and ethics into public life.

NOTES

Introduction

1. See el-Zein 1977; Gilsenan 1982; Asad 1986; Varisco 2005; Kreinath 2012.
2. Scott Leonard and Michael McClure ([2004] 2008), after reviewing various approaches to myths or "ancient narratives that attempt to answer the enduring and fundamental human questions," conclude that each approach peels away a layer contributing to a multifaceted explanation of myth.
3. Shahab Ahmed (2016, 273) argues that Asad's linking of "orthodoxy" to his conception of Islam as a "discursive tradition" is too easily read in a prescriptive fashion that projects the production of orthodoxy as "the definitive purpose of the discursive tradition/Islam." To the contrary, Zareena Grewal (2014), using Asad's concepts of "discursive tradition" and "orthodoxy" in a much more open-ended and dynamic fashion, produces an informative ethnographic study of American Muslim student-travelers' debates and redefinitions of Islamic authenticity.
4. See Williams 1977; Bourdieu 1977; Foucault 1994; Ong 1999, 2002; Daniels 2005, 2013a, 2013b.
5. See Dougherty and Fernandez 1981, 1982; Shore 1991; Boyer 1993; Keller and Keller 1996; Daniels 2009.
6. See Mahmood 2005; Deeb 2006; Hirschkind 2006; Kessler 1978; Ong and Peletz 1995; Peletz 2002; Farish A. Noor 2003; Fischer 2008; Frisk 2009; Hoffstaedter 2011; Sloane-White 2011.
7. In the essay "The Politics of Meaning," Clifford Geertz (1973, 311–41) argues for the use of his interpretative approach to meaning to render political life "intelligible" and thereby theorizing the connection between politics and culture and making the discovery of general cultural conceptions less imprecise. However, many contemporary researchers, following his semantic approach to meaning, have not been able to avoid what he calls "a sort of perfected impressionism" (312).
8. See Witherspoon 1977; Agar and Hobbs 1985; Holland and Eisenhart 1990; Quinn 1982; Strauss 1992.
9. Here, I use cultural models and schemas interchangeably as shared cognitive structures, often stored in long-term memory, that bundle interrelated elements and are used for reasoning about something (see Daniels 2005, 79–80; D'Andrade 2005, 83–84).

1. Sharia in Malaysia

1. For instance, Shaikh 'Abd al-Qādir al-Jīlānī, a twelfth-century Sufi scholar prominent in the genealogies of many Sufi *tarekat* in Southeast Asia, stated, "Cast your lower self [*nafs*] into the Valley of Destiny [*wadi' l-qadar*] until, when its time has come, the top rung of your ladder makes contact with the door of nearness [to the Lord]. You will be welcomed by a face more lovely than all the charming beauty of this world and the hereafter. The fond affection [*mawadda*] between the pair of you will be complete. All obstacles and intermediaries will disappear. Then you will hear its [the lower self's] call for help from the Valley of His Destiny: 'Take charge of the deposits held in trust for you, and make full use of the service I can offer you. I am imprisoned over here, to your detriment or for your benefit.' Your nearness [to the Lord] will plead on its behalf, urging a positive response to its request. At this point the hand of knowledge [*'ilm*] will be extended to it, and the hand of the law [*hukm*] will come to its aid" ('Abd al-Qādir al-Jīlānī 1994, 59).
2. See Daniels 2009; Harnish and Rasmussen 2011; Hardwick 2013; and Laurie Ross 2013.
3. *Kahwin paksa* is still practiced by some and considered part of Malay *adat*. It appears prominently in some genres of popular culture (see Daniels 2013, 128–29).
4. Omer Awass (2017) considers the Al-Madjella to be part of the discursive changes in sharia that took place under European influence in which Muslim scholars began to produce rigidly codified legal works emulating European models of law.
5. I use the actual names of well-known public figures, except when requested to not identify them in all or part of an interview. In such cases, I use a pseudonym or do not name the speaker. For other individuals, I use pseudonyms to protect their identity.
6. Interview with Rahim Thamby Chik, August 2009, Kuala Lumpur, Malaysia.
7. Interview with Yusof bin Jantan, August 2009, Melaka, Malaysia.
8. UNESCO bestowed World Heritage City status on Melaka and Georgetown (Penang) in 2008.
9. Interview with Mohamad Suhaimi (pseud.), May 2000, Melaka, Malaysia.
10. Interview with Rajan (pseud.), January 1999, Melaka, Malaysia.
11. Interview with Abdul (pseud.), October 2010, Penang, Malaysia.
12. Interview with Mohideen (pseud.), November 1998, Melaka, Malaysia.
13. Interview with Robert Seet, February 1999, Melaka, Malaysia.
14. Interview with Haji Hassan (pseud.), August 2012, Kuala Lumpur, Malaysia.
15. Fernando (2012, 301) shows that between 1949 and 1951 the Communities Liaison Committee (CLC), consisting of Malay, Chinese, and Indian elites, held frank discussions addressing several "long-standing intercommunal issues such as Malay backwardness, citizenship and nationality, language and education."
16. Hooker (1983, 180–82) notes that Malaysian Muslim scholars were in the process of Islamizing colonial "Muhammadan" laws in the postwar period. That is, non-Muslim, European, secular definitions of Islamic law were being replaced with substantive laws based on standard *fiqh* texts. However, he remarked that there were serious institutional restrictions to the full realization of these "Islamizing" trends—namely, the absence of an Islamic state, the overriding jurisdiction of secular over sharia courts, and the derivation of sharia court procedural rules and process from the secular

model. This constitutional amendment raising the jurisdiction of sharia courts is one move in the direction of removing the roadblocks to a fuller politico-legal Islamization.

17. I did not witness any performances of these traditional arts in the Kota Bharu; however, Hardwick (2013), an anthropologist and folklorist, reports their continued existence and transformation in rural Kelantan, where they embody diverse senses of personal and normative piety.

18. Interview with Nik Abdul Aziz, July 2012, Kuala Lumpur, Malaysia.

19. Interview with Halim (pseud.), December 1999, Melaka, Malaysia.

20. Malaysian states have enacted sharia family laws that restrict intermarriage between Muslims and non-Muslims. The non-Muslim party is required to convert before marriage.

21. Interview with Ching (pseud.), October 1999, Melaka, Malaysia.

2. Family Law

1. Interview with Zawati, Haryaty, and Aisha (pseud.), October 2010, Putrajaya, Malaysia.

2. In 2008, the Perlis Department of Islamic Religion and the Perlis Shariah High Court decided that Selimah Mat, a Malay woman born a Muslim, was no longer a Muslim at the time of her death and could be buried according to Buddhist rites. Her younger sister claimed Selimah Mat had traveled to Thailand and married a Buddhist and later continued to practice Buddhism up to the time of her death. Similarly, in the case of Nyonya Tahir, the Shariah High Court Negeri Sembilan decided that although she was born a Malay Muslim she was no longer a Muslim at the time of her death. Halimah-ton Shaari, Ngu Teck Hua, and V. Raman (2006) compared newspaper coverage of the Nyonya Tahir and Moorthy cases and found that vernacular newspapers in Malaysia tend to cater to the interests of their particular racial groupings.

3. The civil law would apply to the non-Muslim party regardless of gender, but many of the highly publicized cases of conversion within a civil law marriage involve husbands converting to Islam. The sharia law provision that provides for the dissolution of the marriage is discussed below.

4. On January 27, 2014, the Selangor Department of Islamic Religion (JAIS; Jabatan Agama Islam Selangor) intervened at a wedding in a Hindu temple and arrested the bride, the thirty-two-year-old Zarena Abdul Majid, who was registered as a Muslim and therefore not legally allowed to marry a Hindu man. She claimed that her father registered her and her siblings as Muslims but she was raised as a Hindu after he abandoned the family (SUARAM 2015). This case caused a public uproar among liberal rights activists.

5. In Iran, the minimum age for a girl to marry is thirteen and for a boy is fifteen; in Algeria it is twenty-one for men and eighteen for women; in Jordan it is sixteen for men and fifteen for women; in Libya it is twenty for both men and women; and in Pakistan the minimum ages are the same as in Malaysia, but there are penal sanctions for contracting child marriages. Brunei and many other Muslim societies have not specified any minimum age for marriage (Black, Esmaeili, and Hosen 2013, 117).

6. Zaleha Kamarudin (2007, 79) observes that one of the Malaysian government's remaining reservations concerning CEDAW is that Article 16 (1)(a) conflicts with the sharia law and the laws of Malaysia in which the minimum age of marriage for women is sixteen and for men eighteen.

7. Interview with Hakim Suhaily, December 2010, Kuala Lumpur, Malaysia.

8. See www.e-fatwa.gov.my.

9. Tariq Ramadan (2009) and Jasser Auda (2008), two prominent Muslim philosophers, contend that contemporary jurists should draw on scientific studies before issuing rulings concerning the many areas in which law and science overlap in our contemporary world.

10. Companions or *Sahabat* were pious supporters of Prophet Muhammad who helped him to establish the Islamic way of life and polity from 610, when he began having divine revelations, to 632, when he died. Many of his Companions led and expanded the Islamic community after his passing.

11. Interview with Dato' Wira Syeikh Yahaya, December 2010, Alor Setar, Kedah.

12. *Mas kahwin*, the equivalent of *Mahr* in Arabic, is one of the basic Sunni marriage requirements. *Pemberian* are additional marriage gifts that vary across Muslim societies.

13. Interview with Zaleha Kamarudin, November 2010, Kuala Lumpur, Malaysia.

14. Interview with Zainah Anwar, January 2011, Petaling Jaya, Selangor, Malaysia.

15. In the Sisters in Islam booklet *Islam and Polygamy* (2002), Zaitun Mohamed Kasim, entertaining the question of whether polygamy was part of the Sunna of Prophet Muhammad, writes that he had a monogamous marriage with Siti Khadijah binti Khuwailid for twenty-eight years until her death—only then did he practice polygamy, which was a custom for Arabian society. However, he married mostly elderly widows with the aim of spreading Islam, a rationale that contrasts with reasons behind most polygamous marriages in contemporary Malaysia. Furthermore, Zaitun refers to a *hadith* in which Prophet Muhammad denied permitting his daughter's husband, Saidina Ali ibn Abi Talib, from marrying another woman. This appears to be an imprecise reference to the *hadith* reported in *Ṣaḥīḥ Al-Bukhārī* (1538; Imām Muhammad 1994), which clarifies that the Prophet rejected the marriage of Ali to the daughter of one of his enemies, Abu Jahl. This booklet does not refer to *hadiths* that demonstrate that the Prophet allowed other Muslim men to practice polygamy.

16. Interview with Norani Othman, October 2010, Petaling Jaya, Selangor, Malaysia.

17. Nik Noriani and Norhayati (2004) of SIS argue that many of the *hadiths* traditional scholars selectively draw on to structure marriage and marital relations, which demean and degrade women, are weak and of dubious authenticity.

18. Interview with Norani Othman, October 2010, Petaling Jaya, Selangor, Malaysia.

19. Ibrahim (2015, 213–14) describes Egyptian legislators, in passing Law 25 of 1929, as performing a form of "vertical pragmatic eclecticism" within the Ḥanafi school when they gave judges the authority to extend female custodianship to nine for boys and eleven for girls, shifting from the dominant view of the Ḥanafi school, which was seven for boys and nine for girls. The Law 100 of 1985 increased the ages to ten for boys

and twelve for girls, and Law 4 of 2005 amended this law, fixing the age at fifteen for both boys and girls.

20. See www.e-fatwa.gov.my.

3. Criminal Law

1. *Akikah* (Ar. *'aqiqa*) is a ceremony performed shortly after the birth of a child in which prayers are made for the benefit of the newborn child and often one or two sheep are sacrificed to express gratitude to Allah and for a collective meal.

2. Interview with Hakim Shukri, January 2011, Melaka, Malaysia.

3. See www.e-fatwa.gov.my.

4. Hodgson (1974, 125) notes that Greek Orthodox, Armenian, Jacobite (Syrian), Coptic Christian, and Jewish communities were organized as *dhimmi* millets and given great authority over their own group members under the Ottoman Empire. However, Shiʻi groups that were not assimilated into the official Ḥanafī-dominated Muslim *umma* were overlooked and kept under careful control; but, in some cases Shiʻi judges "were given the same semi-official recognition" as Shāfiʻīs or Mālikīs.

5. Interview with Hakim Suhaily, December 2010, Kuala Lumpur, Malaysia.

6. The Malay category *pondan*, and this judge's translation of it as "transsexual," potentially lumps together a broad range of gender and sexual diversity, including male cross-dressers, homosexuals, bisexuals, and men that identify as women.

7. Anwar Ibrahim was sacked from his position as deputy prime minister of Malaysia in 1998 and subsequently found guilty of fraud and sodomy. He served six years in prison on these charges and was convicted of sodomy again in 2015. Both of his sodomy cases were contentious and highly publicized.

8. Interview with Zawati, Haryaty, and Aisha (pseud.), October 2010, Putrajaya, Malaysia.

9. Interview with Norani Othman, October 2010, Petaling Jaya, Selangor, Malaysia.

10. Holland et al. (2007, 14) defined "dramas of contention" as "conflicts and differences of opinion that captured public attention." Their team of researchers focused on several public political events to highlight critical dilemmas facing American democracy.

11. Interview with Hajjah Haznita, January 2011, Melaka, Malaysia.

12. Hoffstaedter (2011, 179–81) states that religious authorities patrolling for *khalwat* and consumption of alcohol focus on mid-range and cheap hotels and student hangout spots in recreational and parking lots rather than top hotels, bars, and clubs. After a raid on a high-class nightclub in Kuala Lumpur in 2005 in which the children of some of Malaysia's elite were arrested, the government decreed that religious authorities stay away from five-star establishments, arguing that enforcement of sharia laws in these entertainment venues would disrupt tourism and give Malaysia a bad image.

13. Interview with Dato Hj. Hussin, October 2010, Seremban, Negeri Sembilan, Malaysia.

14. Interview with Abu Bakar, November 2010, Kota Bharu, Kelantan, Malaysia.

15. Interview with Datuk Haji Mohamad, November 2010, Kuala Lumpur, Malaysia.

16. The government of Brunei Darussalam issued its Syariah Penal Code Order in 2013 and began the gradual rollout of its implementation in May 2014. It includes *hudud*,

qisas, and *diya* and in some cases applies to both Muslims and non-Muslims (see Daniels 2014b).

17. Interview with Zaleha Kamarudin, November 2010, Kuala Lumpur, Malaysia.

18. In his critique of Kelantan's *hudud* bill, Kamali (1998, 208–10) observes that although the penal code states that it will just be applied to Muslims, it also allows non-Muslims the choice to have *hudud* penalties applied to them. He also notes that the provisions on abetment and conspiracy can be applied to any persons, including non-Muslims, who aid and abet a Muslim to commit any of the offenses in the code. Kamali argues that both of these aspects of the bill violate the Federal Constitution, which declares that sharia laws can only be applied to Muslims. Overall, he criticizes the bill for its legal conformism (*taqlid*) and imitative orientation, and calls for contemporary jurists to engage in *ijtihad* in devising Islamic penal policies that seek to realize the overriding values and objectives of sharia and that fit contemporary social and cultural conditions.

19. In the case of *Siti Fatimah Tan binti Abdullah v. Majlis Agama Islam Pulau Pinang* in 2006, the Shariah High Court reached a different decision after reviewing the plaintiff's life after her conversion for marriage. She grew up in a Buddhist family and was named Tan Ean Hung. Her conversion to Islam was filed in 1998 and she was registered under the name of Siti Fatimah Tan binti Abdullah. The following year she married Ferdoun Aslanian, an Iranian citizen, and after four months of marriage he left her. According to the evidence presented in court, he did not practice Islam and never taught Siti Fatimah anything about the religion. She continued to practice Buddhism and eat pork, and one witness stated that he never saw Siti Fatimah's husband pray in an Islamic fashion although he did see him praying in Buddhist fashion with Fatimah before an image of a Buddhist deity. From this evidence, it was apparent that she did not embrace or practice Islam after formally converting for marriage. The Shariah High Court decided in favor of Siti Fatimah, ruling that she was no longer a Muslim and ordering the Islamic Religious Council to annul the documents of her conversion to Islam.

20. Interview with Zaleha Kamarudin, November 2010, Kuala Lumpur, Malaysia.

21. The words listed as not to be used in reference to non-Islamic religion are *Allah, Firman Allah, ulama, hadith, ibadah, Kaabah, kadi, Illahi, wahyu, mubaligh, syariah, qiblat, haji, mufti, rasul, iman, dakwah, Injil, salat, khalifah, wali, fatwa, imam, nabi,* and *sheikh*. The expressions listed as not to be used in reference to non-Islamic religion are *Subhanallah, Alhamdulillah, Lailahaillallah, Walillahilham, Allahu Akbar, Insyaallah, Astaghfirullahal 'Azim, Tabaraka Allah, Masyaallah,* and *Lahaula Walaquata Illabillahilaliyil Azim*.

4. Economics

1. Wong Chin Huat (2016), a political and social analyst at the Penang Institute, a PKR think tank, writes about *halal* trolleys at hypermarts, a recently launched sharia-compliant airline, and plans for a *halal*-certified train as instances of "communal segregation" that sharpen ethnic and religious divisions as Malay political elites turn toward constructing a more authoritarian state.

2. See Fischer 2008; Sloane-White 2011, 2017; Rudnyckyj 2013; and Elder 2017.

3. Omer Awass (2017) notes that Islamic scholars in the International Islamic Fiqh Academy of the Organization for Islamic Cooperation (OIC) use the term *ṣukūk* to refer to Islamic stocks rather than bonds because they don't consider the latter to be sharia-compliant.

4. See www.e-fatwa.gov.my.

5. Interview with Zainul and Hamidah (pseud.), October 2010, Putrajaya, Malaysia.

6. Interview with Cik Firdaus Koh (pseud.), August 2012, Kuala Lumpur, Malaysia.

7. Interview with Cik Tariq (pseud.), July 2012, Gombak, Selangor, Malaysia.

8. Interview with Dr. Burhan (pseud.), August 2012, Kuala Lumpur, Malaysia.

9. Hallaq (2013, 147) argues that the sharia and its moral economic system are incompatible with modern capitalism. Similar to many of my Malaysian Muslim interlocutors, Hallaq contends that modern Islamic banking and finance "are Islamic merely in name, reflecting nearly nothing of what Islam as a moral system is all about" (151).

10. Interview with Abdul Latif (pseud.), July 2009, Alor Setar, Kedah, Malaysia.

11. Interview with Ustaz Othman (pseud.), July 2009, Alor Setar, Kedah, Malaysia.

12. Global Ikhwan organized a Polygamy Club and Obedient Wives Club to disseminate its teaching of returning wholeheartedly to the Qur'an and *Sunna* for modeling domestic relations. The Obedient Wives Club published a controversial book titled *Islamic Sex: Fighting Jews to Return Islamic Sex to the World* in 2011, which was banned in Malaysia.

13. In some of Imam Ashaari's controversial teachings that led to bans on many of his publications, and to the eventually banning of Darul Arqam, he taught that As-Suhaimi, the founder of Aurad Muhammadiah, received his instruction directly from Prophet Muhammad and would return as the Imam Mahdi and save the Muslim *umma* on the eve of doomsday (Jomo and Ahmad 1992, 84–85; Kamarulnizam 2003, 111). I think Darul Arqam / Global Ikhwan members believed that Imam Ashaari was one of the *Mujaddid* that a *hadith* states will be sent at the beginning of every century to revive and restore Islam.

14. After a successful reelection in 2013, Nik Abdul Aziz retired and passed on the chief minister post to his deputy, Ahmad Yaakob. Following a prolonged illness, he died on February 12, 2015, after which Haron Din became the spiritual leader of PAS.

15. See Gomez 2006; Ramanathan and Ahmad Fauzi 2006; and Daniels 2013a.

16. See Muhammad Syukri Salleh (1999, 244–45) for a discussion of PAS efforts to achieve several preliminary subgoals, including promotion of these three concepts, to prepare for the full execution of sharia laws under the administration of an Islamic state.

17. Douglas Raybeck (1996, 108–41), an ethnographer of Kelantan in the late 1960s, reports the presence of prostitution, nightclubs, and other "shady activities."

18. In 2010, following an extensive investigation into two high-profile cases, the federal anticorruption agency declared that they found no evidence that chief minister Nik Aziz has committed any acts of corruption (*Sinarharian* 2010d).

19. Interview with Cik Wan Azhar (pseud.), December 2010, Kota Bharu, Kelantan, Malaysia.

20. Personal communication with Patricia A. Hardwick, 2011.

21. PAS leaders named this exposition after the Chinese Muslim admiral Cheng Ho, who led a large fleet of ships for the Ming emperor from China to Southeast Asia and other regions during the early fifteenth century.

22. Interviews with Dato' Zainuddin, November 2010, and Wan Nik, December 2010, in Kota Bharu, Kelantan, Malaysia.

23. Interview with Cik Hong (pseud.), December 2010, Kuala Lumpur, Malaysia.

24. In the post–World War II context, socialist ideas had considerable influence on movements in Muslim-majority societies, including those in Southeast Asia. However, in the 1960s and 1970s the Islamic resurgence channeled these movements along more normative Islamic lines, which tended to emphasize Islamic proscriptions against *riba* and *haram* consumption rather than the application of sharia to economic production or the capitalist economic system in general (see S. M. Yusuf 1988).

25. The concept "communities of practice" has been used within a practice-based approach to speak of aggregates of people who engage in some joint activities (Lave and Wenger 1991; Eckert and McConnell-Ginet 1992; Wenger 1998). I attempt to demonstrate how the concept can be used within an "anthropology of knowledge" approach that accounts for the dynamic relationships between knowledge and practice (see Keller and Keller 1996).

26. In Malaysia, where the government is more repressive of new Islamic movements, the mufti of the Federal Territories issued a fatwa banning ESQ, asserting that it promotes free interpretation of the Qur'an and a conception of pluralism suggesting that all religions are the same (*Antara* 2010).

27. See Holland et al. 2007; Gregory 2007; Song 2009; and Zhang 2010.

5. Pro-Sharia Discourses

1. See Kamarulnizam 2003; Liow 2009; Daniels 2013b; and Hardwick 2013.

2. See Singh (2009) and Daniels (2013a) for analysis of Malaysia's twelfth general election of 2008, and Weiss (2013) and Case (2014) on Malaysia's thirteenth general election of 2013.

3. Md. Asham bin Ahmad (2011), a senior IKIM fellow, argues that Muslims should derive the meaning for "moderation" or *wasaṭiyya* from an understanding of the Qur'anic phrase *ummat wasaṭ*, which clearly describes the "middle position" of the Muslim community. Burhani (2012) describes the Nahdlatul Ulama usage of this concept in contemporary Indonesia, which is more theological than the political usage in the post-9/11 United States, where some Muslim groups use it to distinguish themselves from extremists.

4. Keller and Lehman (1991) argue that local people embed two Polynesian metaphysical concepts, *hkano* (material essence) and *ata* (efficacious image), in a larger theory of a domain of knowledge that includes premises about the existence of material and immaterial things.

5. Interview with Nik Abdul Aziz, July 2012, Kuala Lumpur, Malaysia.

6. Hallaq (2013) argues that the properties of the paradigmatic Euro-American nation-state are incompatible with those of the paradigmatic Islamic moral-legal system of governance. He recommends that Muslims avoid adopting the modern nation, with all its immoral baggage, and rather that they organize institutions of Islamic governance

and engage their Western counterparts in language they can understand in the process of positioning the moral as the central domain (168). In the ethnographic case of PAS in Malaysia, it is clear they intend to transform many aspects of the modern nation-state to suit their goals.

7. See *Sinarharian* 2010e, 2010a.

8. See *Utusan* 2010b; *The Star* 2010.

9. IKRAM, the popular name for this organization, is not an acronym. In Arabic, *ikrām* means "honor," "glory," and "generosity."

10. Interview with Zaid Kamaruddin, December 2010, Melawati, Selangor, Malaysia.

11. Interview with Ustaz Zakaria (pseud.), November 2010, Kuala Lumpur, Malaysia.

12. Hallaq (2013, 71) notes that jurists (representing "legislative" power) in premodern forms of Islamic governance were generally private unpaid scholars closer to the common social ranks rather than the higher levels of "executive" power. Describing the position of *ulama* in contemporary Malaysia, Azza Basarudin (2016, 138) states that "they participate in reproducing the religious monopoly and, in that process, are vulnerable to co-optation by regimes of power dependent on their knowledge."

13. Federal Constitution Article 11(1) states "Every person has the right to profess and practice his religion and, subject to Clause (4), to propagate it." Article 11(4), the caveat to this provision, clarifies that "[s]tate law and in respect to the Federal Territories of Kuala Lumpur, Labuan and Putrajaya, federal law may control or restrict the propagation of any religious doctrine or belief among persons professing the religion of Islam." Several states have issued such enactments specifying restrictions on the propagation of non-Islamic religions to Muslims.

14. In June 2015, the PAS congress approved a motion to sever ties with DAP after it distanced itself from PAS president Abdul Hadi Awang over the push to implement *hudud* in Kelantan (*Today* 2015).

6. Contra-Sharia Discourses

1. Aihwa Ong (1989, 1990) argued that Malay women enjoyed relatively high status vis-à-vis men due to a customary emphasis on gender complementarity and bilateral kinship principles. Describing the context when the UMNO-led secular state launched its own "Islamization campaign" amid rising *dakwah* movements in the 1980s, Ong (1990, 272) contends that "the consequence of this struggle of capitalist state versus Islamic *umma* has been an intensification of gender inequality in Malay society." Nevertheless, several kinship studies conducted prior to the Islamic resurgence indicate that the cultural model of asymmetrical gender relations embraced by the UMNO-led state and Islamic NGOs was long rooted in Malay society (Djamour 1959; Firth 1943; Banks 1983). Based primarily on fieldwork conducted in the late 1960s, Banks (1983, 67) explains the presence of both a male-slanted gender hierarchy and the "great freedom of Malay women" by noting that "Malays simply do not see religious law as a coercive instrument, but as a tool for the understanding of the social and natural world and as a guide to the creation of a viable social order. Freedom in certain spheres does not imply equality before the law in all others, nor do unequal laws imply coercive interpretations."

2. Interview with Zawati, Haryaty, and Aisha, October 2010, Putrajaya, Malaysia; and with Zaleha Kamarudin, November 2010, Kuala Lumpur, Malaysia.

3. Sylva Frisk (2009) suggests that an increase in female religiosity has opened up spaces for women to create more authority for themselves in Malaysia. She argues "that women, through the Islamic discourse on piety, are able to negotiate and transform gender relations and actively shape their lives in correspondence to ideals found in orthodox Islam" (23).

4. Interview with Norani Othman, October 2010; and Zainah Anwar, January 2011, in Petaling Jaya, Selangor, Malaysia.

5. SIS has filed for a judicial review of this religious edict, which was entered into a gazette on July 31, 2014 (*Malay Mail Online* 2014c). The fatwas Malaysian muftis issue are published and subsequently become law.

6. Interview with Doctor Ramasamy, August 2010, Penang, Malaysia.

7. Interview with P. Ramakrishnan, August 2010, Penang, Malaysia.

8. Interview with Tan Seng (pseud.), November 2010, Petaling Jaya, Selangor, Malaysia.

7. Individuals: Views, Voices, and Practices

1. Lara Deeb (2006) provides examples of Shia women in Lebanon who performed public piety in other ways but did not currently wear the clothing style most in the community considered expressive of piety. In contrast, Shahram Khosravi (2008, 123) describes how unveiled female Iranian airline passengers on international flights line up for the lavatory to put on their veils and lighten their makeup before landing in Tehran.

2. In January 2015 a national scandal ensued after a video went viral on social media showing three Malay Muslim fans, wearing *tudung*, being physically embraced by members of the Korean idol group B1A4. Some of my Malaysian Muslim friends posted the video on Facebook. According to normative sharia proscriptions, unmarried members of the opposite sex are not supposed to be engaging in such body contact. For many, it was even more shameful for Muslim women wearing hijab to be flouting sharia norms in this manner.

3. In Brunei's Syariah Penal Code, implemented in 2013, any non-Muslim committing *zina* with a Muslim is subject to *hudud* punishment if he or she is proved guilty of this *hadd* offense. Non-Muslim acts of theft, sodomy, and contempt of Prophet Muhammad or any of the prophets of Allah are also punishable.

4. In one narrated *hadith* of Prophet Muhammad, which appears in *Ṣaḥīḥ Al-Bukhārī* and *Muslim*, he stated, "By Him in Whose Hand is my life, when a man calls his wife to bed, and she does not respond, the One Who is above heaven becomes displeased with her until he (her husband) becomes pleased with her" (Al-Imam Abu Zakariya Yahya 1999, 274).

5. Interview with Lili Zohail (pseud.), December 2010, Kuala Lumpur, Malaysia.

6. Interview with Aliza Abu Bakar (pseud.), November 2010, Kuala Lumpur, Malaysia.

7. Interview with Mohamad Zuhaidi (pseud.), July 2012, Kuala Lumpur, Malaysia.

8. These are optional ritual prayers beyond the five daily obligatory prayers that entail prostrations and glorification of Allah and/or supplications. *Hajat* prayers focus on a

particular intention or request for Allah's blessings, and *Istikhārah* prayers ask for Allah's guidance in making a decision. *Tahajjud* prayers are optional prayers of worship that may not involve any request of divine assistance.

9. Interview with Wan Hafizi (pseud.), December 2010, Kuala Lumpur, Malaysia.
10. PERKIM (Pertubuhan Kebajikan Islam Malaysia; Malaysian Muslim Welfare Organization) assists with the process of conversion and provides classes and seminars for new Muslims and those interested in converting.
11. Interview with Cik Firdaus Koh (pseud.), August 2012, Kelana Jaya, Selangor, Malaysia.

Conclusion

1. F. K. Lehman (2000) argues that cultural schemas are used to "'govern' behavior immediately without having to generate from scratch, from the axioms and first principles of our underlying knowledge, a 'solution' to a task at hand. As such, we can think of them . . . as output *theorems of* our underlying knowledge bases." Indeed, the cultural models or schemas I infer from discourses and practices that are used to reason and partially govern behavior can be viewed as these sorts of heuristic mental models of a much broader corpus of knowledge and underlying cognitive system.

GLOSSARY

adat perpatih   matrilineal-based customary patterns
adat temenggong   bilateral-based customary patterns
akhlak   etiquette; ethical conduct
akidah (Ar. ʿaqidah)   religious belief
akikah (Ar. ʿaqiqa)   ceremony for newborn baby
amalan soleh   good works; righteous actions
amanah   something entrusted to someone; to be reliable, trustworthy
aurat   parts of the body to be covered

bahasa Malaysia   Malaysian language; Malay
baju kurung   long skirt and matching tunic
baju melayu   two-piece garment with matching pants and shirt
bangsa   race; ethnic group; people
Bumiputera   indigenous people; natives

dakwah (Ar. daʾwa)   calling people to Islam
dasar   basic foundations and principles
dīn   way of life
diya   financial compensation for offenses against another person

fard kifayah   collective responsibility
fasakh   at-fault divorce
fiqh   jurisprudence
fitrah   obligatory tithe due before the end of the fasting month

gharar   uncertainty

hadhanah   child custody
hadith   Prophetic Traditions
halal   permitted
hamba   slave; servant
haram   forbidden
harta sepencarian   joint marital assets
hidayah   divine guidance
hikmah   wisdom

ḥirāba   highway robbery; banditry
hudud (Ar. ḥudūd)   penalties fixed by the Qur'an and *hadith*; ethical limits
hukum syarak   Islamic law

'ibādāh (M. ibadah)   religious worship
'iddah   three-month period after divorce
ijtihad (Ar. ijtihād)   religious interpretation based on scriptures
ikhlas   inner sincerity
iman   Islamic faith
irtidād   apostasy
islah   Islamic reform
itqan   skill

jenayah   criminal; crime

kadi (Ar. qaḍi)   Muslim judge
kahwin paksa   forced marriage
kalimat   word; phrase
kebaya   long traditional skirt
kenduri   traditional feast
keramat   sacred grave sites or shrines possessing supernatural powers
kesalahan   offense; wrong
khalifah   caliph
khalwat   unmarried people of opposite sex in a secluded place; improper proximity
khutbah   Friday prayer sermons
kopiah   Islamic cap; skullcap
kuliah masjid   religious talks in mosques

liwat   sexual relations between men

masjid   mosque
mas kahwin   required marriage gift from husband to wife
maṣlaḥah (M. maslahah)   benefit; welfare; public good
mas'uliah   accountability
maqasid shariah (Ar. maqāṣid sharī'ah)   objectives of sharia
maysir   speculation
mualaf   Muslim convert
muamalat (Ar. mu'āmalāt)   economic matters
mudarabah   profit-sharing contract
mumaiyiz   age of discernment of right and wrong
munakahat   marriage and family matters
murtad   apostate
musahaqah   sexual relations between women
mushawarah   consultation; negotiation
muzakarah   consultation about a problem

nafkah economic support; maintenance
nasab descent; inherited from family or lineage
nusyuz disobedience

pondan a man posing as a woman
pondok traditional Islamic boarding school

qazaf (Ar. qadhf) slanderous accusation of unlawful sexual intercourse
qisas (Ar. qiṣāṣ) retaliation for offenses against persons

rasuah bribery
riba usurious interest; surplus value without a corresponding gain
riḍa wholehearted consent
ridda apostasy
rojak popular dish with assortment of vegetables and other ingredients; a varied mix of things

sabar patience
sariqa theft
sebat caning
shūrā (M. shura) consultation; collective deliberation
shurb khamr drinking alcohol
silat traditional Malay martial arts
ṣukūk Islamic stocks and/or bonds
suluh (Ar. sulh) marital mediation
sunat recommended behavior based on practices of the Prophet Muhammad
Sunna practice of Prophet Muhammad
surau prayer hall not used for Friday congregational prayers

tajdid Islamic renewal
tajwid pronunciation of Arabic characters
takaful insurance
takfir alleging that a person professing the religion of Islam is an infidel
talaq male pronouncement of divorce
ta'liq contractual marriage promises
taqwa Islamic piety
tarbiah education
tarekat Sufi brotherhoods
taṣawwuf Sufism
taubat repentance
Tauhid Islamic monotheism
tauliah authorization to perform religious instruction
ta'zir (M. takzir) discretionary punishment
telekung long prayer cloak
tudung headscarf

ubudiah   service to Allah
ulama (Ar. 'ulama')   Islamic scholars
umma (M. ummah)   Muslim community

wajib   obligatory
wakaf (Ar. waqf)   Islamic religious endowments
wali   male guardian
Wali Hakim   judge serving as guardian
wasaṭiyyah   middle path; moderation
wasiat   Muslim will

zakat   obligatory tithe based on savings over the year
zinā (M. zina)   unlawful sexual intercourse

REFERENCES

'Abd al-Qādir al-Jīlānī. 1994. *Utterances of Shaikh 'Abd al-Qādir al-Jīlānī (Malfūzāt).* Translated by Muhtar Holland. Kuala Lumpur: S. Abdul Majeed & Company.

Abdul Aziz Bari and Farid Sufian Shuaib. (2004) 2009. *Constitution of Malaysia: Text and Commentary.* 3rd ed. Kuala Lumpur: Prentice Hall.

Abdul Aziz Mohamad. 2007. "Majority Judgment, Lina Joy v. Majlis Agama Islam Persekutuan." *Jurnal Hukum* 24:120–41.

Abdullah Alwi Haji Hassan. 1996. *The Administration of Islamic Law in Kelantan.* Kuala Lumpur: Dewan Bahasa dan Pustaka.

Abdullah Yusuf Ali. 1992. *The Qur'an: Text, Translation and Commentary.* Medina: Ministry of Hajj and Endowments.

Abdullahi Ahmed An-Na'im. 2007. "Negotiating Authenticity and Justice." *Baraza!* 1:3–4.

Abdul Samat Musa. 2003. "An Overview of the Historical Background of Islamic Law and Its Administration under the Federal Constitution." In *Kajian Syariah dan Undang-Undang,* edited by Irwan Mohd Subri, Md. Yunus Abd Aziz, Abidah Abdul Ghafar, Dina Imam Supaat, and Syahirah Abdul Shukor, 95–108. Kuala Lumpur: Kolej Universiti Islam Malaysia.

ACCIN. 2005. *Bantah Penubuhan IFC.* Kuala Lumpur: Secretariat ACCIN.

Agar, Michael, and Jerry R. Hobbs. 1985. "How to Grow Schemata out of Interview." In *Directions in Cognitive Anthropology,* edited by Janet W. D. Dougherty, 413–31. Urbana: University of Illinois Press.

Agrama, Hussein Ali. 2010. "Ethics, Tradition, Authority: Toward an Anthropology of the Fatwa." *American Ethnologist* 37:2–18.

Ahearn, Laura M. 2012. *Living Language: An Introduction to Linguistic Anthropology.* Malden, MA: Wiley-Blackwell.

Ahmad Farouk Musa. 2013. "A Perverse Understanding of Human Rights." July 22, 2013. Accessed December 5, 2015. http://irfront.net/print_version/2892.html.

———. 2015. "Hudud Amputations: An Unethical Proposal." April 29, 2014. Accessed December 5, 2015. http://irfront.net/print_version/3634.html.

Ahmad Fauzi Abdul Hamid. 1999. "Development in the Post-Colonial State: Class, Capitalism and the Islamist Political Alternative in Malaysia." *Kajian Malaysia Journal of Malaysian Studies* 17:21–57.

———. 2005. "The Banning of Darul Arqam in Malaysia." *Review of Indonesian and Malaysian Affairs* 39:87–128.

Ahmad Ibrahim. 1992. "The Malaysian Constitutional System." In *Constitutional Systems in Late Twentieth Century Asia*, ed. Lawrence W. Beer, 507–28. Seattle: University of Washington Press.

Ahmad Ibrahim and Joned Ahilemah. 1987. *The Malaysian Legal System*. Kuala Lumpur: Dewan Bahasa dan Pustaka.

Ahmed, Shahab. 2016. *What Is Islam? The Importance of Being Islamic*. Princeton, NJ: Princeton University Press.

Ali, Wajahat, and Matthew Duss. 2011. *Understanding Sharia Law: Conservatives' Skewed Interpretation Needs Debunking*. Washington, DC: Center for American Progress.

Al-Imam Abu Zakariya Yahya. *Riyād-us-Sāliheen*. 1999. Vol. 1. Translated by Dr. Muhammad Amin. Riyadh: Darussalam.

Allers, Charles. 2013. *The Evolution of a Muslim Democrat: The Life of Malaysia's Anwar Ibrahim*. New York: Peter Lang.

———. 2017. "Anwar and *Maqasid*: Forging a Muslim Democracy." In *Sharia Dynamics: Islamic Law and Sociopolitical Processes*, edited by Timothy P. Daniels, 279–302. Cham, Switzerland: Palgrave Macmillan.

Andaya, Barbara Watson, and Leonard Y. Andaya. (1982) 2001. *A History of Malaysia*. 2nd ed. Honolulu: University of Hawai'i Press.

Antara. 2010. "Religious Leaders Defend ESQ against Malaysian Mufti's Fatwa." July 9. Accessed February 27, 2012. www.antaranews.com/en/news/1278668233/religious -leaders-defend-esq-against-msian-muftis-fatwa.

Anwar Ibrahim. 2007. "Anwar Ibrahim's Media Statement on Religious Freedom." June 2. Accessed November 19, 2013. www.malaysianbar.org.my/letters_others/anwar _ibrahims_media_statement_on_religious_freedom.html.

———. 2012. "Hudud and UMNO's Politics of Desperation." PKR press release. August 25. Accessed October 29, 2013. www.keadilanrakyat.org/.

Asad, Talal. 1986. *The Idea of an Anthropology of Islam*. Occasional Papers Series. Washington, DC: Georgetown University Center for Contemporary Arab Studies.

———. 1993. *Genealogies of Religion: Discipline and Reasons of Power in Christianity and Islam*. Baltimore: Johns Hopkins University Press.

———. 2003. *Formations of the Secular*. Stanford, CA: Stanford University Press.

———. 2011. "Thinking about the Secular Body, Pain, and Liberal Politics." *Cultural Anthropology* 26:657–75.

Astro Awani. 2015. "Hudud: PAS Hopes Private Bill Motion Makes It to Parliament." May 19. Accessed November 1, 2015. http://english.astroawani.com/malaysia-news /hudud-pas-hopes-private-bill-motion-makes-it-parliament-61037.

Auda, Jasser. 2008. *Maqasid Al-Shariah as Philosophy of Islamic Law: A Systems Approach*. Washington, DC: International Institute of Islamic Thought.

Awass, Omer. 2017. "Fatwa, Discursivity, and the Production of Sharia." In *Sharia Dynamics: Islamic Law and Sociopolitical Processes*, edited by Timothy P. Daniels, 31–62. Cham, Switzerland: Palgrave Macmillan.

Azza Basarudin. 2016. *Humanizing the Sacred: Sisters in Islam and the Struggle for Gender Justice in Malaysia*. Seattle: University of Washington Press.

Banks, David J. 1983. *Malay Kinship*. Philadelphia: ISHI.

Black, Ann, Hossein Esmaeili, and Nadirsyah Hosen. 2013. *Modern Perspectives on Islamic Law*. Cheltenham, UK: Edward Elgar.

Boo Su-Lyn. 2014. "Constitution Has to Be Amended for Shariah Court to be Equivalent to Federal Court, Lawyers Say." *Malay Mail Online.* December 12. Accessed November 1, 2015. www.themalaymailonline.com/malaysia/article/constitution-has-to-be -amended-for-shariah-court-to-be-equivalent-to-federa.

Bourdieu, Pierre. 1977. *Outline of a Theory of Practice*. Translated by Richard Nice. Cambridge, UK: Cambridge University Press.

Bowen, John J. 2014. *Religions in Practice: An Approach to the Anthropology of Religion*. 6th ed. Boston: Pearson.

Boyer, Pascal. 1993. "Cognitive Aspects of Religious Symbolism." In *The Cognitive Implications of Religious Symbolism*, edited by Pascal Boyer, 4–47. Cambridge, UK: Cambridge University Press.

Burhani, Ahmad Najib. 2012. "*Al-tawassuṭ wa-l i'tidāl*: The NU and Moderatism in Indonesian Islam." *Asian Journal of Social Science* 40:564–81.

Case, William. 2014. "Malaysia in 2013: A Benighted Election Day (and Other Events)." *Asian Survey* 54:56–63.

Center for Security Policy. 2010. *Shariah: The Threat to America*. Washington, DC: Center for Security Policy Press.

Chandra Muzaffar. 1994. "Reformation of Shari'a or Contesting the Historical Role of the Ulama?" In *Shari'a Law and the Modern Nation-State: A Malaysian Symposium*, edited by Norani Othman, 21–25. Kuala Lumpur: SIS Forum (Malaysia) Berhad.

Christian Post. 2011. "Christians in Malaysia Accept Ruling on Church Raid." November 9. Accessed July 4, 2012. www.christianpost.com/news/christians-in-malaysia-accept -ruling-on-church-raid-61249/.

Colby, Benjamin N., J. Fernandez, and D. Kronenberg. 1981. "Toward a Convergence of Cognitive and Symbolic Anthropology." *American Ethnologist* 8:422–50.

Coulson, Noel J. 1969. *Conflicts and Tensions in Islamic Jurisprudence*. Chicago: University of Chicago Press.

D'Andrade, Roy. 1989. "Cultural Cognition." In *Foundations of Cognitive Science*, edited by Michael I. Posner, 795–830. Cambridge, MA: MIT Press.

———. 1995. *The Development of Cognitive Anthropology*. Cambridge, UK: Cambridge University Press.

———. 2005. "Some Methods for Studying Cultural Cognitive Structures." In *Finding Culture in Talk*, edited by Naomi Quinn, 83–104. New York: Palgrave Macmillan.

Daniels, Timothy P. 2005. *Building Cultural Nationalism in Malaysia: Identity, Representation, and Citizenship*. New York: Routledge.

———. 2009. *Islamic Spectrum in Java*. Burlington, VT: Ashgate.

———. 2013a. "PAS in Kedah: Cultural Politics of Pigs and Development." *Contemporary Islam* 7:155–72.

———. 2013b. " 'Islamic' TV Dramas, Malay Youth, and Pious Visions for Malaysia." In *Performance, Popular Culture, and Piety in Muslim Southeast Asia*, edited by Timothy P. Daniels, 105–33. New York: Palgrave Macmillan.

———. 2014a. "African International Students in Klang Valley: Colonial Legacies, Postcolonial Racialization, and Sub-citizenship." *Citizenship Studies* 18:855–70.

———. 2014b. "Brunei's Syariah Penal Code and Secular Fundamentalism." *Berita* (Autumn):14–21.

———. 2017. "Introduction: Sharia Dynamics and the Anthropology of Islam." In *Sharia Dynamics: Islamic Law and Sociopolitical Processes*, edited by Timothy P. Daniels, 1–27. Cham, Switzerland: Palgrave Macmillan.

Djamour, Judith. 1959. *Malay Kinship and Marriage in Singapore*. London: Athlone Press.

Donohue, John J., and John L. Esposito, eds. 2007. *Islam in Transition: Muslim Perspectives*. 2nd ed. New York: Oxford University Press.

Dougherty, J. W. D., and James Fernandez. 1981. "Introduction." "Special Issue on Cognition and Symbolism I," *American Ethnologist* 8:413–21.

———. 1982. "Afterword." "Special Issue on Cognition and Symbolism II," *American Ethnologist* 9:820–32.

Deeb, Lara. 2006. *An Enchanted Modern: Gender and Public Piety in Shi'i Lebanon*. Princeton, NJ: Princeton University Press.

Eckert, P., and S. McConnell-Ginet. 1992. "Think Practically and Look Locally: Language and Gender as Community-Based Practice." *Annual Review of Anthropology* 21:461–90.

Ee Ann Nee. 2010. "Shariah Confusion." *Malay Mail*, December 6.

Elder, Laura. 2017. "Gendered Accounts of Expertise Within Islamic Finance and Financialization in Malaysia." In *Sharia Dynamics: Islamic Law and Sociopolitical Processes*, edited by Timothy P. Daniels, 171–202. Cham, Switzerland: Palgrave Macmillan.

el-Zein, Abdul Hamid. 1977. "Beyond Ideology and Theology: The Search for the Anthropology of Islam." *Annual Review of Anthropology* 6:227–54.

Farish A. Noor. 2003. "The Localization of Islamist Discourse in the *Tafsir* of Tuan Guru Nik Aziz Nik Mat, Murshid'ul Am of PAS." In *Malaysia: Islam, Society and Politics*, edited by Virginia Hooker and Norani Othman, 195–235. Singapore: Institute of Southeast Asian Studies.

———. 2004. *Islam Embedded: The Historical Development of the Pan-Malaysian Islamic Party PAS (1951–2003)*. Kuala Lumpur: Malaysian Sociological Research Institute.

Feldman, Noah. 2007. "Shari'ah and Islamic Democracy in the Age of al-Jazeera." In *Shari'ah: Islamic Law in the Contemporary Context*, edited by Abbas Amanat and Frank Griffel, 104–19. Stanford, CA: Stanford University Press.

Feener, R. Michael. 2013. *Shari'ah and Social Engineering: The Implementation of Islamic Law in Contemporary Aceh, Indonesia*. Oxford, UK: Oxford University Press.

Fernando, Joseph M. 2012. "Elite Intercommunal Bargaining and Conflict Resolution: The Role of the Communities Liaison Committee in Malaya, 1949–51." *Journal of Southeast Asian Studies* 43:280–301.

Firth, Raymond. 1946. *Malay Fishermen: Their Peasant Economy*. London: Kegan Paul, Trench, Trübner & Co.

Firth, Rosemary. 1943. *Housekeeping among Malay Peasants*. London: Lund, Humphries.

Fischer, Johan. 2008. *Proper Islamic Consumption: Shopping among the Malays in Modern Malaysia*. Copenhagen: Nordic Institute of Asian Studies Press.

Foucault, Michel. 1972. *The Archaeology of Knowledge*. Translated by A. M. Sheridan Smith. New York: Pantheon Books.

———. 1994. "The Subject and Power." In *The Essential Foucault: Selections from the Essential Works of Foucault, 1954–1984*, edited by Paul Rabinow and Nikolas Rose, 126–44. New York: New Press.

Frisk, Sylva. 2009. *Submitting to God: Women and Islam in Urban Malaysia*. Seattle: University of Washington Press.

Geertz, Clifford. 1973. *The Interpretation of Cultures*. New York: Basic Books.Gilsenan, Michael. 1982. *Recognizing Islam: Religion and Society in the Modern Middle East*. London: I. B. Tauris.

Gomez, E. T. 2006. "The 2004 Malaysian General Elections: Economic Development, Electoral Trends, and the Decline of the Opposition." In *Malaysia: Recent Trends and Challenges*, edited by S. Sweek-Hock and K. Kesavapany, 73–99. Singapore: Institute of Southeast Asian Studies.

Gregory, Steven. 2007. *The Devil behind the Mirror: Globalization and Politics in the Dominican Republic*. Berkeley: University of California Press.

Grewal, Zareena. 2014. *Islam Is a Foreign Country: American Muslims and the Global Crisis of Authority*. New York: New York University Press.

Halimah Abdul Rahman. 2009. *Undang-Undang Berkaitan Syariah*. Kajang: Time Edition.

Halimahton Shaari, Ngu Teck Hua, and V. Raman. 2006. "Covering Race and Religion: The Moorthy and Nyonya Tahir Cases in Four Malaysian Newspapers." *Kajian Malaysia* 24:185–201.

Hall, Stuart. 2001. "Foucault: Power, Knowledge and Discourse." In *Discourse Theory and Practice: A Reader*, edited by Margaret Wetherell, Stephanie Taylor, and Simeon J. Yates, 72–81. Thousand Oaks, CA: Sage.

Hallaq, Wael B. 2004. "Can the Shari'a Be Restored?" In *Islamic Law and the Challenges of Modernity*, edited by Yvonne Yazbeck Haddad and Barbara Freyer Stowasser, 21–53. Walnut Creek, CA: Altamira Press.

———. 2009. *Shari'ah: Theory, Practice, Transformations*. Cambridge, UK: Cambridge University Press.

———. 2013. *The Impossible State: Islam, Politics, and Modernity's Moral Predicament*. New York: Columbia University Press.

Harakah. 2010a. "Bajet penyayang harapan baru rakyat Kelantan." November 22–25.

———. 2010b. "Budget 2011: Separate Halal, non-Halal Revenue." October 25–28.

———. 2010c. "Expo Cheng Ho: Amat bererti buat Kelantan." November 26–28.

Harding, Andrew. 1996. *Law, Government and the Constitution in Malaysia*. London: Kluwer Law International.

Hardwick, Patricia A. 2013. "Embodying the Divine and the Body Politic: *Mak Yong* Performance in Rural Kelantan, Malaysia." In *Performance, Popular Culture, and Piety in Muslim Southeast Asia*, edited by Timothy P. Daniels, 77–103. New York: Palgrave Macmillan.

Harnish, David D., and Anne K. Rasmussen. 2011. "Introduction: The World of Islam in the Music of Indonesia." In *Divine Inspirations: Music and Islam in Indonesia*, edited by David D. Harnish and Anne K. Rasmussen, 5–41. New York: Oxford University Press.

Hasbullah Awang Chik. 2014. "Life after Al-Arqam Sees Global Ikhwan Expand on Halal Business." *Malaysian Insider*. December 21. Accessed October 24, 2015. www .themalaysianinsider.com/.

Hefner, Robert W. 2010. "Religious Resurgence in Contemporary Asia: Southeast Asian Perspectives on Capitalism, the State, and the New Piety." *Journal of Southeast Asian Studies* 69: 1031–47.

Hill, Jane H. 2008. *The Everyday Language of White Racism*. Malden, MA: Wiley-Blackwell.

Hirschkind, Charles. 2006. *The Ethical Soundscape*. New York: Columbia University Press.

———. 2011. "Is There a Secular Body?" *Cultural Anthropology* 26:633–47.

Hodgson, Marshall G. S. 1974. *The Gunpowder Empires and Modern Times*. Vol. 3 of *The Venture of Islam: Conscience and History in a World Civilization*. Chicago: University of Chicago Press.

Hoffstaedter, Gerhard. 2011. *Modern Muslim Identities: Negotiating Religion and Ethnicity in Malaysia*. Copenhagen: Nordic Institute of Asian Studies Press.

Holland, Dorothy, and Margaret Eisenhart. 1990. *Educated in Romance: Women, Achievement, and College Culture*. Chicago: University of Chicago Press.

Holland, Dorothy, D. M. Nonini, C. Lutz, L. Bartlett, M. Frederick-McGlathery, T. C. Guldbrandsen, and E. G. Murillo, Jr. 2007. *Local Democracy under Siege*. New York: New York University Press.

Hooker, M. B. 1983. "Muhammadan Law and Islamic Law." In *Islam in South-East Asia*, edited by M. B. Hooker, 160–82. Leiden: E. J. Brill.

Hussin, Iza R. 2016. *The Politics of Islamic Law: Local Elites, Colonial Authority, and the Making of the Muslim State*. Chicago: University of Chicago Press.

Ibrahim, Ahmed Fekry. 2015. *Pragmatism in Islamic Law: A Social and Intellectual History*. Syracuse, NY: Syracuse University Press.

Imām Muhammad al-Bukhārī. 1994. *Summarized Ṣaḥīḥ al-Bukhārī*. Translated by Dr. Muhammad Muhsin Khan. Riyadh: Maktaba Dar-us-Salam.

Islamic Renaissance Front. 2012a. "Agree to Disagree: Book Banning Frenzy Must End." June 6. Accessed December 5, 2015. http://irfront.net/print_version/1672.html.

———. 2012b. "End the Smear Campaign." November 8. Accessed December 5, 2015. http://irfront.net/print_version/2480.html.

———. 2012c. "Lessons from the On-going Demonization of DAP." August 10. Accessed December 5, 2015. http://irfront.net/print_version/2130/html.

Izutsu, Toshihiko. 1966. *Ethico-Religious Concepts in the Qur'ān*. Montreal: McGill University Press.

Jakarta Globe. 2009. "Indonesian Man Sentenced to Jail and Caning in Malaysia for Drinking Alcohol." September 15. Accessed October 30, 2015. http://jakartaglobe .beritasatu.com/archive/indonesian-man-sentenced-to-jail-and-caning-in-malaysia -for-drinking-alcohol/.

———. 2011. "Malaysian Muslim NGOs: Act against Christian Proselytizers." August 15. Accessed July 4, 2012. http://jakartaglobe.beritasatu.com/archive/malaysian-muslim -ngos-act-against-christian-proselytizers/.

Jamilah Kamarudin. 2015. "JAKIM Supports PAS Hudud Bill, Stiffer Punishment." *Malaysian Insider*, April 24. Accessed November 1, 2015. www.themalaysianinsider.com /malaysia/article/jakim-supports-pas-hudud-bill-stiffer-punishment.

Jomo, K. S., and Ahmad Shabery Cheek. 1992. "Malaysia's Islamic Movements." In *Fragmented Vision: Culture and Politics in Contemporary Malaysia*, edited by Francis Loh Kok Wah and Joel S. Kahn, 79–106. Honolulu: University of Hawaii Press.

Jurnal Hukum. 2006a. "Dalam Perkara Permohonan Keluar Islam Muhamad Ramzan Maniarason." *Jurnal Hukum* 22:181–89.

———. 2006b. "Permohonan Perisytiharan Status Agama Janisah binti Abd Rahim @ Bigul." *Jurnal Hukum* 22:67–69.

Kamali, Mohammad Hashim. 1998. "Punishment in Islamic Law: A Critique of the Hudud Bill of Kelantan, Malaysia." *Arab Law Quarterly* 13:203–34.

———. 2000. *Islamic Law in Malaysia: Issues and Developments.* Kuala Lumpur: Ilmiah.

———. 2006. *An Introduction to Sharī'ah.* Kuala Lumpur: Ilmiah.

Kamarulnizam Abdullah. 2003. *The Politics of Islam in Contemporary Malaysia.* Bangi, Selangor: Universiti Kebangsaan Malaysia.

Kelantan State Economic Planning Unit. 2009. *Kelantan Facts and Figures, 2008/2009.* Kota Bharu: Kelantan State Secretariat.

Keller, Charles M., and Janet Dixon Keller. 1996. *Cognition and Tool Use: The Blacksmith at Work.* Cambridge, UK: Cambridge University Press.

Keller, Janet Dixon, and F. K. Lehman. 1991. "Complex Concepts." *Cognitive Science* 15:271–91.

Kerajaan Negeri Kelantan. 2007. *Kelantan Menerajui Perubahan.* Kota Bahru: Urusetia Penerangan Kerajaan Negeri Kelantan.

Kessler, Clive S. 1978. *Islam and Politics in a Malay State: Kelantan, 1838–1969.* Ithaca, NY: Cornell University Press.

Khosravi, Shahram. 2008. *Young and Defiant in Tehran.* Philadelphia: University of Pennsylvania Press.

Kreinath, Jens. 2012. "Toward the Anthropology of Islam: An Introductory Essay." In *The Anthropology of Islam Reader*, edited by Jens Kreinath, 1–41. New York: Routledge.

Lambek, Michael. 2000. "The Anthropology of Religion and the Quarrel between Poetry and Philosophy." *Current Anthropology* 41:309–20.

Lave, J., and E. Wenger. 1991. *Situated Learning: Legitimate Peripheral Participation.* Cambridge, UK: Cambridge University Press.

Lehman, F. K. 1997. "Cognitive Science Research Notes." Unpublished paper.

———. 2000. "Cultural Models (and Schemata) and Generative Knowledge Domains: How Are They Related?" Paper presented at the American Anthropological Association Annual Meeting, San Francisco.

Leonard, Scott, and Michael McClure. (2004) 2008. "The Study of Mythology." In *Magic, Witchcraft, and Religion*, edited by Pamela A. Moro, James E. Myers, and Arthur C. Lehman, 51–62. Boston: McGraw-Hill.

Lever, John. 2016. "Re-imagining Malaysia: A Postliberal Halal Strategy?" In *Halal Matters: Islam, Politics and Markets in Global Perspective*, edited by Florence Bergeaud-Blackler, Johan Fischer, and John Lever, 19–37. New York: Routledge.

Liow, Joseph Chinyong. 2009. *Piety and Politics: Islamism in Contemporary Malaysia.* Oxford, UK: Oxford University Press.

Luttrell, Wendy. 2005. " 'Good Enough' Methods for Life-Story Analysis." In *Finding Culture in Talk*, edited by Naomi Quinn, 243–68. New York: Palgrave Macmillan.

Mackeen, Abdul Majeed Mohamed. 1969. *Contemporary Islamic Legal Organization in Malaya.* Monograph Series 13. New Haven, CT: Yale University Southeast Asia Studies.

Mahmood, Saba. 2005. *Politics of Piety: The Islamic Revival and the Feminist Subject.* Princeton, NJ: Princeton University Press.

Malay Mail Online. 2013. "Court of Appeal Quashes 'Allah' Judgement." October 14, 2013. Accessed October 14, 2013. www.themalaymailonline.com/malaysia/article/court-of -appeal-quashes-allah-judgment.

———. 2014a. "By Ignoring Custody Orders, IGP Liable for Contempt of Court, Bar Council Says." June 12. Accessed June 14, 2014. www.themalaymailonline.com/malaysia /article/by-ignoring-custody-orders-igp-liable-for-contempt-of-court-bar-council-say.

———. 2014b. "CFM: Only BN Can Drive Peace Deal in Interfaith Row." January 26. Accessed January 28, 2014. www.themalaymailonline.com/malaysia/article/cfm-only -bn-can-drive-peace-deal-in-interfaith-row.

———. 2014c. "Despite MB's proposal, Selangor Mufti Says 'Will Only Entertain SIS If They Repent.'" November 6. Accessed November 6, 2014. www.themalaymailonline .com/malaysia/article/despite-mbs-proposal-selangor-mufti-says-will-only-entertain -sis-if-they-re.

Malaysiakini. 2010. "Nik Aziz: Politik Melayu kukuh jika Umno tukar dasar." July 18. Accessed November 26, 2015. www.malaysiakini.com/news/137649.

———. 2011. "Tidak apa jika saya tidak dilahirkan sebagai Melayu." February 27. Accessed November 26, 2015. www.malaysiakini.com/news/157222.

———. 2013. "Fathul Bari mahu tindakan pada Nik Aziz." April 9. Accessed November 26, 2015. www.malaysiakini.com/news/226323.

———. 2014. "PM: Use Apex Court to Resolve Custody Disputes." June 12. Accessed June 14, 2014. www.malaysiakini.com/news/265546.

Malaysian Digest. 2011. "NGO Plans to Monitor Churches to Prevent Proselytizing of Muslims." August 11, 2011. Accessed August 17, 2011. www.malaysiandigest.com/.

Malhi, Amrita. 2014. "We Hope to Raise the 'Bendera Stambul': British Forward Move-ment and the Ottoman Caliphate on the Malay Peninsula." In *From Anatolia to Aceh: Ottomans, Turks and Southeast Asia*, edited by Andrew Peacock and Annabel Teh Gallop, 221–40. Oxford, UK: Oxford University Press.

Manning, Christel J. 1999. *God Gave Us the Right: Conservative Catholic, Evangelical Protestant, and Orthodox Jewish Women Grapple with Feminism*. New Brunswick, NJ: Rutgers University Press.

Marranci, Gabriele. 2008. *The Anthropology of Islam*. Oxford, UK: Berg.

Martinez, Patricia. 2008. "Muslims in Malaysia: Notions of Human Rights Reform, and Their Contexts." In *Islam and Human Rights in Practice*, edited by Shahram Akbarza-deh and Benjamin MacQueen, 118–41. New York: Routledge.

Masami Mustaza. 2010. "Concern over Marriage of 14-Year-Old Girl." *New Straits Times*, December 6.

Mauss, Marcel. 1973. "Techniques of the Body." *Economy and Society* 2:70–88.

Mawdūdī, Sayyid Abul A'lā. 2011. *First Principles of Islamic Economics*. Edited by Khurshid Ahmad. Translated by Ahmad Imam Shafaq Hashemi. Leicestershire, UK: Islamic Foundation.

Md. Asham Ahmad. 2011. "Moderation in Islam: A Conceptual Analysis of *Wasaṭiyyah*." *TAFHIM: IKIM Journal of Islam and the Contemporary World* 4:29–46.

Mearns, David James. 1995. *Shiva's Other Children: Religion and Social Identity amongst Overseas Indians*. New Delhi: Sage.

Moustafa, Tamir. 2013. "Liberal Rights versus Islamic Law? The Construction of a Binary in Malaysian Politics." *Law and Society Review* 47:771–802.

Muhammad Syukri Salleh. 1994. "An Ethical Approach to Development: The Arqam Philosophy and Achievements." *Humanomics* 10:25–60.

———. 1999. "Establishing an Islamic State: Ideals and Realities in the State of Kelantan, Malaysia." *Southeast Asian Studies* 37:235–56.

Najib Tun Abdul Razak. 2010. *Mendaya Bangsa Meneraju Kemakmuran*. Kuala Lumpur: UMNO.

Netto, Anil. 2007. "Changing Dynamics in Malaysia's Multi-cultural Society." In *Working for Democracy: Footprints from Civil Society in Malaysia*, edited by Womens Development Collective, 99–122. Petaling Jaya: Women's Development Collective.

Nik Abdul Aziz. 2010. *Rebah, Bangkit dan Terus Bangkit*. Kota Bharu: Unit Komunikasi Menteri Besar (UKMB Resources).

Nik Noriani Nik Badlishah, ed. 2003. *Islamic Family Law and Justice for Muslim Women*. Kuala Lumpur: Sisters in Islam.

Nik Noriani Nik Badlishah, and Norhayati Kaprawi. 2004. *Hadith on Women and Marriage*. Petaling Jaya: Sisters in Islam.

Norani Othman. 2005. "Introduction: Muslim Women and the Challenge of Political Islam and Islamic Extremism." In *Muslim Women and the Challenge of Islamic Extremism*, edited by Norani Othman, 1–10. Petaling Jaya: Sisters in Islam.

Norhafsah Hamid. 2012. *Trying to Be Muslim*. Kuala Lumpur: A. S. Noordeen.

———. 2015. "Sharia Family Law in Malaysia: Gender Equality, Is It a Myth?" Unpublished paper.

Ong, Aihwa. 1987. *Spirits of Resistance and Capitalist Discipline: Factory Women in Malaysia*. Albany: State University of New York Press.

———. 1989. "Center, Periphery, and Hierarchy: Gender in Southeast Asia." In *Gender and Anthropology: Critical Reviews for Research and Teaching*, edited by Sandra Morgen, 294–305. Washington, DC: American Anthropological Association.

———. 1990. "State versus Islam: Malay Families, Women's Bodies, and the Body Politic in Malaysia." *American Ethnologist* 17:258–76.

———. 1999. "Cultural Citizenship as Subject Making: Immigrants Negotiate Racial and Cultural Boundaries in the United States." In *Race, Identity, and Citizenship: A Reader*, edited by Rodolfo D. Torres, Louis F. Miron, and Jonathan Xavier Inda, 262–93. Malden, MA: Blackwell.

———. 2002. "The Pacific Shuttle: Family, Citizenship, and Capital Circuits." In *The Anthropology of Globalization*, edited by Jonathan Xavier Inda and Renato Rosaldo, 172–97. Malden, MA: Blackwell.

Ong, Aihwa, and Michael G. Peletz. 1995. "Introduction." In *Bewitching Women, Pious Men: Gender and Body Politics in Southeast Asia*, edited by Aihwa Ong and Michael G. Peletz, 1–18. Berkeley: University of California Press.

Özyürek, Esra. 2006. *Nostalgia for the Modern: State Secularism and Everyday Politics in Turkey*. Durham, NC: Duke University Press.

Peletz, Michael G. 2002. *Islamic Modern: Religious Courts and Cultural Politics in Malaysia*. Princeton, NJ: Princeton University Press.

———. 2013. "Malaysia's Syariah Judiciary as Global Assemblage: Islamization, Corporatization, and Other Transformations in Context." *Comparative Studies in Society and History* 55:603–33.

Pervez, Saulat. 2011. "Shariah: What Everyone Should Know about Shariah." *The Message International* (September–October): 24–26,.

Peters, Rudolph. 2005. *Crime and Punishment in Islamic Law*. Cambridge, UK: Cambridge University Press.

Qiadah. 2010. *The Land of Dinar and Dirham*. 7th ed. Kota Bharu: Perbadanan Menteri Besar Kelantan.

Quinn, Naomi. 1982. "'Commitment' in American Marriage: A Cultural Analysis." *American Ethnologist* 9:755–98.

Ramadan, Tariq. 2009. *Radical Reform: Islamic Ethics and Liberation*. New York: Oxford University Press.

Ramanathan, K., and Ahmad Fauzi. 2006. "Inter-party Competition and Electoral Campaigning in Rural Malaysia: The Pendang and Anak Bukit By-Elections of 2002." Working Paper 15, Institute of East Asian Studies, Universiti Malaysia Sarawak, Kota Samarahan.

Raybeck, Douglas. 1996. *Mad Dogs, Englishmen, and the Errant Anthropologist*. Long Grove, IL: Waveland Press.

Riddell, Peter. 2001. *Islam and the Malay-Indonesian World*. Honolulu: University of Hawai'i Press.

Riswandi Razak. 2010. "Pengikut Syiah tuntut perlindungan Suhakam." *Sinarharian*, December 28.

Roff, William R. 1998. "Patterns of Islamization in Malaysia, 1890s–1990s: Exemplars, Institutions, and Vectors." *Journal of Islamic Studies* 9:210–28.

Ross, Laurie M. 2013. "Performing Piety from the Inside Out: Fashioning Gender and Public Space in a Mask 'Tradition.'" In *Performance, Popular Culture, and Piety in Muslim Southeast Asia*, edited by Timothy P. Daniels, 13–43. New York: Palgrave Macmillan.

Ross, Lawrence. 2013. "Demi Agama, Bangsa, dan Negara: Articulating Malay-ness through Silat in Malaysia." In *(Re)producing Southeast Asian Performing Arts, and Southeast Asian Bodies, Music, Dance and Other Movement Arts: Proceedings of the 2nd Symposium of the ICTM Study Group on Performing Arts of Southeast Asia*, edited by Mohd. Anis Md. Nor, 256–65. Manila: Philippine Women's University.

Rudnyckyj, Daromir. 2009. "Spiritual Economies: Islam and Neoliberalism in Contemporary Indonesia." *Cultural Anthropology* 24:104–41.

———. 2013. "From Wall Street to *Halal* Street: Malaysia and the Globalization of Islamic Finance." *Journal of Asian Studies* 74:831–48.

Salime, Zakia. 2011. *Between Feminism and Islam: Human Rights and Sharia Law in Morocco*. Minneapolis: University of Minnesota Press.

Scott, James. 1979. *The Moral Economy of the Peasant: Subsistence and Rebellion in Southeast Asia*. New Haven, CT: Yale University Press.

Screpanti, Ernesto. 1999. "Capitalist Forms and the Essence of Capitalism." *Review of International Political Economy* 6:1–26.

Shad Saleem Faruqi. 2007. "Constitutional Perspectives on Freedom of Religion." *Baraza!* 1:5–8.

Shanon Shah. 2007. "Can Personal Expressions of Faith Be Treated as Crimes against the State?" *Baraza!* 1:14–15.

Shore, Bradd. 1991. "Twice Born, Once Conceived: Meaning Construction and Cultural Cognition." *American Anthropologist* 93:9–27.

Sinarharian. 2010a. "Bangga sebagai Melayu Islam Malaysia." September 23.

———. 2010b. "Kelantan buka pintu perdagangan." November 15.

———. 2010c. "Konsep ketuanan Melayu wajib ditinggalkan." November 28.

———. 2010d. "Nik Aziz bebas rasuah." December 16.

———. 2010e. "Nik Aziz diminta jelas kenyataan." September 22.

———. 2011. "Konsisten perjuangkan Islam." August 18.

———. 2012a. "Haji tidak perlu segera: Nik Aziz." June 15.

———. 2012b. "Haram batal haji kali pertama: Mufti." June 15.

———. 2012c. "Kekang gerakan liberalism: Jais serius tangani gerakan ideology songsang serang pemikiran umat Islam." July 1.

———. 2012d. "Melayu perlu bersatu." August 1.

———. 2012e. "PAS Selangor sokong gesaan tangguh haji." June 14.

———. 2012f. "Tidak boleh tangguh haji karena pilihan raya." June 16.

Singh, Bilveer. 2009. "Malaysia in 2008: The Elections That Broke the Tiger's Back." *Asian Survey* 49:156–65.

Sloane-White, Patricia. 2011. "Working in the Islamic Economy: Sharia-ization and the Malaysian Workplace." *Sojourn: Journal of Social Issues in Southeast Asia* 26:304–34.

———. 2017. *Corporate Islam: Sharia and the Modern Workplace.* Cambridge, UK: Cambridge University Press.

S. M. Yusuf. 1988. *Economic Justice in Islam.* New Delhi: Kitab Bhavan.

Song, Jesook. 2009. *South Koreans in the Debt Crisis.* Durham, NC: Duke University Press.

Sperber, Dan. 1974. *Rethinking Symbolism.* Cambridge, UK: Cambridge University Press.

Strauss, Claudia. 1992. "Models and Motives." In *Human Motives and Cultural Models,* edited by Roy D'Andrade and Claudia Strauss, 1–20. Cambridge, UK: Cambridge University Press.

SUARAM. 2009. *Malaysia Human Rights Report, 2009.* Petaling Jaya: SUARAM.

———. 2015. *Malaysia: Human Rights Report Overview, 2014.* Petaling Jaya: SUARAM.

Suara Perkasa. 2010a. "Ketatkan syarat dapat warganegara." November 1–15.

———. 2010b. "Tin arak di bangunan SUK." December 1–15.

The Star. 2010. "Nik Aziz's Statement draws Criticism from Alwi." September 20. Accessed November 26, 2015. www.thestar.com.my/story/?file=/2010/9/20/nation/7066325&sec=nation.

Thompson, Eric C. 2007. *Unsettling Absences: Urbanism in Rural Malaysia.* Singapore: NUS Press.

Today. 2015. "With PAS-DAP Split, Pakatan's Putrajaya Dream Now Laid to Waste, Analysts Say." June 11. Accessed September 27, 2015. www.todayonline.com/print/1305831.

Tripp, Charles. 2006. *Islam and the Moral Economy: The Challenge of Capitalism.* Cambridge, UK: Cambridge University Press.

Utusan. 2010a. "Nik Aziz tak bangga jadi bangsa Melayu?" September 19. Accessed November 23, 2015. ww1.utusan.com.my/.

————. 2010b. "Mursyidul Am Pas dibidas tidak bangga berbangsa Melayu." September 20. Accessed November 23, 2015. ww1.utusan.com.my/utusan/.

Varisco, Daniel M. 2005. *Islam Obscured: The Rhetoric of Anthropological Representation*. New York: Palgrave Macmillan.

VNC. 2009. "Malaysia: Court of Appeals Upholds the Caning Sentence of Kartika." August 25. Accessed October 30, 2015. www.violenceisnotourculture.org/content /malaysia-court-appeals-upholds-caning-sentence-kartika.

Wallis, Cara. 2013. *Technomobility in China: Young Migrant Women and Mobile Phones*. New York: New York University Press.

Wehr, Hans. (1960) 1979. *A Dictionary of Modern Written Arabic*. 4th ed. Edited by J. Milton Cowan. Ithaca, NY: Spoken Language Services.

Weiss, Meredith L. 2006. *Protest and Possibilities: Civil Society and Coalitions for Political Change in Malaysia*. Stanford, CA: Stanford University Press.

————. 2013. "Malaysia's 13th General Elections: Same Result, Different Outcome." *Asian Survey* 53:1135–58.

Wenger, E. 1998. *Communities of Practice: Learning, Meaning, and Identity*. Cambridge, UK: Cambridge University Press.

Wilkinson, R. J. 1908. *Papers on Malay Subjects, Part I: Malay Law*. Kuala Lumpur: FMS Government Printer.

Williams, Raymond. 1977. *Marxism and Literature*. Oxford, UK: Oxford University Press.

Witherspoon, Gary. 1977. *Language and Art in the Navajo Universe*. Ann Arbor: University of Michigan Press.

Wong Chin Huat. 2016. "Deepening Divisions as Malaysia Stays Mired in Racial Politics." *Today Online*. January 4. Accessed January 4, 2016. www.todayonline.com/world/asia /deepening-divisions-malaysia-stays-mired-racial-politics.

Yusoff Hashim. 1977–78. "Hukum Kanun dan Undang-Undang Melayu Lama Dalam Sejarah Kesultanan Melaka." *Jurnal Sejarah Jilid* 15:130–53.

Zaitun Mohamed Kasim. 2002. *Islam and Polygamy*. Petaling Jaya: Sisters in Islam.

Zaleha Kamarudin. 2007. "Harmonising the International Human Rights Law the Rights of Women in Malaysia: Milestones since Independence." In *Malaysia at 50: Aspirations and Challenges*, edited by Syed Arabi, 75–89. Gombak, Selangor: International Islamic University Malaysia.

Zhang, Li. 2010. "Postsocialist Urban Dystopia?" In *Noir Urbanisms: Dystopic Images of the Modern City*, edited by Gyan Prakash, 127–49. Princeton, NJ: Princeton University Press.

Zuliza Mohd Kusrin, Zaini Nasohah, Mohd al-Adib Samuri, and Mat Nor Mat Zain. 2013. "Legal Provisions and Restrictions on the Propagation of Non-Islamic Religions among Muslims in Malaysia." *Kajian Malaysia* 31:1–18.

INDEX

Inter-Faith Commission (IFC), 158, 160,
165, 224
Internal Security Act, 80
Iran, 77, 141, 233n5
IRF (Islamic Renaissance Front), 110,
163–67, 222
islah, 168
Islam: anthropology of, 6–10; operational
definition of, 7
Islamic Banking Act, 41, 115
Islamic bureaucracy, 40–41, 74, 92, 111
Islamic Circle of North America
(ICNA), 4
Islamic Insurance Act, 41, 115
Islamic natural law, 170
Islamic state: Darul Arqam concept of, 123,
125; PAS concept of, 43–44, 130, 136,
148–49, 155, 174; secular activists'
opposition to, 175–77, 228; small
corporate, 121, 125
Islamization: corporate, 121–22, 219;
cultivation of pious dispositions and,
182, 189, 196, 209, 217; Islamic NGOs
and, 110, 121, 123, 128, 182, 189, 195–96,
219; PAS campaign of, 110, 131, 133, 162,
182, 189, 195–96, 219; precolonial, 23;
religious bureaucracy and, 74, 99–100,
107–8, 182, 189, 195–96, 219, 232n16;
UMNO campaign of, 46, 93, 99–100,
115, 133, 162, 182, 195–96, 219, 232n16,
239n1. *See also* sharia-tization
itqan, 130, 207
Izwan Abdullah, 60

J
Jaafari, 80. *See also* Shia
Jabatan Agama Islam: apostasy and, 106,
233n2; arrest of Shia Muslims, 80, 179;
criticism of liberalism, 171; investigative
unit, 82, 85, 109, 233n4; seizure of prayer
hall, 156; stress on public instruction,
94, 182; SUARAM human rights report
and, 179
JAKIM (Department of Islamic Development Malaysia), 17, 48–61, 77, 89,
100–101, 107, 117, 155, 166
Japan, 138
Jasser Auda, 234n9
jenayah, 41, 77

Joint Action Group for Gender Equality,
93
jurisprudence. See *fiqh*

K
kalimat Allah controversy, 160, 224
Karpal Singh, 175–76
Kartika Sari Dewi Shukarno, 93
Keller (Dougherty), Janet D., 11, 13–15,
238n4
keramat, 79
kesalahan, 77
Ketuanan Islam (Islamic sovereignty), 148,
158, 224
Ketuanan Melayu (Malay sovereignty), 145,
158, 174, 224
Ketuanan Rakyat (people's sovereignty), 171
khalifah, 70, 121, 130, 159, 167
khalwat, 81, 84–85, 190, 197, 235n12
khul', 72
khutbah, 17, 155
kitabiyah, 61
Korea, 138, 240n2
kuliah masjid, 17, 155–56

L
Lebanon, 8, 184
legal codes: from English law, 32; of
postcolonial period, 41–43, 61,
79, 115; of precolonial Islamic
kingdoms, 23
Lehman, F. K., 14, 241n1, 238n4
li'an, 72
liberal pluralism: global flows of, 9, 111–12,
164; liberal Muslim reformers' vision of,
164, 168, 173; Muslim and non-Muslim
clashes and, 30, 93, 108–9, 111, 224–26;
religious neutrality and, 164, 178;
secular human rights advocates' vision
of, 178, 221
liberal rights: Article 121(1A) and, 42,
177; marriage and divorce and, 65, 68,
71–72, 227; Muslim converts and, 58,
177, 224; sharia criminal laws and, 92,
107, 221–22; sharia economics and, 115,
226
Lim Kit Siang, 174–75
Lina Joy, 54, 57, 105, 172, 222
liwat, 81, 84

M

ma-ash, 125
Mahathir Mohamad, 42, 46, 93, 136, 146, 152, 178
mahmudah, 123
Majlis Agama Islam, 48, 58, 104, 106, 236n19
mak yong, 131
Malay identity, 24, 45–46
Malayness, 23–24, 27, 41, 45, 50, 152
Malay rights organizations, 110, 147–48, 174. *See also* PERKASA; GERTAK
Malaysian Chinese Association (MCA), 36
Malaysian Chinese Muslim Association (MACMA), 157
Malaysian Consultative Council on Buddhism, Christianity, Hinduism, and Sikhism (MCCBCHS), 160
Malaysian IKRAM Organization, 121, 157
Malaysian Indian Congress (MIC), 36
Malaysian Indian Muslim Association (PERMIM), 157
Malaysian Islamic Renewal Organization (JIM), 121, 157–58
Malaysian Ulama Association, 157, 160
Malaysian Youth Movement (ABIM), 124, 157, 172
Mālikī, 71–72, 103, 226, 235n4. See also *fiqh*
maqasid sharia, 64, 70, 74, 166, 171–72
marriage, 23, 57, 61–62, 65, 66–67, 125, 224
maslahah, 64, 71, 74, 121
mas'uliah, 130, 134, 207
Mauss, Marcel, 182
Mawdūdī, Abul A'lā, 140
maysir, 115
mazmunah, 123
Middle East, 118–19, 126, 141, 237n3
modernity: European, 33, 77, 94, 112, 164, 166; Islamic, 53–54, 75, 94, 111–12, 116, 146, 150, 183, 186, 216, 226–27, 238n6; liberal pluralist, 69, 93, 112–13, 164, 166, 168, 173, 178–81
Moorthy Maniam, 58, 165
Morocco, 167
mualaf, 108, 155, 192–93. *See also* conversion cases
muamalat, 41, 116
mudarabah, 115, 124

mufti: contesting PAS scholars, 153–55; developing Muslim ethical values, 87; national council of, 40; Nik Aziz on, 44; ruling on child custody, 74; ruling on child marriage, 63–64; ruling on Darul Arqam, 79–80; ruling on ESQ, 238n26; ruling on SIS, 171, 240n5; rulings on economic matters, 116
Muhammad Morsi, 156
Muhammad Syukri Salleh, 122
Mujaddid (Renewer of Faith), 129, 237n13
mumaiyiz, 73
munakahat, 41
muncikari, 81
murabahah, 115
murtad, 50–51, 91, 110, 112, 191–92, 196, 222–23, 225; born Muslim, 54–55, 57, 105, 165, 233n2; Muslim converts, 58, 106–7
musahaqah, 81
mushawarah, 70
musibah, 214, 216
Muslim Professionals Forum, 121
mut'ah, 72

N

nafkah, 56, 68
Najib Razak, 60, 100, 109, 145–46, 162, 227
nasab, 104
National Council for Islamic Affairs Fatwa Committee, 40, 63, 80, 116, 120, 223
National Front (*Barisan Nasional*), 147–48, 151, 220, 222
Nazarudin Kamaruddin, 94
Negeri Sembilan Administration of Islamic Affairs Enactment of 2004, 102
neoliberalism, 9, 118, 129, 141, 143
Nigeria, 77, 98
Nik Abdul Aziz, 89, 132–33; concept of Islamic state, 43–44, 130, 132–34, 148–49, 223; debate with government scholars, 153–54; on development 113, 129, 134, 137–38; on Malay race, 150, 174
non-Islamic religion laws, 41
Norani Othman, 68–69, 71, 92–94, 166–67. *See also* SIS
Nurul Izzah Anwar, 169
nusyuz, 13, 69, 193–94
Nyonya Tahir, 233n2